The Magical Life
of Marshall Brodien

The Magical Life of Marshall Brodien

Creator of TV Magic Cards and Wizzo the Wizard

JOHN MOEHRING

McFarland & Company, Inc., Publishers
Jefferson, North Carolina, and London

LIBRARY OF CONGRESS CATALOGUING-IN-PUBLICATION DATA

Moehring, John, 1942–
    The magical life of Marshall Brodien : creator of tv magic cards and Wizzo the Wizard / John Moehring.
        p.   cm.
    Includes index.

    ISBN-13: 978-0-7864-3182-3
    softcover : 50# alkaline paper ∞

    1. Brodien, Marshall. 2. Magicians — United States — Biography. 3. Wizards — United States — Biography.
I. Title.
GV1545.B76M64   2007
793.8092 — dc22   2007025301

British Library cataloguing data are available

©2007 John Moehring. All rights reserved

No part of this book may be reproduced or transmitted in any form or by any means, electronic or mechanical, including photocopying or recording, or by any information storage and retrieval system, without permission in writing from the publisher.

Cover photograph: Marshall Brodien with the rice bowl trick from his magic show

Manufactured in the United States of America

McFarland & Company, Inc., Publishers
   Box 611, Jefferson, North Carolina 28640
   www.mcfarlandpub.com

Acknowledgments

I will forever be grateful to Marshall's wife, Mary Doyle Brodien. Without the timeline she had already crafted from the boxes full of news clippings, letters, documents, and photos, putting rhyme and reason to Marshall's stories and tales would have been impossible.

Thanks to WGN-TV producer Al Hall, writer Don Sandburg, and archivist George Pappas, all of whom confirmed that those wild and crazy things Marshall claimed went on during the four decades of Chicago's *Bozo Show* were indeed true.

My friend Dexter Cleveland kick-started the project by insisting that I email him at least two chapters a month and, when I felt like I had reached the last chapter, writer and proofreader Lindsay Smith offered to give the manuscript its first test ride. Jay Marshall, the beloved Dean of the Society of American Magicians, was able to read the first draft some months before he passed away in 2005, and both Marshall and I are grateful for his advice and encouragement.

Marshall also wishes to thank his friend Ken Mate for fixing numerous facts, Chuck Romano for assistance with photographs, attorney Stewart Berks for reading the manuscript to be sure we were portraying people in the right light, and Doug McKnight, who gave us helpful suggestions in our search for a publisher.

Table of Contents

Acknowledgments   v
Preface   1

1. Whatever Happened to Wizzo?   3
2. Sellers of the Secrets   9
3. Riverview Park   20
4. First Pitch on the Tube   31
5. Odd Fellows and a Tall Tale   34
6. Cicero, the Mob, and Beyond   38
7. Trouping with an Alligator   50
8. Carnival Knowledge   56
9. Abracadabra, You're Drafted   63
10. A Spell of Hypnosis   68
11. Straitjackets and Shenanigans   74
12. Nightclub Necromancer   88
13. The Cairo   98
14. Bozo's Circus   108
15. New Girlfriend and a Prize Fight   113
16. Pass on the Playboy   120

17. Presto! Less Hypno	123
18. Taking on Trade Shows	130
19. *The Mike Douglas Show*	136
20. A Movie and a Trip to the Moon	141
21. Doody, Doody, Do	144
22. TV Magic Cards	150
23. Eicoff Enters the Scene	162
24. Friends in the Biz	167
25. The Best Partner Is No Partner	173
26. Old Chicago	178
27. The Restaurateur	181
28. Visit from the FBI	188
29. DBA Marshall Brodien Magic Co.	192
30. Circus Daze Over	196
31. Home Shopping	200
32. Ships Ahoy	203
33. Mansion for Sale	205
34. A New Bozo	207
35. Check, Please!	210
36. ToTo's	214
37. Ventures in Toyland	217
38. Viva Las Vegas	225
39. A Shot at Producing	230
40. Marshall Meets his Match	234
41. Magic Boom of the '90s	239
42. Farewell to 40 Years of Fun	245
43. Sh-h-h-h... It's a Secret	250
44. Pressing On	254
Index	259

Preface

This book is a collection of fascinating reminiscences that perhaps should never have been committed to paper.

The tales begin in the 1940s, when a young magician named Marshall gets a job demonstrating at a magic shop in the Chicago Loop. He's soon performing in the sideshow at Riverview Park. By age 19, he's amazing nightclubbers and mobsters who frequent the Magic Lounge in Cicero with his magic tricks. He headlines for three years as a stage hypnotist at Chicago's posh Cairo Supper Club. He pioneers the use of big-scale illusions on tradeshow floors across America. For 27 years, he appears on WGN-TV's *Bozo Show* as Wizzo the Wizard. And, oh yes, along the way, Marshall goes on television and pitches and sells millions of dollars worth of TV Magic Cards and TV Magic Sets, eventually becoming the undisputed leader in the mass marketing of magic to several generations of wannabe magicians.

So, why shouldn't these reminiscences be published? It's because most of them are unbelievable, but they really are true. Even when you hear his recollections straight from his mouth they sound and seem impossible. But I have listened to them all, researched and substantiated them, and discovered that the truth is indeed more astonishing than fiction.

"Not today" became a punch line of sorts that was bantered about while I did the interviews and gathered the information for this book. Over the course of the two years that I listened to Marshall recount the hundreds of anecdotes about his unconventional life and fantastic career as a magician, that two-word retort often served as a useful on-the-spot editing tool.

I first heard Marshall's wife, Mary, utter, "Not today," in a restaurant one evening after dinner, just before Marshall launched into his story of how an unsavory character once held him at gunpoint, demanding the secret of his vanishing birdcage trick. Naturally, after being married to Marshall for over a decade, Mary had heard this story, as well as countless others, many, many times. Thus, when Marshall posed the question, "Did I ever tell you about the time I did the birdcage trick for this mob guy?" Mary's witty response of, "Not today," really meant, "Yes, I've heard the story many times before and I'm going to hear it again and everybody's going to be entertained and laugh a lot."

I had heard about the birdcage a half-dozen times, but that night there were two or three people at the table who hadn't. So, once again, I listened, marveling at Marshall's consummate storytelling skills and, of course, I was genuinely laughing, along with everyone else, as if this were the first time I'd heard about the time Marshall did the birdcage trick for the mob guy.

From that evening on, whenever Marshall prefaced his telling of a particular incident with a question — such as, "Have I told you the one about the time in the Army when I hypnotized a soldier and made him think he was stuck to a toilet seat for an hour?"— the standard answer was, "Not today." But it was quickly followed by, "Why don't you tell me about it again?" That's because a re-telling usually brought forth a couple of previously forgotten details that gave the original version a relevant place in the bigger jigsaw puzzle-like work I was assembling.

The Magical Life of Marshall Brodien is a biography, and while Marshall has supplied the main narrative, some of what appears between quotation marks comes from his recollections of what others said at the time. And though the names of several persons featured in the book have been changed to protect their privacy, I still like to think of it as a work of believable nonfiction.

— John Moehring
Fall 2007

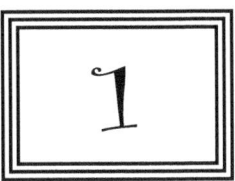

Whatever Happened to Wizzo?

When the phone call came from WGN-TV, Marshall Brodien was at work in his home office in Geneva, Illinois, designing new tricks for the "Marshall Brodien 25 Trick Magic Sets" that would soon be on the shelves of Costco stores everywhere.

Jeff Hoover, segment producer for the Chicago superstation's *WGN Morning News,* was on the phone. He wanted to tell Marshall about an unusual call the switchboard had received. A couple of mornings prior, the *Morning News* had carried a report on street magician David Blaine's death-defying publicity stunt in London. Blaine, who'd previously been buried alive under a tank of water for a week and, on another occasion, frozen in a block of ice in New York's Times Square, was now starving himself in a sealed Plexiglas box hanging above the River Thames.

The news update of Blaine's bizarre stunt of October 2003 prompted an elderly sounding lady viewer to phone the station: "Watching that David Blaine do those strange things reminded me of the crazy magician who used to be on the *Bozo Show*. I was calling to ask whatever happened to Wizzo?" The operator was at a loss, but the lady on the line was persistant. "Let me tell you something," she said. "That Wizzo was weirder than Mr. Blaine could ever want to be."

Marshall Brodien portrayed Wizzo the Wizard on WGN-TV's *Bozo Show* for 26 years, retiring the mystical zany character in 1994. The highly popular children's show ran another seven years before the plug was finally pulled. When the primetime special *Bozo: 40 Years of Fun* aired, Wizzo came back to join in the farewell fling. But after that show, Wizzo's wacky magic had become but a flickering memory of a bygone era of fun-for-fun's-sake children's television.

Jeff Hoover told Marshall, "As soon as the guys on the news desk heard about that woman's call, it got everybody talking about you. The cameramen, the floor crew, even people in the cafeteria were asking, 'Whatever happened to Wizzo?' Everybody down here wants to know what you've been up to since you left the station."

Marshall, in his inimitable unassuming manner, mentioned to Jeff that the Society of American Magicians had recently honored him at their centennial celebration in New York City, where he gave a talk, recounting his show-business beginnings as the sideshow barker at Riverview Park ... the years of doing tricks for the mob bosses in Cicero ... his long-running hypnotic show at the Cairo Supper Club ... the fun years of pitching millions of decks of TV Magic Cards and magic sets on television ... the craziness of doing literally thousands of hours of magic skits on *Bozo's Circus*, which became later known as the *Bozo Show*....

Jeff politely interrupted and said, "Marshall, I was calling to find out if we could get you down here for an interview on the *Morning News*."

"Yeah, that might be fun," Marshall said. "I could come on the show and do a few magic tricks...."

"As Wizzo?" Jeff asked.

"Oh, no. I don't do him anymore," Marshall said with a laugh. "Anyway, I think Wizzo left town a long time ago, took all his money and invested in condos in Arobia or somewhere far away."

"Seriously, what would it take to get you to appear as Wizzo just one more time?" Hoover asked. "His fans are calling."

Wizzo the Wizard, as he first appeared on WGN-TVs *Bozo's Circus*, July 31, 1968. The Arabian Nights costume was orginally designed for Marshall when he performed for the American Gas Association's magic-themed trade show exhibit at Chicago's McCormick Place. *Marshall Brodien Collection.*

"No. I don't think so," Marshall said. "I said I would never put the costume on again. However, I will come on the show as Marshall Brodien and talk about Wizzo."

"Couldn't Wizzo come on and talk about Marshall Brodien? Please, Marshall, you have to do it. Just say yes."

"No," Marshall said, "and Wizzo says no."

But Hoover wouldn't give in. "Tell me what it would take to get you to do Wizzo one last time? We'll come out and pick you up in a limousine. Bring you down here. Roll out the red carpet. Whatever it takes. You know everybody loved Wizzo. I still crack up every time I think of the way he rolled his eyes and said, 'Doody, doody, doo' to make the magic happen. What a thrill it would be for everybody to see he's alive and well and as funny as he always was."

Reflecting back to that day, Marshall says, "Jeff Hoover was so enthusiastic and such a nice guy that I just couldn't say 'no' to him any more, so I told him, 'Let me think about it, and I'll call you back.'" He hung up the phone and brooded it over for over 24 hours, and when he finally did call back, he said, "After giving it some serious consideration I've decided I'll do it."

Jeff couldn't believe what he'd heard. "Wizzo lives!" he shouted. "This is great. We'll put you in the exact same dressing room that Wizzo used to put on his makeup. The *Bozo Show* dressing room is still vacant. In fact, the old wardrobe trunk is still there and Bozo and Wizzo photos are still on the walls. Thank you, Marshall, this is going to be super!"

• • •

"It was five o'clock in the morning when I sat down in the dressing room," Marshall recalls. "As I started putting on the costume and the makeup, I looked in the mirror and asked myself, 'Why am I doing this?' But as soon as I got out on the set and starting doing some of the fun on-camera magic bits with entertainment critic Dean Richards and co-anchors Larry Potash and Roseanne Tellez, everything was fine. Basically, Jeff had told me to just go out there and be Wizzo ... be crazy. 'Have some fun,' is what he said."

Meteorologist Paul Konrad was midway through a weather update, standing in front of the chroma-keyed map of Chicagoland, when on strolled Wizzo. He greeted Paul with a garbled "Doody, doody, doo," then started pulling yards upon yards of bright colored streamers from his mouth. Konrad was laughing so hard he couldn't finish the forecast. For the next two hours, Wizzo scurried about the studio, popping on camera when least expected, causing strange things to happen every time he uttered those nonsensical words, "Doody, doody, doo."

The wacky Wizard knotted together a couple of silk scarves and stuffed them into the top of traffic reporter Robin Baumgarten's blouse. He took a third scarf and made it disappear, telling her, "The hanky-poo will invisibly fly to the imaginary land of Arobia, then magically journey back here and appear between your two ... hanky-poos, of course." Robin giggled as Wizzo fished out two corners of her scarves and handed them to Konrad and sportscaster Mike Barz. They were instructed to give the scarves a tug, and when they did, they were amazed, but not nearly as astonished as Robin. Tied between the scarves was not the hanky-poo that had made the invisible roundtrip to Arobia, but instead, a silky white brassiere.

At the midpoint of the *WGN Morning News* program, which is watched every weekday by 450,000 Chicago-area households, Dean Richards walked over to Brodien and said, "You won't believe the action on the switchboard. They just called back to say they've had over 40 calls. We don't get that many calls when the politicians and home-run heroes show up." For his finale that morning, Wizzo coaxed reporter Larry Potash into removing his birthday-present necktie for a laugh-filled presentation of the classic cut-and-*eventually*-restored necktie trick.

By the end of the three-hour program, the switchboard was blinking and beeping like an overheated NASA mission-control panel. The calls from Wizzo and *Bozo Show* fans and friends had swamped the automated answering system and continued even after the *Morning News* went off the air.

Later that afternoon, when Jeff Hoover called Brodien to again thank him for doing the show, he told Marshall that the WGN-TV switchboard had not been that jammed since the morning of September 11.

• • •

The weekend after Marshall's appearance on the *Morning News* program, the Wizard's costume was given a cursory dry-cleaning and was carefully fitted back onto the mannequin in the basement of his home. The life-size mustachioed likeness of Wizzo stands next to a six-foot-high colorful cabinet that's known among magicians as the Mismade Lady, a stage illusion where a female assistant is divided into four segments then miraculously put back together in a perplexing manner.

If you dared open one of the four hinged doors of the Mismade Lady cabinet and peeked inside, you'd find a few odd, foam-stuffed prop body parts of Cooky the Clown, the loveable character created for the *Bozo Show* by Marshall's dear friend Roy Brown. That's because in the heyday of the comedy-magic act of Marshall Brodien & Cooky, it was Cooky who crawled into the box instead of a lovely young lady, which resulted in a whole lot of amusement along with the amazement.

While the description of how Brodien presented the Mismade illusion may sound like a museum guide's spiel, it's akin to what you might hear and see if you visited his home. You see, Marshall Brodien, a.k.a. Wizzo the Wizard, has magically transformed the spacious 1,000-square-foot lower level of his suburban home into a wondrous gallery of his show-business past and present.

Across from the Mismade Lady illusion is a glassed-in cabinet that's chock full of memorabilia from the *Bozo Show*, displaying even the sleek golden Emmy statue that Brodien was awarded for his contributions to the popular children's show. Filling the shelves of another lighted étagère are props that range from a chrome-plated 1960s automotive part that Marshall mysteriously levitated while performing trade shows for Bethlehem Steel; to an antiquarian birdcage trick that Harry Houdini gave to Marshall's mentor, stage and nightclub magician Jack Gwynne; to the still-sealed bottle of rare "Louis the 13th" cognac that was a gift for doing an evening of magic at mob boss Jackie Cerone's home; to one of the original decks of TV Magic Cards, the item that sold millions and forever made famous Brodien's sales slogan: "Most magic tricks are easy ... once you know the secret."

Vintage posters of Thurston, "The World's Greatest Magican"; Kar-Mi, the mystic who "Swallows a Loaded Gun Barrel and Shoots a Cracker from a Man's Head"; Alexander, "The Man Who Knows"; and Carter the Great, Sorcar, Gwynne, and others cover one wall of a comfortable sitting area. The other two walls are lined with almost 100 framed eight-by-ten photographs that capture well over a half-century of Marshall Brodien's robust performing career. He's shown doing magic and drawing huge crowds in front of the sideshow at Chicago's Riverview Park. There are black-and-white photos of him at age 19, eating fire and performing card tricks at the Magic Lounge in the mafia-managed town of Cicero. While in the Army, he's pictured upside down, escaping from straitjackets, as well as doing a command performance for General Wyman, the Commanding General of the U.S. Continental Army. Scads of volunteers are performing crazy stunts during his hilarious nightclub shows of hypnotism. The aisles at trade shows are packed with buyers as he does his customized product pitches at trade shows. And countless are the photographs of Marshall with the politicians, celebrities, show-business folks, and magicians he's befriended and worked with over the years.

But the impact of the man's myriad accomplishments doesn't register until you start to wind your way through the aisles of magical merchandise that Brodien has created and marketed. Stacked from floor to ceiling, no matter which way you turn, are all the different magic sets and packaged tricks that have sold at retail since 1970.

They begin with the huge variety of items pitched on television by TV

Magic, Ltd. There are the many sets, kits, and tricks marketed by the Marshall Brodien Magic Company that were found in retail chains nationwide into the 1990s. There's a specialty set designed for Bill Bixby when he was *The Magician* on TV, another for Blackstone Jr., and there are the dozens upon dozens of products produced for Siegfried & Roy and Lance Burton in Las Vegas. A corner is filled with themed-magic products created for the Disney movies, *Aladdin, The Hunchback of Notre Dame,* and *101 Dalmatians.* There are the custom magic sets designed for exclusive distribution in Target, K-Mart, Sam's Club, JC Penney, and other discount retailers. Even special sets were produced for numerous pitches on the Home Shopping Network and QVC. Rounding the final aisle of this remarkable collection, you discover the shelves of contemporary magical merchandise Brodien has designed and brought to market while serving as a consultant for Harmony Toy, which by the turn of the century was bought out by Cadaco. These diverse lines of magic product have often been responsible for generating $5- to $6-million worth of sales annually.

Marshall Brodien, with his overwhelming output of magical product during the last-half of the 20th century, has influenced more people to take up magic — either as a fascinating hobby or a rewarding profession — than any other magician in history. Robert Lund, the founder of the American Museum of Magic, once attributed Brodien's success to "his ability to perceive television as the most effective selling tool ever invented." Others insist that Brodien's achievements as a TV personality and successful pitchman of prestidigitation can be chalked up to a lifetime of lucky breaks, being in the right place at the right time. Marshall himself will simply smile and tell you, "It's easy, once you know the secret..."

But don't be fooled by that ingenious one-liner that captured the attention of millions and made millions. The true story of Marshall Brodien's road to success has been a long and arduous one — one that's been paved with both persistence and determination.

Sellers of the Secrets

The red and black-striped Chicago Transit streetcar came to a stop near the intersection of North Clark and Diversey Parkway. With mother Mildred in tow, young Marshall stepped out and hurried across the street to the curb. A mere half-block away was the gateway to enchantment — the door to the magic shop.

The magic shop was actually a narrow-as-an-arrow novelty store wedged between a delicatessen and the grand entryway of the Parkway Theater, a modern movie palace where vaudeville would hang on — accompanying the films and defying television — for another decade. However, on this particular Saturday afternoon in 1944, Marshall wasn't out to catch the double-feature matinee showing of Abbott & Costello's *Ride 'Em Cowboy* and *Tarzan's Secret Treasure* starring Johnny Weissmuller. He was on a mission of a different sort.

He had convinced his mom that this squanky shop of candy and cigars, notions and lotions, novelties, toys, newspapers, and perhaps an under-the-counter punch-card game, was one of the few places on the planet that trafficked in the arcane secrets of magic. The garish red-and-yellow lettering on the lackluster plate glass door read, "Jokes & Tricks Sold Here!" That was evidence enough he was at the gates of Mecca.

At the bottom of the shop's display window was an array of boxed tricks from the S.S. Adams Company, a manufacturer of magical props located in what Marshall saw as the far-off, mystical land of Asbury Park, New Jersey. There were Cups & Balls, Imp Bottles, Linking Rings, Phantom Cards, and Rice Bowls. Fanciful labels with drawings of mustachioed wizards transformed the flimsy cardboard containers into mini treasure chests. Atop one box was an item called the "Money Maker Machine." Its stubby printing rollers had been halted midway in the miraculous process of changing a piece of white paper into a genuine greenback. More amazing was the fact that the device only cost a dollar.

Less than a year before his first visit to the magic shop, Marshall had witnessed a performance by a lady magician at his elementary school. Her program was filled with wonders. Silk handkerchiefs changed colors, a pitcher full of milk poured into a paper cone disappeared, and with a wave of a wand, a length of rope that was cut into pieces was magically restored. Then and there, Marshall realized that education meant more than reading, writing, and arithmetic. There were secrets of magic to be learned.

When the magic bug bites, most kids head for the library to check out the first book they can find on the subject. Others pester their parents or a grandmother, letting it be known that a magic set is on the Christmas wish list. Before Marshall had time to think about pursuing either of those paths, a schoolmate named Robert Jordan casually told him about the little store next to the Parkway Theater that sold magic tricks.

Gallantly holding the shop door open for his mother, Marshall surreptitiously patted his left buttock, checking that his wallet was still there. He'd accumulated $6, saving the nickels, quarters, and half-dollars earned from delivering newspapers and polishing shoes outside taverns. Little did the wannabe wizard know that the cost of his first magic fix would be exactly six bucks.

"It was because of the demonstrator," he says. "He did each of the tricks so well that I had to have them all. I bought the Ball and Vase, a Handkerchief Vanisher, a Chinese Prayer Vase, and a couple other secrets he showed me. Again, it was because this guy behind the counter made all the tricks look so easy to do."

That day not only kick-started the career of a magician, it was also the beginning of Marshall's fascination with how a pitchman can deliver things you never dreamed you needed.

• • •

Though not quite a teenager, Marshall desired to know anything and everything about the world of magic. Two friends in the neighborhood were into magic as a hobby, but the moment their interests waned, Marshall was there to see if he could beg or buy their tricks for his ever-growing repertoire. He practiced diligently, and it wasn't long before he was doing shows for birthday parties, schools, Cub Scout meetings, and just about any group that would sit still long enough.

One morning after breakfast, after he completely fooled his mother with a new coin trick he'd been working on, it dawned on Marshall that he should be charging a fee for his performances — maybe as much as $4 or $5. At the same time, he realized if he were to do that he'd definitely need more professional-looking props. It was time to venture downtown, where the "real magic shops" were located.

After World War II, the Windy City had unquestionably become a magic center of the United States. *The Sphinx*, a then-popular monthly magazine for magicians, had an article in the April 1947 issue that spotlighted "The Dealers of Chicago." Listed were Joe Berg, Laurie Ireland, Sam Berland, Ed Miller, and National Magic, which was Jim Sherman's shop in the Palmer House. Photos of the interiors of their shops, all packed with customers, were captioned, "Chicago magic dealers are happy, well-fed, and contented, with competition being the least of their worries."

With the money Marshall had saved from doing shows around his neighborhood, he visited Joe Berg's emporium at 30 West Washington. Berg had run magic shops in Chicago since the mid-1920s, and he considered this his nicest shop to date. Carpeting covered the showroom floor. The walls were oak paneled and the custom shelving was crammed with the latest apparatus, as well as some rarities. Glass display cases packed with more props and accessories were arranged in such a way to create a "U" of demonstration-counters. There was a backroom with a fully equipped shop for manufacturing magic and, by 1947, Berg had made a business arrangement with the great Dutch stage conjuror Okito (Theo Bamberg) to work as a prop builder and demonstrator.

Marshall began to hang out at Berg's, more so on Saturday afternoons when the local magicians and the pros working the Chicago-area theaters and nightclubs stopped in. With a little eavesdropping he learned of the latest tricks, miracles that hadn't yet made it to the pages of Berg's catalog.

It wasn't long before Joe knew Marshall by name and considered him a regular. When he purchased a new trick Marshall usually had the pleasure of having Joe himself explain how the effect was presented, graciously sharing a performance tip or two beyond what was revealed in the mimeographed instruction sheet sold with the trick.

Yet, the privilege of shopping where the pros shopped often had a drawback — especially if you were a teenager. Keeping the secret of how the trick worked became less of a priority than keeping the secret of *how much* the trick cost... "Don't tell me you've spent another $5 for one of those magic tricks!" Marshall's mother would shout, as he was caught sneaking a new purchase up the back stairway of their third-floor apartment on North Avenue. "You know, you're just throwing your money away, again."

And when Marshall yelled back, "Mom, I can assure you that I would not waste $5 on a new magic trick," he was telling the truth. The magic props that he was now buying for his act were in the $10 to $20 range. The bigger stuff came from Abbott's Magic Company. The plant where everything was manufactured was in Colon, Michigan, but they had a branch store in Chicago above the Woods Theater on West Randolph.

"A magician by the name of George Coon managed the place," Marshall recalls. "He sold me my first set of Hippity-Hop Rabbits." This "sucker trick" featured plywood cutouts of black and white bunnies that magically transposed, even though the method led spectators to believe they knew the secret. For the double-bluff climax, the rabbits changed to red and yellow, leaving most of the audience bamboozled.

As winter blew into Chicago in 1948, the solo trips to the Loop became more frequent. One icy afternoon, Marshall opted not to hit the shops of Berg's or Ireland's. Instead, he headed for a place called Finer Amusements at 159 North Wabash. "It was an arcade owned by Bobby Baer and Gene Wilhelm, but I heard they had a well-stocked trick counter there. The day I dropped in, Bobby Baer was trying to show a customer how to perform a new trick. It was something I'd bought at Berg's. In fact, I was already doing it in my shows. So I introduced myself and said, 'Here, let me show you how to do it. It's real simple.' Because I knew the secret and could make the trick work for the customer, Bobby rang up a quick sale. He laughed and told me to get behind the counter and show this person some more magic. The guy ended up buying $20 worth of tricks."

Marshall purchased the Hippity-Hop Rabbits trick when he was 16, about the same time he decided to have his first professional photograph taken. *Marshall Brodien Collection*

2. Sellers of the Secrets

Baer appreciated young Brodien's gung-ho enthusiasm, especially his ability to take a simple trick and convince people off the street that they just might have as much fun with magic as Marshall did. Bobby asked him if he would be interested in working for the store. There were several people standing around the counter and Marshall remembered being quite surprised at the offer. However, a one-word answer — "Sure!" — popped out of his mouth. After he'd demonstrated and sold a few more tricks, he turned to Bobby and told him that he could only work afternoons and on weekends. He said he was only 14 and just entering high school.

For the next 11 months, Marshall sold magic tricks from four o'clock in the afternoon till nine at night, and he worked double shifts on Saturdays and Sundays. He loved demonstrating. Where else could you have the opportunity to learn the secrets of all the latest tricks and get paid to practice them?

• • •

In November of 1949, Bobby Baer closed down Finer Amusements and relocated his operations to 19 West Randolph Street. Naturally, Marshall followed him in the move. "The new place was in a much better location with more traffic," Marshall says. "We were across the street from the Oriental Theatre, and the famous Marshall Field's department store was just around the corner."

A two-story high, chase-lighted marquee out front heralded the arrival of "Baer's Treasure Chest." Two smiley-face bears wearing cartooned straw hats gazed down on the store's double doors, as if to lure fun seekers inside. Black, 12-inch-tall moveable letters announced BOOKS, RECORDS, TOYS, JEWELRY, and SOUVENIRS for sale. A neon sign in the window made it known there was a GAME ROOM that featured PIN BALLS WITH FLIPPERS. A three-foot-square panel in the upper-left corner of the sign indicated the Treasure Chest was also the home of "Chicago's Magic Center."

In reality, the store was a bigger, grander arcade for Bobby Baer. He had added rows of ski-ball games, a shooting gallery, and had more than doubled-up on his count of flashing, flipping, pinging, and bell-ringing, coin-consuming arcade machines. And because of a bit of political gamesmanship known only to Baer and certain city councilmen, the new amusement palace was the only arcade licensed within the bustle and hustle of Chicago's Loop.

There truly was more space devoted to the magic department. Two glass-topped showcase counters filled with pocket tricks stood in front of a floor-to-ceiling shelf that was stocked with Chinese Sticks, Card Penetration Frames, Die Boxes, Chick Pans, and other parlor and stage-sized effects. In addition to Brodien, Tom Rainey and Don Theobald managed the counter,

The Treasure Chest, which was located at 19 West Randolph in the heart of the Chicago Loop, is where Marshall got his first job demonstrating magic. *Marshall Brodien Collection*

rotating their shifts so there was always a magician on duty. And it wouldn't be too many months before the Treasure Chest would be hiring seasoned pros such as Don Alan, Ed Marlo, and Okito to demo on Saturdays.

Wheeling and dealing behind the Magic Center counter instilled something of an entrepreneurial spirit in Brodien, who was now 15. Saving up a couple of his weekly paychecks, he acquired a penny-arcade game called a

Marshall demonstrating at the Treasure Chest's Magic Center, the upstairs shop that catered to the pros. *Marshall Brodien Collection*

Kicker & Catcher and, almost overnight, put the mechanical money grabber on the take.

"One evening on my way home from the Treasure Chest, I stopped at this bookstore at 4100 West North Avenue, about a block from where I lived. Because a lot of young people came in there to buy comic books, I knew this would be a great place for my little machine." The owner was willing to give it a try, agreeing to a 50/50 split of the pennies. "All the kids, as well as a lot of adults, lined up to play the game. We were soon splitting $15 to $20 every week."

One of the souvenir counters at the Treasure Chest offered some rather attractive earrings that sold for 59¢ a pair. Marshall became acquainted with the man who supplied them, and he soon started buying them in quantity for 25¢ a pair. When he made his weekly stop at the North Avenue bookstore to split the Kicker & Catcher pennies, he would visit a nearby notions store and drop off a dozen or so pairs of the earrings. "The proprietor paid me about 75¢ apiece for them, then marked them up to $1.25 or $1.50."

A cheap mimeographed-and-stapled pamphlet in one of the Treasure Chest's bookracks showed how to make a gimmicked-card version of the Three Card Monte, a sleight-of-hand game played by street hustlers. Brodien felt that this easy-to-do version of this well-known trick just might sell. Taking inexpensive playing cards, he spent many a late night cutting and taping the card-flap gaff that was necessary to do the dirty work. After printing up some simple instructions, Marshall created an artwork envelope package for his product. The little bookstore on the corner sold them as fast as he could make them. Marshall's Monte proved to be such a hot item that even the Treasure Chest stocked them.

For those who put stock in signs and omens, it could be said that Brodien's homemade trick cards were fortune-telling cards of sorts — foretelling a fortune to be made in packaging and marketing magic tricks.

• • •

As Marshall began his second year of part-time demonstrating at the Treasure Chest, he found himself more and more in demand as a performer. Dozens of downtown businessmen would watch the young wiz in action and ask, "What would you charge to do a show at my kid's birthday party this weekend?" After winning a Friday night talent contest at the Parkway Theater in the spring of 1950, he started getting calls to do school shows. The school assemblies led to more parties. Marshall Brodien needed business cards.

Rather than look for a printer, Marshall learned the craft of printing. At the nearby Manley Trade and Vocational School, there was a teacher who was fascinated by magic. All Marshall had to do was perform a few tricks and the instructor showed him how to set type and let him to use the school's offset press to print his own business cards and flyers.

Marshall created a one-sheet brochure with the bold header: "For Entertainment, book BRODIEN THE MAGICIAN in his FOOLIES of 1950."

There was a dramatic photo of Marshall, and the copy advised: "Streamlined Magic, Laughs, and Surprises from Start to Finish. Comedy and mystery — the ingredients for the kind of entertainment America likes best — are blended in a streamlined show full of laughs and surprises. His illusions can be performed anywhere. All the effects can be seen from any distance in the room or hall. It's magic, but it's modern."

The up-and-coming Mr. Brodien was now demanding a fee of $10, with a buck added on if he had to arrange his transportation. When the client didn't provide a ride, he usually traveled by bus or streetcar, toting his act in two special yellow carrying cases he'd constructed.

Although Marshall was too young to drive an automobile, by a peculiar set of circumstances, he soon found himself in possession of a valid Illinois driver's license. "There was this gentleman named Schultz who always came into the Treasure Chest on Sundays to pick up jokes and tricks. We called him Schultz the Undertaker. I think he worked for the city, maybe a coroner. I just remember that he always had envelopes full of documents sticking out of his coat pockets."

One morning, in the course of talking about the latest tricks, Schultz asked Marshall where he lived. "When I told him that I lived out north of town and took the streetcar to work, he asked me, 'You need a driver's license?' Because I was only 15 and didn't have a car, I said, 'Not really.' After that, I sort of forgot about it."

The next time the friendly undertaker walked in the store, he headed straight for the magic counter. He reached into his overcoat pocket and, with a summons-serving gesture, handed Marshall a folded page of paper. "Just fill in all the blanks," Schultz said, giving him a ballpoint pen. It was a driver's license application. "When you get to the blank space that asks for the year you were born, be sure to write in 1933."

Marshall was born in 1934, but for "year-of-birth" line, he did as requested and entered 1933. Schultz smiled and said, "That looks pretty official to me. Now all you gotta do is sign it." That done, he carefully folded the completed form, stuck it back into his pocket-file of papers, tipped his dark brown fedora and said, "This won't take too long, but don't hold your breath."

Within a week, Marshall was holding his very own official driver's license. This was in the days before licenses carried photo identification, but what made it undeniably official was the notarized signature of a deputy of the State of Illinois Highway Department. Of course, Brodien was grateful to Schultz. He remembers saying to himself, "Now I have to figure out how to drive." That dilemma quickly disappeared the day a skinny kid everybody called "Stosh" came to work at the Treasure Chest.

Stosh applied for work as a part-time demonstrator at the magic counter.

He was an amateur magician, but he did things that pros couldn't. That's because he stayed up till three or four in the morning, drinking beer and practicing intricate sleight of hand with coins and cards. Yet, Stosh always showed up to work on time. He had a car.

Upon hearing of Marshall's newly acquired driver's license, Stosh not only volunteered to teach him how to drive, but let him use his automobile to practice. "One thing was for sure," Marshall says, "while I was learning to drive, I didn't have to worry about getting stopped by the cops for not having a driver's license."

• • •

Another character who showed up at the Treasure Chest was a man simply known as Professor Stevenson. "He was in his late 40s or early 50s," Marshall remembers, "and I'm really not sure where he was from. He just told us he was a stage hypnotist, passing through Chicago."

Some freshly printed flyers were the Professor's only credentials. Inch-high letters stated, "YOU WILL NEVER FORGET PROF. STEVENSON, HYPNOTIST." His piercing eyes stared outward from the page. The copy beside his picture informed of an "Amazing, Instructive, Amusing, Weird, and Entertaining Program." Printed near the bottom of the sheet was *For Engagements, Phone:* _____, and the space was blank. Apparently the Professor was stopping at a hotel or rooming house that didn't have guest phones in the rooms.

The phone number of the Treasure Chest was rubber stamped in the blank space when Bobby Baer allowed Stevenson to place a stack of the flyers on the Treasure Chest's magic counter. Maybe it would help the Professor pick up a show or two. After two weeks, it was fairly obvious that the Professor wasn't getting any calls, because he jumped at Bobby's job offer to help out on weekends by demonstrating behind the counter.

At the time, Marshall was more interested in magic than mesmerism. Yet, he was curious as to how "stage hypnotism" worked. "I never saw Stevenson perform, but I was always asking questions. He told me about some of the bits he did, how you make a hypnotized person laugh and cry onstage, and how you could make people feel as if they were hot or freezing cold." It was invaluable information that Marshall would remember, even though it would be four or five years before a need for such arcane knowledge would arise.

• • •

Brodien quit high school the year he turned 16.

"It didn't make my mother very happy," Marshall remembers. "In fact, she said that she was disappointed when I told her I wanted to work full time at the magic shop downtown."

He hadn't reported to his new position at the Treasure Chest for too many mornings before he received a piece of not-too-welcome mail. The return address was the Chicago Public Schools System. Marshall was officially informed that all high-school dropouts, even if they were gainfully employed, were required to attend a continuation school until they were 17 years old.

Marshall dutifully signed up at Logan Continuation School, where he was scheduled for a one-day-a-week class for a year. "By the second or third week, I hated it. Going to school only one day a week didn't seem like it was worth the effort." His feeling of futility was something he had expressed to his teacher from day one.

As it turned out, his instructor, Mr. Stanley Murphy, liked magic. And he appreciated it when Marshall arrived early to show him new tricks that had come into the store. It wasn't long before Mr. Murphy asked Marshall if he would put on a magic show for the rest of the students at Logan. Since Mr. Murphy had five different groups of students weekly, it meant Marshall would have to be at the school all week. This was definitely a farfetched request from Murphy, knowing that Marshall didn't even like being there for his one day of class.

Brodien made a counter proposal. He would put on an elaborate full-hour magic show for all five groups for five days in a row — only if he didn't have to show up for classes at Logan for the rest of the year. When Marshall made the nervy suggestion that Murphy simply sign-in for him on the weekly records, the teacher laughed ... at first.

"But as I told him about my position with this growing company in a new downtown location, and how I was doing exactly what I wanted to do with my life — which was to go into the magic business — and how *he* might be the one holding me back, I was able to persuade him to do it. Mr. Murphy finally said, 'Okay, do the five shows and go your way, but you can't tell anybody.'"

On December 4, 1950, Marshall received a letter signed by Stanley F. Murphy, Assistant Director of the Logan Continuation School: "On behalf of the students and faculty, thank you for the splendid performances staged at our school. Everyone was entertained. We predict that you will go places in the not too distant future. You are approaching success very fast. Again, glad to have you for the repeat performances."

As Christmas approached, bells were ringing on the cash registers at the Treasure Chest. Brodien had become the number one demonstrator as far as sales. He did all the training, stocked the shelves, and was even creating the window displays with the magic products. In addition, he was picking up lots of holiday shows, perhaps because he was the only teenage magician in the Windy City who could boast of having his own printed playbills and posters.

Riverview Park

A good-natured guy by the name of Don Lieberman came into the Treasure Chest on the Fourth of July of 1951. The locals who frequented the magic counter knew Don by his nickname of "Mickey the Mook," a chain smoker and perpetually unemployed trickster. "He said he was opening at Riverview Park," Brodien recalls, "working as the magician in the sideshow. He told me, 'Come out and see me anytime. Just ask for me at the ticket box. I'll get you in.'" On his next day off, Marshall hopped a trolley to Riverview.

The 72-acre amusement park, which opened in 1904 and flourished on Chicago's northwest side through both World Wars, was located at 3300 Western Avenue, on the bank of the Chicago River. Riverview Park enjoyed the reputation of being the world's largest amusement park, and its noisy two-mile midway was filled with over 100 rides, including six roller coasters. Screams of the thrill-seekers often drowned out the recorded brass-band music that was piped into the loudspeakers that lined the walkways. The air was always filled with the mouthwatering smells of freshly popped popcorn and sweet swirling cotton candy, and hot dogs grilling and French fries frying. There was a myriad of carnival games, dark rides, fun houses and mazes, shooting galleries and arcades, souvenirs and concessions, more rides and games, and even two kiddie-lands. Riverview was a sensory overload for all ages. The park's billboard and radio-advertising slogan, "Laugh your troubles away at Riverview," had been heeded by generations of Chicagoans for almost a half-century.

Marshall headed straight for the Palace of Wonders, the Congress of Oddities, the sideshow, or, as it was referred to by anyone who'd spent a day at Riverview, the freak show. Bright yellow, vivid green, and traffic-stopping red canvas banners with artwork of the performers — all emblazoned with the

3. Riverview Park

exclamations "ALIVE!" and "STRANGE" and "IN PERSON!" — surrounded the platform in front of the building. A gaudy representation of a magician wearing a tailcoat was painted on the billboard-sized banner behind the stage. Other bally panels featured cartoonish artwork of the sideshow's cast of curiosities — the World's Fattest Man, the Four-Legged Girl, the Armless Wonder, Monkey Girl, and Electro the Human Dynamo.

"I went up to the ticket seller and told her I was there to see the magician," Marshall says. "She told me she didn't know anything about a magician in the show, but I might want to ask Dick Best, the man who was in charge." She pointed toward a heavy-set gentleman who, frowning at the noonday sun, was walking out the exit door of the building.

"Mr. Best, I'm looking for a guy named Don Lieberman, some people call him 'Mickey the Mook.' Does he still work here?"

"No," Best said. "That so-called magician disappeared on me. He didn't show up for work the other day, his stuff is gone, and we haven't seen him since."

Seizing what seemed like an opportunity, Marshall asked, "Well, does that mean you need a magician? A replacement?"

Dick Best squinted and sized up the clean-cut, not-quite-17-year-old kid, and said, "I don't know. You're awful young-looking for a magician." As they stepped into the shade of the nearby building, Best elaborated on the facts of life of working a ten-in-one show — an attraction where patrons see all ten acts for the price of a single admission. Soon to be deemed politically incorrect, the ten-in-one was already notorious as being "the beginning of the end" for retired circus and show-biz anomalies.

With a definite tone of discouragement in his voice, Best said, "The sideshow's a real grind. There are 20 shows a day, starting at noon, and you don't even think about going home till almost midnight. Not much of a way for a teenager to spend the summer."

Unfazed, Marshall replied, "I know I could do a good job for you." He waited a beat, and said, "I tell you what. I'll work a week for nothing. Just let me show you what I can do."

Best grinned and said, "I don't want you to work for nothing, but I will give you a chance to show me your stuff in front of an audience. Come back tomorrow with your props."

Marshall mounted the stage the next day with a six-minute act of mostly sucker tricks, the Egg Bag, Chinese Sticks, and Hippity-Hop Rabbits. He had the crowd yelling and screaming, and more important, laughing. "Dick Best liked my personality, the way I worked with the people. He shook my hand and said, 'I've put you on the payroll; you're here to stay.'"

Later that afternoon, Brodien stopped by the Treasure Chest to tell Bobby

Baer about the successful audition at Riverview Park. Bobby was happy that Marshall would be spending the rest of the summer working before crowds of living, breathing, ticket-buying customers. It was the only way to hone an act, get some chops. Bobby assured Marshall that when the amusement park closed in September, he'd still have his job at the Treasure Chest.

From the time he was taken under wing at the store on Wabash Avenue, Marshall always considered Bobby to be a father figure. He was more than a first employer; he was a mentor. Countless would be the times that Bobby encouraged Marshall to take any and every job that furthered his performing career.

And it wouldn't be long before Baer would give young Marshall his first opportunity to pitch magic on television — an endeavor that would have far-reaching implications.

• • •

Once the slick-haired, ruddy-complexioned, silver-tongued talker outside the Palace of Wonders had convinced the tip (the crowd he'd accumulated) that the show inside was worth a quarter of a dollar, tickets were hawked with great haste. Spectators pressed into "the odditorium" (as it was called by one of the talkers), where there was no air conditioning, no seating. Ten four-foot-high platform stages lined the two longest walls of the steel-frame, concrete-floored building. The audience stood to watch each performer — gawking and politely applauding their strange and bizarre bits of show business — before being herded toward the next stage.

Brodien's magic spot provided some lighter than usual moments for the ten-in-one attraction, a few more laughs than most Riverview Park patrons expected from the freak show. Marshall says, "Because I auditioned with comedy magic material and Best liked it, and because we had mostly young people coming to see the show, I kept all of my tricks interactive." He even added a comedy finale to his six-minute act. The Goofus Plant was an exotic artificial potted plant that refused to grow, even though it was profusely watered throughout the act. When Marshall's allotted time was about up, and just as he was about to direct the audience to the next stage, the prop pot went berserk. "Flowers bloomed and coiled-up snakes sprang into the front row. The people loved the surprise."

From time to time, the sideshow talker worked inside and featured the Blade Box, a carnival illusion that was used in conjunction with the presentation of Serpentina the Snake Girl. The pseudo-reptilian persona would walk on stage wearing a silk robe and slither into a coffin-like cabinet, as a talker explained, "This remarkable lady has the ability to shape her body and skin

Marshall's stage in the ten-in-one show at Riverview Park, where he featured the alarming and amusing Goofus Plant. *Marshall Brodien Collection*

into that of a snake." Over a dozen blades were plunged through the box. The knife-like edges that protruded from the bottom of the box were less than two inches apart. It looked utterly impossible that Serpentina could have snaked herself between the blades.

The talker invited "those who desire to look into the box and see the strange and unusual position of the girl" to step up onto the platform. Advising that this viewing privilege would cost an additional 25¢, he reached between the blades and removed Serpentina's silk garment and tossed it aside. "Not to be vulgar," he said, "but you cannot see through the material." He urged those interested to move quickly and have their quarters ready. "We make no apologies, this is the way the girl makes her living." Those who paid a quarter to walk by and see how Serpentina was twisted betwixt the blades also discovered that she had been wearing a swimsuit beneath her robe.

As the last week of the season approached, Dick Best asked Brodien if he would be interested in becoming a talker next year. "You're young, you have a good sense of humor, and you look honest," he said. "Having you out front next year will give the joint a facelift. And, of course, you know you can make more money as a talker."

Marshall had listened to the sideshow talkers for the last month and already knew the ballyhoo by heart. So, a few days before the park closed down, when Dick asked him to go out front and give it a try, he was more than ready.

"I performed the Pillory Escape, an illusion that talkers used to draw a crowd." An attractive girl was tied to a wooden post with different lengths of rope. As the ropes were knotted it was explained that the girl was so secure it was impossible for her to escape. "Yet, I told the people, 'When I give the command she will mysteriously walk away from the post, just as if she was never tied to it. And, if the girl fails to escape from the cross in three seconds from the time I say go, I will give everyone a free ticket to the show.'" Marshall then went into the pitch for the show, describing the strange, odd, and unusual freaks of nature that were alive and inside the Palace of Wonders. "And it only costs a quarter. That's right, the price of a lousy hot dog. You know you can't get a good hot dog today for a quarter. If you do, it's a lousy one. Here you get to see all the acts, there's no wait, no delays, for only 25¢. One act follows right after the other. It's a continuous show. Twenty-five cents takes you all the way through. And the ticket box is right over there...." Without breaking the pace of his pitch, Marshall slowly counted, "One, two, three...." The knotted and tangled rope fell to the stage floor, and the girl walked toward the sideshow entrance. "There she goes!" he uttered. "The first act is about to go onstage. There goes the music! Get your tickets right over there. The show is about to begin!"

Marshall's ballyhoo had drawn a crowd of 100 or more people and they were lined up to buy tickets. When he stepped down from the stage and wiped his brow, Dick Best shook his hand and said, "You're a natural! Next season, you work out front."

• • •

When Marshall showed up at Riverview Park in late April of 1952 to begin his second season, he didn't take the trolley to work. He'd saved up enough money, working all winter at the Treasure Chest, to buy a car.

"Raymond John, a friend who lived in the neighborhood, called me and said that he had a 1941 Dodge he wanted to sell. I remember paying $150 for the ten-year-old car, but it ran beautifully." Marshall also sported a brand-new (for him) tuxedo, a used one he bought for $15 from his magician friend, De Yip Loo. Another friend, Don Theobald, who'd worked behind the counter at the Treasure Chest, replaced Marshall as the ten-in-one show's magician.

"As the new talker, I'd alternate with another spieler on the stage outside the sideshow building, working a half hour on, and a half hour off. I got a raise, was now making $100 a week, and I continued to do lots of magic out front, adding the Guillotine to stop traffic."

Another crowd builder was the Reversible Girl. Pointing to a long-haired shapely lady standing with her back to the audience, Marshall would solemnly warn the crowd, "Watch the Reversible Girl." Then he'd go into his spiel, telling of the incredible cast of characters in the sideshow, punctuating the pitch with the command, "Watch the Reversible Girl..." He would wax more

Marshall's second and third seasons at Riverview Park found him working outside as the talker for the freak show. *Marshall Brodien Collection*

and wane of the wonders inside. "Watch the Reversible Girl…" Once you stopped, looked, and listened to Brodien's hypnotic pitch, you were hooked. And when he said, "Watch the Reversible Girl" for the fourteenth time — and the lady, without ever showing her face, simply walked through the entrance to the sideshow — you found yourself following, reaching into your pocket or purse for that quarter. Skip that ice-cream cone, bag of roasted peanuts, and another ride on the roller coaster. The 25¢ spent at the sideshow was a one-way ticket to a realm beyond reality…

"You'll see Priscilla the Monkey Girl with long black shaggy hair just like a monkey … two rows of teeth in the upper jaw like the anthropoid ape … pouches in the sides of her mouth where she can store food for days at a time if necessary.

"She's married to Emmett the Alligator-skinned Man … covered from the top of his head to the toes of his feet with rough, tough corrugated hide laid out in checks and squares like that of a crocodile … his skin is so rough and tough you couldn't penetrate it with the sharpest knife … sheds his skin twice a year like the crocodile … on a hot day he keeps his body moist in cold water.

"You'll see Amarico, the Anatomical Wonder … the man with the disappearing stomach … watch him make his stomach disappear so completely that he'll place a football in the cavity, button up his shirt … you can't tell the football is there. He'll stretch his skin 14 inches away from his body, let it snap back like an elastic rubber band… He'll twist and turn his body into more shapes than a pretzel and at times he will amaze you.

"You'll see Tony Marino, the man who swallows swords, sabers, key-hole saws, wrecking bars, stove pokers, bayonets, and lighted neon tubes. You'll see the Three-Legged Man with 13 toes … watch him kick a football with his third leg.

"You'll see the World's Fattest Man, Tiny Carter … weighs 679 pounds … it takes seven girls to hug him and a box car to lug him. Girls, if you're looking for a husband, there's a big fat chance for you right here … he'll keep you shady in the summer and warm in the winter. Cecil B. DeMille picked him for the movie *The Greatest Show on Earth*, not because he's the fattest man on earth, he's the only fat man who entertains you … he sings like a mocking bird and when you see him do the Charleston, all 679 pounds, if you don't laugh there's something wrong with your laughing apparatus … you're dead … you better go see your undertaker!

"You'll see Jackie Hoyt Jenkins, the Armless Wonder, a boy born to go through life with no sight of arms or hands … he does everything with his feet … operates a typewriter, paints with oil colors, threads a needle and sews, shuffles and deals a deck of playing cards, plays musical instruments, and operates carpenter's tools. But when you see him take a cigarette paper with one foot, a sack of tobacco in the other, and roll a perfect cigarette with his feet, if your hands don't burn with applause there's something radically wrong. The average man can't roll a cigarette with two hands ... here's a boy who does it with his feet.

"You'll see Betty Lou Williams, the world's only living double-bodied, four-legged girl.... born to go through life with the body of her twin sister growing from the pit of her stomach. When she walks out on the platform, as close to you as you are to me, prepare for the shock of your lifetime.

"You'll see Grace McDaniels, the mule-faced woman, with the head, face, features, and characteristics of a gigantic Georgia mule. When she removes the heavy black veil — not to be vulgar, but because you can't see through the material — and you see in the flesh not something stuffed, mummified, made of wax, or made up for the occasion to fool you, but created by the hand of God, born of a human mother the same as you or I ... a sight you'll go away talking about for the longest day you live ... something your mother's never seen.

"You'll see Electro the Human Dynamo ... struck by lightning at the age of five ... could not speak or hear for three years ... doctors and scientists examined this girl and claimed her body is immune to electricity. You'll watch her light up neon tubes, shoot sparks from her hands, and light torches at her fingertips. She could light up this entire auditorium if she wanted to."

Oftentimes, as Marshall wound down his bally and went into the ticket pitch explaining that "a ticket only costs a quarter, the price of a lousy hot dog," a shill (someone working with the show) would push their way up to the booth, fake the purchase of a ticket, then rush inside. It was a sure bet that the rest of the folks would follow. After all, the talker was warning, "Hurry, hurry, because there's only room for a few more. The show's about to begin. Hurry, because there's always the chance it could be standing room only at the Palace of Wonders."

And so went the seductive spiel to sell tickets. By summer's end, young Mr. Brodien had delivered his syncopated sideshow come-on close to 2,000 times. Yet, he was always ready to "dance onstage" one more time. That was a phrase used when it was time for a ten-in-oner to mount the platform and do their thing. They used to shout, "Be back in a few minutes — I gotta go dance onstage."

• • •

Labor Day weekend was a busy time of the year for Riverview Park. The crowds that showed up were often bigger than the throngs that turned out

Brodien with sideshow operator Dick Best, when his ten-in-one freak show toured with the Canadian National Exposition in 1952. *Marshall Brodien Collection*

for the Fourth of July. The park would be closing down for the season and, for the tens of thousands of Chicagoland kids who had to go back to school, it was the final fling of summer. For Marshall, it meant a welcome return to his job of demonstrating and selling tricks at the Treasure Chest.

At the same time, September signaled the start of the fair and carnival season for the cast of Dick Best's freak show. They would play under canvas for another dozen or so weeks, giving the performers some bonus time before heading south for the winter, usually to Georgia or Florida. Since Brodien had done such an admirable job all summer as the sideshow talker, Dick asked him if he'd like to work the first leg of the fall tour.

Marshall asked Bobby Baer if it'd be okay to report to the magic shop a month late. Bobby graciously said, "Sure, go make a few extra bucks. You'll have fun going on the road for the first time. But just make sure you're back by Halloween." In the jokes, gags, and magic trick business, Halloween is the retail season that rivals Christmas.

"Dick asked me to be the talker when the sideshow played the Canadian National Exposition in Toronto, Ottawa, and Quebec. Since it was basically the same acts I had worked with all summer, and I knew all the spiels and what to say to get audiences into the tent, it sounded like the job was going to be a piece of cake. That was until I got there. All of the people walking up and down the midway only understood and spoke French. And I didn't do either."

But that did not hinder Brodien from giving the sideshow the biggest and best ballyhoo its owner had ever heard or seen.

"With magic there are few language barriers," Marshall maintains. "The magic and illusions that I performed out front were universal. I stopped traffic and built the tip." And Monsieur Brodien had picked up enough fractured French to lure the crowds inside the tent: *"Écrivez cette manière pour la grande exposition, un congrès collossal des merveilles. C'est la plus grande exposition anormale sur terre. Un billet est seulement vingt-cinq cents. Hâte, hâte. Écrivez cette manière pour la grande exposition...."*

Granted, Marshall was not standing atop a dais promoting a cultural attraction such as the symphony or the ballet at the Canadian National Exposition. But who would ever have believed that an 18-year-old high school dropout could bring such savoir-faire to a ten-in-one freak show?

• • •

Upon returning from his Canadian sideshow ventures, Marshall discovered that the magic business at the Treasure Chest was booming. Bobby Baer had taken over the upstairs space occupied by Abbott's Magic Company of Colon, Michigan and had created a new "store within the store," calling it the Chicago Magic Center Pro Shop. Abbott's was closing down its retail branches across the United States, and Baer made a deal to continue as an exclusive distributor of Abbott-made props and tricks. In addition, the shelves were stocked with effects from such prestigious magic manufacturers as Merv Taylor, Petrie & Lewis, Silk King Studios, and Golden Gate Magic.

Whenever professionals or serious amateurs entered the Treasure Chest and needed to know of things beyond Stripper Decks, Thumb Tips, or plastic Ball Vases, they were escorted upstairs to the Pro Shop. Marshall and Tom Rainey were the pros in charge. A four-foot high signboard with changeable letters always listed the magical effects of the week. And the dynamic duo was always ready to demonstrate any one of them at the drop of a top hat.

Also, Theo Bamberg, the crafty Dutch magician who had traveled the globe as Okito, had become a regular fixture at the Pro Shop. For over 12 years, he had been under the employ of respected Chicago dealer Joe Berg, crafting beautiful pieces of conjuring apparatus. But now that Berg had relocated to Hollywood, Okito made the Pro Shop of the Treasure Chest his headquarters. He was hired to demonstrate, however, magicians really came into the shop to hear his tales of the good old days of performing during the Golden Age of Magic.

Despite the half-century generation gap, Okito, well into his 70s, and Marshall, not yet 20, became the best of buddies. They palled around after they got off work and on weekends Okito accompanied Marshall when he went to work at Riverview Park. "He would spend time with me backstage at the sideshow. He knew a lot of the acts working there, including Lady Nina who, with her husband, did a horoscope reading show." Okito took great delight in introducing Marshall to his friends and acquaintances as "my long-lost illegitimate son."

Marshall found the elder Okito to be a great resource for learning about magic's myriad mysteries, yet it was only a matter of time before Marshall would come up with an illusion that would completely mystify the grand master.

First Pitch on the Tube

By early 1953, black-and-white television sets were in 4.5 million households across America, double the number from the previous year. Programs like *Dragnet*, *I Love Lucy*, and *The Ed Sullivan Show* were no longer dependent on local and regional syndication and were realizing commercial sponsorships through the major networks.

While Treasure Chest owner Bobby Baer wasn't too keen on what the Madison Avenue ad agencies were doing on network television, he did see a potential for selling his wares on local stations. He asked Marshall if he would help him put together a commercial — a spot peddling something that would cause customer awareness of his magical emporium on West Randolph Street. They chose the venerable Cups and Balls, the classic effect that involves the vanishing, reappearance, and transposing of small balls from under three cups.

After watching Marshall's stock performance of the Cups and Balls, the Rocklin Irving & Associates ad agency scripted a three-minute commercial. Arrangements were made to shoot the 16mm black-and-white spot at WGN's studio 6A on the morning of February 28. The routine was so well rehearsed it turned out to be a one-take shoot. After all, Brodien had been demonstrating the trick over the counter every day for the past two years.

"*Hello, folks. I'm known as Marshall the Magician, and I represent Chicago's Magic Center at 19 West Randolph Street, America's largest magic and novelty company, right across the street from the Oriental Theatre. Now, if you will give me your undivided attention, I'll show you the most baffling trick in America today ... the Cups and Balls. You take the one, two, three solid plastic cups, and one, two, three cotton balls. The object of the trick is to make the balls penetrate the solid cups....*"

After two minutes of razzle-dazzle demo, Marshall glided into the part of the pitch where ordering the trick seemed like the only logical thing to do: "There is positively no sleight of hand required to do this trick. It comes in a beautifully decorated box complete with full instructions, telling you exactly how this trick is done! Whether you're six or sixty, you can do this trick! And when you go to a party and you can't sing or dance or tell funny stories, do a little magic! The Cups and Balls trick sells for only $1, and you may order by mail right now from the Chicago Magic Center, 19 West Randolph Street, Chicago 1, Illinois. Enclose your name and address and $1 for each set you want. That's the Chicago Magic Center, 19 West Randolph Street, Chicago 1, Illinois. Or if you're going downtown today or tomorrow, come into America's largest magic and novelty store, the Chicago Magic Center, located in the Treasure Chest at 19 West Randolph ... directly across from the Oriental Theatre. We are open seven days a week, from 9:30 in the morning till midnight. And a professional magician is always present to help you!"

The Rocklin Irving agency scheduled the spot to run for a week — mornings, afternoons, and during the late-night movies on WGN-TV. Envelopes containing a dollar bill — sometimes four quarters taped to a sheet of paper with the return address — poured into the Treasure Chest. Baer and Brodien were more than busy filling the mail orders. More overwhelming was the number of people who popped into the Treasure Chest to pick up the trick. Many wanted to stop their cars at the curb, run in and grab one before heading home to the suburbs. Since there was a no-parking, no-standing zone in front of the store, a traffic cop had to be dispatched to the scene to control traffic. He would direct customers to a parking lot a block away, where one-hour parking was available for $1. And more often than not, the friendly attendant offered parkers a chance to participate in a punch card game. For a quarter, you could play the cardboard pick-a-number game, and if the odds were with you, win back the buck, or perhaps several more, that you paid for parking.

Less than a month after the Cups and Balls commercial aired, a representative from the ad agency called the shop, asking for Marshall. They wanted to hire him to do another TV spot, this time for an upholstery company.

More than happy to do the job, Marshall reported to WGN's studios, wearing a sharp three-piece suit, and within 30 minutes had whipped out another three-minute spot. *"Hello, I'm Marshall Brodien, here to tell you how Lincoln Upholstery will re-upholster your sofa, no matter what the size, and a matching chair for only $39.95.... There are thousands of materials and fabrics to choose from, and there is free pick-up and delivery within 50 miles of Chicago.... All you have to do is call Randolph 6–8600. That's RA6–8600. Plus if you call this number immediately and are among the first 300 to place your order, you will receive from Lincoln Upholstery this $29.95 indirect-television light table,* *with automatic cigarette lighter and flip-flop ashtrays, as a free gift.... Go to your phone right now and call Lincoln Upholstery at Randolph 6-8600. That's R— A—six—eight—six hundred."*

After Lincoln Upholstery, Marshall did two more commercials for Colefinder Lincoln-Mercury, one with him levitating a girl in the middle of the auto dealer's showroom. Peddling products via the tube was fun and easy money for Marshall. But spring had sprung, and it was time to return to Riverview Park for another season of pitching the freaks.

Odd Fellows and a Tall Tale

Brodien worked as the outside talker on Dick Best's freak show at Riverview for one more season. He enjoyed the association with the peculiar performers, especially when they shared their sideshow savy. "Sword-swallower Tony Marino and fire-eater Ogee O'Saturday, 'The White Hindu,' gave me a show business lesson that I never forgot. They told me, 'Anything you see someone else do, you can learn to do it ... but only if you make your mind up to do it.' Well, that year, I had made up my mind to learn from these experts how to eat fire and swallow swords."

Tony Marino was a veteran circus and carnival performer, fire eater, knife thrower, and sword swallower, who had been working with the Riverview Park sideshow for a season. He made Marshall a confidant and showed him the basics of sword swallowing. Although fakirs in India, China, and the Middle East had been sticking blades and daggers down their throats for centuries, it wasn't until the 1893 Chicago World's Fair and a Mongolian midway marvel by the name of Genghis Shama that sword swallowing became a staple of the American sideshow.

Ogee O'Saturday told Marshall that the only secret to fire eating was to believe the flames were not hot, and if he would practice with that in mind he would learn how.

"Ogee insisted on being introduced onstage as The White Hindu," Marshall remembers, "even though in casual conversations backstage he was always Ogee. His performance out on the bally platform was extremely strong. He would take a two-inch-wide strip of steel and put a blowtorch to it. A crowd always gathered as I explained, 'The White Hindu is about to lick this strip of red hot metal, just like you or I would lick a lollipop. And before he does that, he will stick the nozzle of that blazing blowtorch into his mouth.'"

As the blazing blue flame of the blowtorch turned the steel from red to white hot — Marshall would turn away, cup the microphone close to his mouth, and solemnly say, "Exactly five men have killed themselves trying to accomplish this feat.... Three years ago, when we were down in Sarasota, Florida, a man came up on the platform and said that he could do it. He tried, but he nearly died.... Ladies and gentlemen, direct your undivided attention to The White Hindu, as he puts that blowtorch into his mouth, just like you or I would drink a hot cup of coffee."

When Ogee opened his mouth and stuck the fiery nozzle inside, there

By age 17, sword swallowing and fire eating had become part of Brodien's ever-expanding repertoire. *Marshall Brodien Collection.*

was a tremendous *swoosh* sound, as the flames flared out almost a yard on each side of his face. Then, when Ogee touched the near-molten metal to his tongue, the crowd heard a sizzle. "Even though his tongue had become callused and cauterized from doing this over and over, year after year, you could still hear and smell flesh burning and see smoke every time he did it."

When it was the White Hindu's turn to take to the ten-in-one stage, he passed flames from hand to hand and extinguished blazing torches that were lowered into his mouth. For his finale, he would lean over the edge of the stage and, with a burst of flame from his mouth, light a cigarette that was held between a spectator's lips.

Marshall not only learned Ogee's feats of fire manipulation, but also turned them into wondrous pieces of performance magic, something other magicians took note of. When the Society of American Magicians held their national convention in the Windy City that June, they were quick to book Brodien as a performer. The opening night gala called *Carnival of Illusions* was staged in the grand ballroom of the Sherman Hotel, and Marshall was a natural as the master of ceremonies. He also did his fire eating and sword swallowing in an hour-and-a-half production that headlined Clarke "The Senator" Crandall, "Silent Sam" Berman, and the world-famous Jack Gwynne, who performed such sideshow illusions as the Girl Without a Body and the Three-Legged Lady. Brodien even agreed — as part of his $50 contract — to bring along an armful of sideshow bally panels he borrowed from Dick Best, which gave the hotel ballroom a carnival atmosphere.

• • •

When Riverview closed for the season in 1954, Marshall made the decision not to return to the magic counter at the Treasure Chest. He had accepted an offer to work full-time doing close-up magic at a nightclub in Cicero. But first, he had to fulfill an obligation he'd made to Dick Best. He'd promised to work as the sideshow talker for a week at the Pennsylvania State Fair.

The day before opening day, Brodien rode to Allentown with Dick and his wife. After finding a hotel room and unpacking his suitcase, he walked over to the fairground site to watch the crew laying out the sideshow tent. He was surprised when he looked up and spotted his friend Ted Evans. Before shaking hands, Marshall went straight into his ballyhoo for the world's tallest man: *"Once inside the tent, you will meet Ted Evans, The English Giant ... the man who was a star in Cecil B. DeMille's motion picture,* The Greatest Show on Earth. *He's ten-feet, four-inches tall, wears a size-24 shoe, and it takes ten yards of fabric to make a suit for this remarkable man."*

Dick had not told Marshall that the ultra-tall British gentleman, with whom he'd worked with during his first season at Riverview, was joining the show. Since the fair wasn't scheduled to open until noon the next day, Ted asked if Marshall wanted to catch a movie at a nearby drive-in theater. Brodien said sure, never thinking about what kind of vehicle a ten-foot-tall man might drive. "Boy, was I surprised, when we walked across the parking lot to his car. He was driving a 1948 Packard sedan that had the front seat completely removed. We had to enter through the back doors. As we took off, I was sitting beside him in the back seat. I couldn't even start to reach the dashboard, but Ted's hands were way up there, shifting gears and steering the automobile."

When Ted drove up to the admissions booth at the drive-in, the attendant was somewhat bemused. The left-front driver's window remained securely rolled up, while a man sitting in the back seat handed her the money for the tickets.

"It was sort of chilly that night and about halfway through the movie, the windshields started to fog up. I told Ted that I'd go find something to clean the windows. But he said, 'Stay where you are. I'll get it with this rag.' He crawled out, and without taking a step from where he stood beside his open door, wiped the windshield dry, as well as the windows on all sides of the car." The silhouette of the English Giant towering over the Packard sedan must have been a bizarre sight for moviegoers parked in the rows behind them. Three or four cars flashed on their headlights. Evans simply grinned and gave a big show-biz wave, which resulted in some applause, laughter, and a cacophony of good-natured horn tooting.

The remainder of the week with the sideshow in Allentown would become the last time Brodien worked with a freak show. These attractions were starting to be considered exploitative and politically incorrect. However, Marshall contends that the freak show was an honest form of entertainment. It is true that most of its performers were simply paid to be gawked at, shamed in public, and often ridiculed. But in that cruel world outside the freak show, their lives would have been the same and they wouldn't have received a penny for their injustices.

"Freak shows gave otherwise hopeless human beings a chance to work and be productive," Marshall says. "These people were happy and enjoyed what they did; they traveled, met people, and made a decent living." For example, Marshall tells of how Betty Lou Williams, the Four-Legged Girl, who came from a poor family in Georgia, changed her destiny once she made the decision to become a sideshow freak. Unable for years to get a job in the real world, she started making good money the very day she entered the carnival world. Over the years, she saved enough to buy her destitute parents a house they could otherwise never have afforded, and she put her sister and two brothers through college.

6

Cicero, the Mob, and Beyond

"From the time I turned 19," Marshall says, "I was making regular trips to the Magic Lounge on Cermak Road, in Cicero. I would go there after I got off work at the Treasure Chest. Sometimes I'd tag along with the other magicians who gathered at the magic counter near closing time. Since I was usually with an older crowd, the people at the lounge rarely questioned that I was underage. They believed my claim that I had just turned 21."

The reason for Marshall's frequent visits to the neighboring Mafia-run suburb of Cicero wasn't because of its free-flowing booze, the striptease joints with women of negotiable affections, or the ubiquitous slot machines and card and dice games. It was to see Senator Crandall.

Clarke "The Senator" Crandall, a recalcitrant, bespectacled gentleman with an enormous handlebar mustache and a knack for mixing drinks with sardonic humor and devious deceptions, was the house magician at the Magic Lounge. The 100-seat saloon was established in 1946 by legendary Chicago bar-magician Johnny Paul. However, when piano-playing George Banning, a former police chief of a nearby suburb, bought the place in 1953, Crandall became the Magic Lounge's main man of mystery and mirth. Johnny Paul moved around the corner to a snazzy bowling alley with a show-bar, where he continued his brand of trickery and tomfoolery until 1959, when the mob set him up as the resident magician at the Showboat in Las Vegas.

There was a stage over the back bar of the Magic Lounge, and once or twice a night, Senator Crandall would give the band a long break and perform stand-up comedy magic. But his forte was close-up magic, minor miracles that were executed right under the noses of patrons sitting at the tables or at the bar. Jay Marshall, a debonair, globetrotting wizard who four decades

Clarke Crandall, better known as "The Senator," shared the spotlight with Brodien at the Magic Lounge. *Marshall Brodien Collection*

later would be appointed the Dean of the Society of American Magicians, says of Crandall, "Along with his deft sleight of hand, The Senator mumbled such a line of nonsense, non sequiturs, sheer truth, and gross exaggeration that people were known to forget the trick he was doing because they were guffawing at his humor."

Marshall met Senator Crandall earlier in 1954, when they worked

Cicero's Magic Lounge, where Marshall worked nightly for two years, until the mob turned the nightclub into a strip joint. *Marshall Brodien Collection*

together on a show for a Society of American Magicians convention in Chicago. And the more Marshall hung around the Magic Lounge, the more The Senator took a liking to him. It wasn't long before the old-fartish cranky conjuror and the young-pup sideshow talker were sharing secrets.

One of the bar tricks that Marshall was quick to learn was dice stack-

6. Cicero, the Mob, and Beyond

Stand-up comedy magic behind the bar at the Magic Lounge. *Marshall Brodien Collection*

ing. The magician tosses four ordinary dice onto the bar and asks a customer to name any number they see on the top of any one of the spotted cubes. Inverting a leather dice cup, he then proceeds to sweep up the dice, one by one, with the mouth of the upside-down cup. When the cup glides to a stop on the bar top and it's lifted, all four dice are precariously balanced one atop the other. On the face of the top die, staring at the perplexed patron, is the very number of spots chosen.

Late that summer, when Crandall received an invitation to go to London for some television work in conjunction with the celebration of the Golden Jubilee of the British Magical Society, he voted for Brodien to be his fill-in. "I can't stand this kid," Crandall said. "It's because he's a boy wonder. Somebody ought to think about hiring him."

"I was pretty excited about the possibility of working somewhere other than Riverview Park or the Treasure Chest," Marshall says. "George Banning asked me to get behind the bar and do a few tricks, an audition of sorts. He liked what I did. The people were laughing, shouting, 'Show us another one,' and they were ordering more rounds of drinks." Right there on the spot, Banning promised Brodien three months of work while Crandall went off to Great Britain.

• • •

Vice thrived with official indulgence in Cicero throughout the 1950s. Under blind eyes of the local police, several Cook County sheriffs, and selected politicians, it was the mob, or "The Outfit" as they preferred to be called, that controlled the town's rackets. Al Capone and his gangsters may have turned to legends, but the same saloons, strip shows, corrupt games, and much more were still there and reigned over by mob bosses, namely Sam Giancana and Joey Aiuppa.

"Across the street from the Magic Lounge was the Towne Hotel," Marshall remembers. "It was Capone's old headquarters, but became the home of the Turf Club, a swinging nightclub. Once inside, if you wanted to gamble, all you had to do was go through a side door and at the end of a long hallway was a huge casino with dice and card games of every sort." Another Cicero gambling establishment was the Rainbow Lounge, run by Al Capone's brother. Just about every bar on the streets of Cicero had slot machines, and most of them had dice games.

Also opposite the Magic Lounge was The 4811, a far-beyond-burlesque striptease club where the girls danced totally nude, then sat between shows and drank with the customers. Then one night, the Feds raided the joint, shutting it down for what many people thought was for good. But three nights later, the mob reopened the doors to the club. It was in the same exact location, but with the new name of The 4813.

Except for revenues from the slot machines that were regularly moved in and out of the backroom by the mob, George Banning's Magic Lounge made most of its money dispensing booze with music and magic. Every night, singing-bartender Jumping Joe Pistone and accordionist Manny Quartucci joined Banning at the piano, and they kept the joint jiving till near dawn. The witty wizardry of Senator Crandall and Marshall at the Magic Lounge provided a certain comic relief from the various vices of sinful Cicero. Prominent members of the mob, including Joey Aiuppa, Frank "The Immune" Diamond, and Jackie "The Lackey" Cerone frequented the lounge because it was a genuinely fun place. But early on, Marshall learned that Mafia types could be a tough crowd.

"One slow night, not too long after Crandall had taken off for England," Marshall remembers, "George Banning sent me over to do a trick for these three serious-looking men sitting at the end of the bar. I was prepared to do the Vanishing Birdcage, but decided I'd do it with a little different presentation for these guys."

Holding the empty wire cage between his hands, Marshall approached the men. He singled out one of them—a short, round-faced man who wore a black suit, gray shirt and a black tie, and a black fedora with a gray band. He would later be introduced as "Gumpy." Brodien told Gumpy, "Tap the little birdcage three times and a bird will appear."

"Well, this guy rapped the cage three times, waited a couple of seconds, looked up at me and said, 'There's no friggin' boid in dere.'"

Marshall asked him to try again. Gumpy slapped the side of the cage three more times. Nothing happened. "Hey! There's still no boid in your cage."

"Here, just hold it," Marshall said. When Gumpy reached for the birdcage, it disappeared faster than a lightning bolt.

The three men were speechless. With mouths agape, they stared at Marshall's empty hands. Gumpy turned to his friends and asked, "Where's da friggin' boidcage?"

"The kid's a magician," one of them said. "It's magic."

"Yeah, it might be magic," the other said, "but Gump wants to know where the cage went to."

"I can't tell you," Marshall said. "It's a magic secret."

With that, Gumpy reached into his coat, slowly pulled out a large-caliber gun, clicked the hammer, and pointed it right between Brodien's eyes. "Like I wuz sayin' ... where's dat friggin' boidcage?"

"I made that birdcage come out of my sleeve faster than it ever went up there," Marshall now says with a grin. Getting out of a pickle, even with the mob, was easy ... once you knew the secret.

• • •

George Banning dismissed the disappearing-birdcage incident as "just a little Sicilian flare-up" and told Marshall, "Gump's a real wacko. You might want to stay clear of him, especially when he's had a drink." But that was easier said than done. Every time the pug-ugly gangster came into the lounge he'd have a drink or three.

"Hey, magish! Get over here. Show dis broad a trick." Gumpy was sitting at the bar next to a dynamite-looking blonde with a full balcony, and he was demanding a command performance from "my friend, the magish."

"I walked over to the bar where they were sitting," says Marshall. "I introduced myself to his date and started performing a routine with some sponge rabbits. Gumpy just turned and looked the other direction."

Some 30 seconds later, the lady was crying out, "How'd you do that? I don't believe it!" She swiveled around toward Gumpy, yanked on his coat sleeve, and asked, "How'd he do that? Tell me how he did it!"

"How you 'spect me to know? Huh? I'm not lookin' at what you're lookin' at." Gumpy then asked Marshall, "What's dis crazy broad talkin' about? Huh? I wuz lookin' over there, tryin' to talk to Carmie." Gumpy turned back to ask bartender Carmen Manno if he knew which horse won the ninth race at Sportman's Park. He told Marshall, "Magish, do another one for her. I tink she likes your tricks."

Marshall took out a pack of playing cards, asked the lady to choose one, remember what it was, then had her shuffle it back into the deck. Pointing out how high the ceiling of the lounge was, he hurled the pack of cards upward — an act that produced yet another scream of "How did you do that?" Stuck to the ceiling was the card she had selected. Again, she yelled at Gumpy, "Honey, please tell me how he does it." Without taking his eyes off the racing form he held in his hands, Gumpy said, "Magish, I tink it's time to leave us alone. Get da hell outta here."

"After that second experience with Gumpy," Marshall says, "every time I saw him coming in the front door of the club, I would head for the coffee shop across the street."

The Aloha Restaurant, a counter-and-booth hamburger joint where Marshall usually took his breaks, was distinctively different from most grab-a-bite-and-run restaurants. It had a doorman ... of sorts. Vinnie "The Hat" always stood just inside the front door. He didn't have a uniform and he never helped patrons find a seat; instead, he nodded to those customers who seemed to have business in the backroom. Vinnie was the lookout for the Aloha's gambling operation.

"Vinnie was very interested in magic and, whenever I came in for a coffee or a sandwich, he always wanted me to show him a trick or two. One time, I didn't have any props on me, so I asked him if he had a deck of cards. He rushed out to the backroom to get one."

Brodien told the doorman to break the seal on the brand-new pack of cards, remove them from the box, and give them a thorough shuffle. As Marshall took back the mixed-up deck and spread them from hand to hand, he commented, "There's something funny about these cards ... I'll show you what I mean. Just take out any one."

Vinnie took a card and before he could turn it over, Marshall said, "Seven of Diamonds." Vinnie stuck the Seven back in the deck and selected another card. And again, before he could peek at it, Marshall said, "That's the Five of Spades." Another one was picked. "The King of Diamonds." Vinnie threw the King on the table and reached for a card near the bottom of the deck. "Ace of Hearts," Marshall said.

6. Cicero, the Mob, and Beyond

"Jeeezus! How tha hell you doin' that?"

Marshall winked and said, "Marked cards." Actually, he had been forcing the cards on Vinnie, but thought he'd have some fun.

"Marked cards? What da hell?" Vinnie looked like Vesuvius about to errupt. "Holy shit! Marked cards! Somebody's cheatin' da friggin' house." He started for the backroom.

"I chased after him," Marshall says. "And stopped him just before he went through the door. I told him that I was just kidding. The cards weren't really marked. I was making him pick those cards. After he finally calmed down, I had to show him how the Classic Force worked." Each time the cards were spread and the spectator made what seemed like a free choice, it was in fact the magician who controlled the selection.

Although Marshall never reported to the Magic Lounge until after eight o'clock, one evening, because of the light traffic, he showed up in Cicero about an hour early. He decided to sit at the bar and have a cup of coffee with Carmie Manno.

"You don't have to worry about Gumpy giving you a hard time," Carmie said, as he brought the cream and sugar. "Last night, he was coming out of the 1000 Club in Chicago, when a car pulled up and he was shot."

Sensing it was something mob related, Marshall said, "Oh, really? I'm sort of sorry to hear that he might not be coming back for a while...."

"Trust me," Carmie said, "he's not coming back ... he was shot eight times."

• • •

In April of 1955, when Senator Crandall returned from England, the Magic Lounge threw a gala welcome-home party for him. Shaking hands with Brodien, The Senator quipped, "Don't worry, kid, I just came back to visit my material."

Marshall had already signed a summer-long contract to be the talker for a new daytime attraction at Riverview Park. However, George Banning was insistent that the "boy wonder" keep working nights at the club, sharing the spotlight with The Senator. If Marshall did as George desired, it meant that immediately after his six o'clock show at the amusement park, he would have to barrel through hectic Chicago traffic to get to the Magic Lounge by eight. But the ever-ambitious Mr. Brodien didn't care. He was young and eager to entertain. And, knowing the amount of money he'd be earning working the two jobs, he went out and bought a ritzy white Ford Fairlane convertible. The drive from Riverview to Cicero would be a breeze.

The show at Riverview came about because of Marshall's connection

Even a patron's dog at the Magic Lounge is amazed by Marshall's performance of the Cups and Balls. *Marshall Brodien Collection*

with Al Szasz, a professional wrestler who owned a performing chimpanzee, a boxing kangaroo, and a wrestling bear. "Al had been approached by Al Dobritch, the booking agent for the *Super Circus* TV show who wanted to put together a tent show called *Super Circus Animal Acts*," Marshall explains. "In addition to showcasing his talented animals, Szasz's wife, Ada Ash, a wild young lady who dyed her hair bright pink and hyped herself as the 'World's Strongest Woman,' was going to wrestle alligators. They wanted me to be the talker for the show and more or less *bribed* me into doing it by telling me that I could perform some illusions later on, when they took the show on the road."

The prospect of expanding his performing capabilities to include more big-scale tricks was motivation enough for Marshall to start building an illusion he always wanted to own — the Blade Box. "Basically, I took a pattern of the configuration of the Blade Box at Riverview Park — something I had traced on a large sheet of paper during my last season with the sideshow — and with the help of a girlfriend, I improved the design. I had her lie on her side on the plywood bottom panel and, using wood cutouts for the blades, figured out a more deceptive pattern for the slots where the metal blades pass through the box. They were much closer together."

After lugging sheets of plywood and building supplies up the three flights of stairs to the back porch of his house on North Avenue, Marshall began construction of his Blade Box. "My mother got all kinds of complaints from the neighbors over the non-stop sawing and hammering noises." A plumber's shop cut and threaded the lengths of one-inch-diameter steel pipe, which were flanged and attached to the box as legs. The end product was a bit cumbersome, because the pieces wouldn't come apart. "To this day, I can't remember how I got it down the back steps and over to a friend's warehouse, where it was painted."

While the Blade Box was being artistically painted with a colorful Chinese dragon bearing scales, claws, and fangs of fiery red, emerald green, and imperial gold, Marshall began construction of his second illusion — a death-defying Electric Chair. This illusion was an imposing device that allowed the magician to pass thousands of volts of electricity through a young lady's body, enabling her to illuminate light bulbs with her fingertips. She would be able to take the torches that Marshall used in his fire-eating act and set them aflame with the tip of her tongue. Once these two illusions were completed, Marshall would possess a pair of mysteries that would not only amaze audiences wherever he traveled, they would also totally baffle a couple of the best minds in magic, namely Okito and the great Jack Gwynne.

But for now, at least until Labor Day rolled around, his afternoons would be spent at Riverview Park, hyping the wonders of the *Super Circus Animal Acts* show, announcing the wrestling matches with a big brown bear, refereeing boxing bouts with a kangaroo named Pogo, and helping Ada Ash corral her alligator, a lackadaisical reptile that preferred sunning on the bank of the nearby Chicago River to the rigors of show business.

• • •

Out at the Magic Lounge that summer, Brodien was creating a sensation as "The Human Torch." He had added fire eating to his stand-up act and his behind-the-bar stunt of transforming himself into the "Human Cigarette Lighter"— performing the daredevil bits he'd learned from sideshow-worker Ogee O'Saturday — was garnering raves from the Windy City show-biz and night-life columnists. "Flame-dousing Brodien pleases patrons at Lounge," proclaimed a headline in the *Chicago Sun-Times*. "Magician lights up the night," said another.

One night, a night that George Banning just happened to have taken off, a well-dressed stranger who simply identified himself as "Tony B" showed up to have a talk with Marshall B. "Basically, this guy came in to offer me the nightclub," Marshall says.

Tony B. said, "We can change da name of the place to Marshall Brodien's Magic Lounge. Nice, huh? You run it like you wanna. We take care of da books. Everybody looks at it like it's your joint. Whatta you think?'

Not knowing what to do, Brodien told the mobster he needed a little time to think about it. He said that he was about to be drafted and couldn't let them know anything until he heard from the draft board. In the meantime, Marshall gave his good friend, the "Mayor of Randolph Street," a call. Bobby Baer, who'd long been involved with the mingling of politics and the ways and means of the mob, whether it be within the Chicago Loop or on the streets of Cicero, told Marshall, "Don't do it. If your name is on the place, and if there is any trouble or anyone ever gets shot there, and the police or FBI finds out your name's on any of the licenses, you will be the one who goes to jail."

Brodien never had to worry about giving a decision to Mr. B. A couple of nights later, actually a slow night when Senator Crandall was off, a creepy looking man dressed more like a street thug than a mobster showed up at the bar. He asked Carmie if George Banning was around. Carmie seemed to know the man and was a little uneasy when he left the bar and went to the office to tell George he had a visitor. Accordionist Manny Quartucci must have also sensed trouble; he stopped playing, put his accordion down, and stepped off the stage.

When George came to the bar, there was neither a hello nor a handshake. The man simply said, "I'm here for the money."

As soon as George told him, "I don't have it," the guy started toward him, yelling, "It's Sunday! You said you'd have it tonight. I need the freakin' money, and I need it right now!"

George ran to the cash register, where a chrome-plated revolver was kept under the cash drawer. "When we saw him going for the gun," says Marshall, "Manny and I went sailing over the bar and headed for the door. The guy kicked George to the floor before he could get to the gun. He grabbed a bottle of Schenley's — I'll never forget the brand of whisky — and smashed it on the edge of the back bar, then shoved the jagged-glass bottleneck right up to George's throat. That was when Carmie yelled, 'Jimmy, don't do it!'"

Jimmy must have been the thug's name, because he heeded Carmie's cry. He dropped the broken bottleneck to the floor, and took a step back. "Okay, you lucky scumbag," he told George. "I'll be back tomorrow. And you better have every freakin' nickel of da money."

Marshall never heard anything more about Jimmy and never knew if he showed up again. However, in less than a week, when Rose Paul was in the club one evening, she approached Marshall and told him that she was taking over — real soon. She asked if Crandall and Brodien wanted to stay around and work for her. They both said yes.

With the same ease that the mob shuffled jukeboxes and slot machines around the joints in Cicero, they discarded George Manning and turned the place over to the ex Mrs. Paul, who as it turned out was an extremely close friend of mob king pin, Joey "O'Brien" Aiuppia.

When Brodien and Crandall reported to work the next night, a new neon sign out front let it be known that they were at Rose's *Original* Magic Lounge.

Trouping with an Alligator

The Senator agreed to hold down the fort at the Magic Lounge for six weeks, while Brodien took his act on the road. As promised, Al Szasz had lined up a string of fair and carnival dates for his under-canvas trained-animal show, and Marshall would be the talker in addition to having a spot for doing some magic and illusions. They planned to hook up with Gem City Shows out of East St. Louis. The first date on the route card was a five-day run at the Mississippi Valley Fair in Davenport, Iowa.

"I spent most of the afternoon packing my illusions and loading the equipment needed for the show," Marshall says. "The sun was setting as Al and Ada went over the final checklist. Then Al tossed me a ring full of keys and said, 'Here, you can drive the truck with Pogo. We'll take the station wagon and pull the trailer with the alligator.'"

Marshall couldn't exactly put his finger on the clause in his contract that specified he had to chauffeur a boxing kangaroo cross-country, but then again, his contract with Al was little more than a friendly handshake.

As Ada coaxed her reprehensible reptile into the trailer, Marshall crawled into the cab of the truck loaded with Pogo. He adjusted the rearview mirror, started the engine and turned on the headlights, then peered through the little screen window over his shoulder to see if the kangaroo was ready to roll. "It was dark and quiet back there ... so quiet I figured that Pogo might sleep the whole trip."

Marshall clicked on the radio and was surprised it worked. Searching for a music station, he came across a weather forecast. Temperatures in the lower 40s were expected for most of the Midwest that evening. He clicked on the heater, which, naturally, didn't work.

Szasz's '52 Ford gator wagon pulled around the side of the truck, and

7. Trouping with an Alligator

Ada rolled down her window and shouted, "Drive carefully! See you at the fairgrounds about midnight!" As Al shot out the driveway and onto the blacktop highway, he gave the steering wheel a tap for a farewell toot.

To Pogo, that honk of the horn was like the sound of the bell for round one. He was up and sparring, throwing punches. "It was a three-and-a-half-hour drive from Chicago to Davenport," Marshall says, "and for three of those hours, that kangaroo did nothing but bounce up and down, back and forth, and all over the walls of that rickety old truck."

As Marshall drove through Moline, Illinois, just before crossing the Mississippi River bridge over to Iowa, Pogo's wild-and-crazy, bouncing-and-boxing spree suddenly ceased. Marshall slowed down, sensing something was wrong. "Then I smelled it. It was absolutely terrible. Pogo had dropped a load. And the stench made the Chicago stockyards seem like a garden of roses." Marshall couldn't roll down the windows because it was near freezing outside. He pressed on, figuring he only had a few more miles to go. But the putrid odor was overwhelming. Tears welled up in his eyes. Then, something miraculous happened. Right there on the westbound stretch of Interstate Highway 32 leading into Davenport, Brodien had a vision. He saw the exit sign for the Mississippi Valley Fairgrounds. Hallelujah!

He swerved to the right, put the pedal to the metal and sailed down the exit ramp. He pulled off the access road and onto the gravel right of way, where he parked the truck. Throwing open the door, he jumped into the chilly-but-gloriously-fresh air. Marshall walked the rest of the distance to the fairgrounds.

Al Szasz had been there for at least an hour. He'd already rounded up a crew of gazonies (itinerant carnival laborers), and the canvas was unfolded and spread over the frosty grass. They had the corners staked and were almost ready to raise the tent when Marshall appeared.

Al laughed at Marshall's tale of woe. Al's oft-used retort of "shit happens" had particular relevance that morning. He sent one of his roustabouts back to the highway to drive the truck back to their spot on the midway, where Pogo and the rest of the rather rank cargo were unloaded.

• • •

By daybreak, Al and his crew were adding the final touches to the façade of the show tent, hanging the colorfully painted bally panels and banners. A young man with a PRESS card pinned to his Chicago Cubs baseball cap wandered up. He was from WOC-TV, a station that covered the Quad Cities of Davenport and Bettendorf in Iowa, and Moline and Rock Island in Illinois. He told Al he was scouting for interesting news stories to publicize the fair,

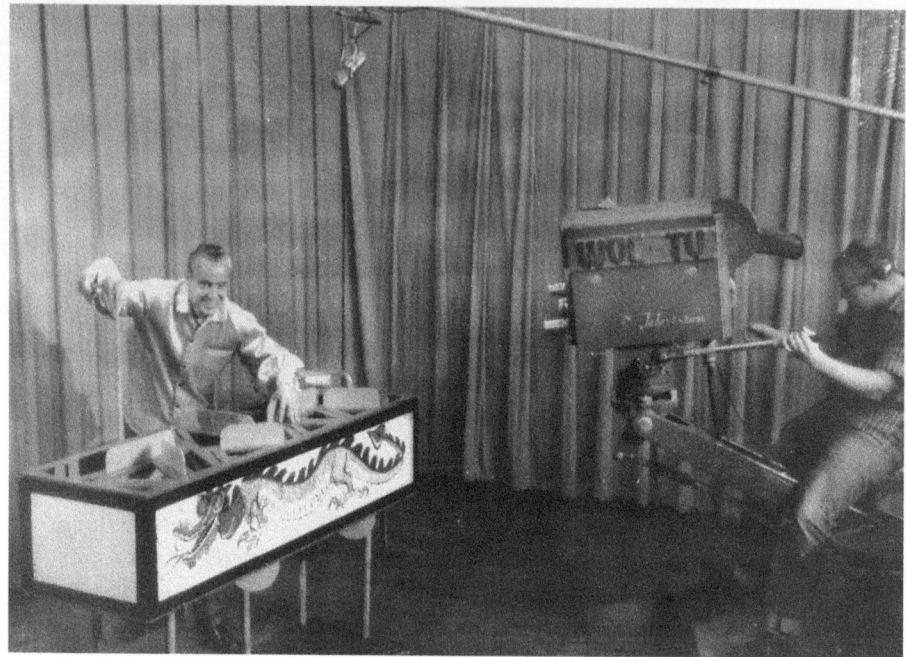

Marshall's specialty designed Blade Box made its first television appearance in the mid-1950s on WOC-TV in Davenport, Iowa. *Marshall Brodien Collection*

and the "Pogo the Boxing Kangaroo" banner had caught his eye. The reporter asked Al, "What would you think about having Pogo on the five o'clock news tonight? It would be a great plug for your show, and it would get some crowds out here over the weekend. All you have to do is get the kangaroo over to the station, which is only a couple of miles away."

With the unpleasant Pogo-in-the-truck experience still lingering on his mind (and noses of some folks), Al wasn't too eager to transport that kangaroo anywhere anytime soon. "You know what might be even better?" he suggested to the TV newsman. "This year, we are traveling with one of the world's greatest magicians, Marshall Brodien, and he has two new astonishing illusions that have never been exhibited west of the Mississippi. What if Mr. Brodien came over to the station and premiered these illusions on WOC-TV?"

The reporter liked the idea, they packed up the Blade Box, and Marshall drove over to the station in time for the five o'clock news. A girl was placed in the coffin-like box and 15 steel blades were plunged through it — each blade only inches from the other — leaving no imaginable way for her to be inside. When it came time for the "blow off" (the moment in a sideshow where an extra quarter is charged "to see the strange and unusual position of

7. Trouping with an Alligator

the girl"), Marshall went into a little different spiel. Speaking directly into the camera, he said, "Ladies and gentlemen, if you would like to discover how this young lady twists around the blades and shapes her body into that of a serpent, you must see Al Szasz's *All-Star Animal Show* at the Mississippi Valley Fair this weekend. You'll see Pogo the Boxing Kangaroo, direct from Australia. You'll witness the lovely Ada Ash wrestle an Amazonian alligator. And, as a special added attraction, you'll not only see my show of magic and illusions, you'll learn the secret of Serpentina, the lovely lady in the Blade Box of Mystery." Of course, what Brodien neglected to tell the folks out there in TV-land was that there was an extra charge to take a gander at the pseudo-reptilian lady lying in his brand-new Blade Box.

After a weekend at the Missouri State Fair in Sedalia, the formidable team of Al, Ada, and Marshall played their show at a half-dozen smaller county fairs and carnivals across Missouri and Illinois. Because bad weather caused the cancellation of a date in Kankakee, Illinois, they returned home to Chicago a few days earlier than scheduled. Unfortunately, this provided Al and Ada with the opportunity to send Marshall on another animal-transport mission.

• • •

At the end of each season, Ada's alligator was taken to the zoo in Columbus, Ohio, where it was boarded for the winter.

Because the truck with the water-tank trailer was in the shop for repairs, Al asked Marshall if he'd do him a favor and drive the reptile over to the zoo. Marshall said yes, but with one condition. Ada had to accompany him and help with some of the driving. It was a 350-mile trip. They taped the alligator's jaws shut for safety's sake and gingerly placed him in the spacious trunk of Marshall's convertible.

"It was past midnight when we left town," Marshall says. "I had volunteered to drive first while Ada slept in the backseat. I remember wondering what I was going to say if a copper stopped us. Ada's dyed-pink hair was rolled up in bright-green plastic curlers, and it was a pretty freaky sight.

"About two hours into the trip, I heard what I thought was Ada snoring. It was annoying because it kept getting louder and louder." The snoring he heard was actually ripping and tearing noises. The alligator had freed its mouth and was chomping his way through the upholstery and springs of the backseat.

"Hey, wake up!" Marshall shouted, looking in the rear-view mirror. "The alligator's getting out! He's coming through the backseat of my car!"

"You sonnovabitch!" Ada yelled. She put a halt to the creature's aggressiveness by punching him squarely between his beady eyes. "Get your scaly ass back in the trunk!" The gator hissed and sluggishly backtracked, as Ada said, "I think we better stop and tape his mouth again."

"We were on the outskirts of Fort Wayne, Indiana," Marshall remembers, "and I pulled into this little all-night gas station. I got out, stretched my legs, and told the guy on duty to fill it up. Ada walked toward the rear of the car and I told her, 'When I open trunk, you hold him still and I'll tape his mouth shut.' I glanced over at the attendant, realizing he was probably thinking we were a couple of kidnappers."

When Marshall did open the trunk, the alligator, dazzled by the bright lights, lunged forward and hissed. The attendant's eyes popped wide open. He dropped the gas nozzle and started screaming, "Hey, man! That's some kind of he-ist-tor-i-cal monster you got there! I best go call the police."

Marshall eventually calmed the attendant, convincing him that the monster was merely a trained alligator being returned to the zoo. After wrapping about a yard of duct tape around the reptile's jaws, Marshall slipped the attendant a $20 bill, and they were on their way.

"We laughed like crazy for the next hour, making up these crazy scenarios of how that poor fellow was going to tell his boss about this one." After all, it's not too often that a mild-mannered guy driving a shiny white convertible with a pink-haired chick in the backseat and a hissing prehistoric-looking creature in the trunk stops at your service station at two o'clock in the morning.

• • •

Once he had settled back into the nightly grind of doing bar magic at the Magic Lounge, Brodien tried to persuade Rose Paul to let him perform an illusion or two during his stand-up act. "I remembered there was this trapdoor in the stage that would be great to use with illusions. When Johnny Paul, Rose's ex, owned the place, he did a trick where he'd cover Rose with a cloth and she'd disappear. Then a minute or so later, usually in the middle of one of Johnny's jokes, she'd come busting in the front door."

Rose had to remind Marshall that the trapdoor was "more than less out of commission" because of something Senator Crandall had done.

Not long after Johnny moved out and opened his new place a few blocks away, Crandall came up with an absurd piece of shtick (a comic vaudeville bit) utilizing the trap. In the middle of The Senator's long-and-involved cut-and-restored rope routine, a waiter from The 4811, a striptease club across the street, holding a large round tray full of drinks, would rise through the trapdoor. He'd look out at the audience and ask, "Where are all the girls?" Then he'd look over toward The Senator, shake his head and say, "Oh, I'm terribly sorry. I must be in the wrong place."

7. Trouping with an Alligator

In his inimitable deadpan style, Senator Crandall would mumble, "Yeah, The 4811 is on the other side of the street," as he continued with his rope trick. The waiter shrugged his shoulders and slowly descended through the hole in the stage.

Johnny Paul heard about Crandall's bit and was peeved. Not because it was a funny gag, but because patrons knew about the elevator and the secret trapdoor — his old vanishing-lady stunt was being exposed. Early one morning, after the lounge closed down for the night, Johnny broke in, tore out the motor, welded shut the trapdoor, and brought an end to The Senator's clever piece of nonsense.

Despite the fact there was no longer a trap, and even though everybody felt the stage was too small for big illusions, Marshall still pushed to include the Blade Box and the Electric Chair in his show. The big stuff drew crowds at the fairs and carnivals. Why couldn't it do the same at the Magic Lounge? Then, just about the time he'd convinced Rose to let him start trying out the illusions, the Outfit let it be known they had designs on doing something different at the Magic Lounge.

Late one night, after everyone had left the club and they were about to lock the doors, a well-dressed tough guy walked in, spotted Marshall and asked, "You're that magician, right?" When he said yes, Marshall was informed, "This is your last night, 'cause you're not working here no more. You take your magishing stuff wit you tonight. And don't come back. Comprendre?"

Within 24 hours, the place was completely transformed into a full-blown strip joint, where the girls danced totally nude. While the City of Chicago may have had ordinances that prohibited exotic dancers from going beyond pasties and g-strings, in Cicero anything and everything went. The place was still called Rose Paul's *Original* Magic Lounge, but Mrs. Paul was nowhere to be seen. Mob kingpin Joey Aiuppia had planted his friend Rose somewhere else. Magicians were "no more" at the Magic Lounge, and the tricks onstage were of a totally different nature.

Carnival Knowledge

After the mob's presto-chango job on the Magic Lounge, Marshall found himself out of work for the excruciatingly long period of 24 hours. Al Szasz called to let him know that Gem City Shows had booked their animal-and-magic show for a carnival in East St. Louis, Illinois. It was a three-day-weekend run that started the next morning. This meant they would have to drive overnight in order to have the show tent up and ready.

Marshall also got a phone call from Tony Christie, one of the bartenders still at the Magic Lounge. "He told me he was quitting and he and his brother Joe Christie, the owner of the Central Club, were planning to buy the Beacon Inn on the south side of Chicago. They wanted to turn it into a nice show bar — a place where people could bring friends, enjoy a few drinks and have some laughs." Tony asked Marshall if he wanted to work behind the bar doing close-up magic. Marshall said the was interested and told him they'd talk as soon as he got back.

• • •

"When Al and Ada and I arrived at the fairgrounds and started loading in the show, we discovered that because we had packed in such a rush, we'd forgotten a part of the tent. The 25-foot-wide piece of canvas for the back wall was missing." Al asked one of the workers where he might find a panel of canvas that size. He was told that Hedy Jo Star, the proprietor, owner, and operator of the strip show on the midway, might be able to help out.

The burlesque, striptease, and girlie shows that traveled with carnivals and played the fair circuits were always given a conspicuous location at the end of the midway. So, when Szasz dispatched Brodien to find Hedy Jo Star's *French*

8. Carnival Knowledge 57

Follies show, he knew in what direction to head. "Hedy Jo's office-trailer, which doubled as the backstage dressing room for the girls, was parked behind the tent. I knocked on the door, and when she opened it I introduced myself and explained our canvas dilemma. She told me not to worry, she would have 'one of her boys' bring over the piece we needed. Even though she was in work clothes, getting ready for tomorrow's opening, she was pretty sexy looking."

By the next morning, Al and Marshall had rigged the tent with the borrowed canvas and their first show was scheduled for one P.M. At about a quarter till, Brodien stepped onto the platform out front and began his ballyhoo. As he expounded on the wonders of the animal-and-magic show inside, he looked down the midway and noticed a girl in a skintight black dress was coming his way.

It was Hedy Jo and she was dressed to kill. Actually, because she was the talker for her own *French Follies* show, she was dressed to sell — tickets, of course. After his spiel, Marshall stepped down and invited Hedy Jo to come in and see their show. "She told me she couldn't because she had to be back for her first show, which was at noon. When she turned to leave, I thanked her again for sending over the canvas. She said, 'You're more than welcome. I'm glad I could help out a handsome young man like you.' Then, as she walked away she laughed and said, 'I'll be seeing you later.' Well, that made me a little fidgety. When I told Al that I thought this Hedy Jo Star really liked me, he just said, 'You're imagining things.'"

• • •

Early the next morning, Brodien and the Szaszs were having breakfast at a diner across the street from the fairground, when in walked Hedy Jo. "She scooted into our booth and sat next to me," Marshall says, "without even asking if we minded if she joined us." After they finished eating, Marshall asked Hedy Jo if she wanted to see some magic. "I did a coin trick and the sponge rabbits, and she must have liked them because she asked if I could do another one. I said, 'Sure, do you have a dollar bill I could borrow?' She said, 'No, but I have $100.'"

Marshall took out a matchbook, lit one of the matches and touched it to Hedy Jo's $100 bill. It instantly went up in a flash of flame. Looking surprised, Marshall asked, "You have another one of those?" When she said she sure did, and reached for her purse, he had to tell her that he was only joking. Marshall suggested that she look underneath the ashtray over by the napkin dispenser. Her $100 bill was there.

When Hedy Jo excused herself to go to the ladies room, the owner of Gem City Shows, who'd been sitting at a nearby table, walked over and said,

"Ya'll sure look like you're havin' a big time." Then he looked toward the restrooms, lowered his voice and asked, "How well do you know Hedy Jo Star?"

Marshall said, "I only met her yesterday, but she seems like a nice lady."

"Then you really don't know her," the carnival owner said, grinning and flashing a left front tooth that had a gold inlay in the shape of a crescent moon. When Marshall said that he might be "getting to know Hedy Jo a little better, a little later," he told Marshall, "Just be careful, boy. That woman's not a woman. It's one of them female impersonators. Matter of fact, that whole show is full of them boy-girl types."

"Well, when Hedy Jo came back from the restroom, I kept kidding around with her and showing her a couple more tricks, but I was nervous, sort of shaking inside. I couldn't wait to get out of there."

As they crossed the street and walked toward the fairground, Hedy Jo put her arm through Marshall's and asked, "What are you doing later tonight?"

"I sort of stammered and said that I wasn't sure. She told me, 'After the show, the girls and I usually go across the river to St. Louis, where we work as B-girls in this bar called the Sheboom Room. You might want to come over and have some fun.' I tried to use the excuse that I was underage and couldn't get into bars. She told me not to worry. They could get me in with no problem.

"The last thing I remember Hedy Jo saying was, 'I'm sure we'll meet up later.'"

Later that night, 15 minutes before Al and Marshall's next-to-last scheduled show, a fierce thunderstorm hit. Violent gusts of wind lashed through the tent. Sheets of ice-cold rain dropped from the clouds like a waterfall, making it impossible to see more than ten yards down the midway.

Marshall, Ada, and Al took refuge in the cab of the truck. Listening to the radio, they heard that the front gates of the fairgrounds were closed due to flooding. A tornado warning was in effect. The weather was predicted to be even worse tomorrow.

"That was when Al said, 'Let's get the hell out of here.' We tore down the tent and were ready to go in record time. Not that I especially wanted to, but I didn't have the chance to say goodbye to Hedy Jo." Al returned the rain-soaked piece of canvas to her trailer.

Not in his wildest dreams or nightmares could Marshall ever imagine it would be almost two years to the date when Hedy Jo's wanton remark, "I'm sure we'll meet up later," would prove true.

• • •

Upon his return from the fair date in East St. Louis, Marshall drove over to the South Side to talk with Joe and Tony Christie, the new proprietors of

8. Carnival Knowledge

the Beacon Inn at 6330 South Pulaski Road. Joe, who'd run the Central Club at 63rd and Central, had taken the suggestion from brother Tony, who'd been a bartender at the Magic Lounge, that they try to persuade Marshall to be their new behind-the-bar wonder worker.

The Beacon was a corner tavern that had survived for years on local traffic. But with the Christies' infusion of a kitchen with a chef who served decent meals, musical entertainment by accordionist Manny Quartuzzi, and a magician behind the bar who made people laugh, they soon found they were getting patrons from the adjoining neighborhoods.

"The owners realized that a good show drew people," Marshall says. "And because I was getting great responses with the close-up magic, it wasn't long before Joe and Tony agreed to build a stage behind the bar, so I could do stand-up shows. I started performing my Blade Box and the Electric Chair, and during the Christmas holidays that year we packed the place."

• • •

In early January of 1957, Marshall got a phone call from Vic Torsberg, a former pro magician who worked for National Magic Company. Torsberg was the president of Chicago Assembly of the Society of American Magicians and was coordinating the production of an annual public show, sponsored by Assembly and the local club of the International Brotherhood of Magicians. They wanted Brodien to appear on the show. A week later a letter of agreement was mailed that stated: "Fee will be $50, and since we have a carnival theme we want you to do your Electric Chair and Blade Box."

Other performers on the February 22 show staged at Chicago's Eighth Street Theatre were Marshall's friend Senator Crandall, who served as the master of ceremonies; Johnny Platt, a magician who worked regularly at the LaSalle Hotel, but appearing on this show as Hadji Baba; comedy magician Billy Bishop; Bruno, an act from Holland; Al Torsten & Ellen from Germany; and illusionist Jim Sommers & Company. Vic Torsberg performed his Charlie Chan black-art act.

The production, advertised and promoted as *A Carnival of Wonders*, was perfect for Marshall's sideshow fire eating and sword swallowing. However, the two items that had the magicians in attendance abuzz were Electra, "the girl who lighted everything from fluorescent tubes to flaming torches with her fingertips," and Serpentina the Mystery Girl, Brodien's glib-tongued presentation of the Blade Box.

After the show, Marshall's friend, Okito, came backstage to congratulate him, saying, "As you know, I have been a magician for many, many years, but I am totally puzzled by your new Blade Box. You must show me how it

A 1957 performance of Marshall's Electric Chair illusion for the *Carnival of Wonders* revue at Chicago's 8th Street Theater. *Marshall Brodien Collection*

is done." The great Jack Gwynne, who Marshall had first watched on the stage of the Oriental Theatre when he was 14, was with Okito, and he said, "I, too, am baffled by the configuration of the blades."

It was truly a thrill for Marshall to show his two idols the workings of his Blade Box. Gwynne was so impressed with the improvements that he asked if he could utilize the method and have one made for his own act. Of course, Marshall said yes, and he let their mutual friend, Dee Yip Loo, build the Blade Box, which Jack featured in his nightclub and circus act for the next three years.

• • •

Marshall had been running fancy free of Uncle Sam's Army for a few years too many, and he was finally drafted at age 22. It was April Fools Day, and he had exactly two weeks to get things in order, before reporting for his physical exam.

A week before the dreaded date, while Marshall was working his final nights at the Beacon, he had a visit from a mysterious young man who introduced himself as Ken Knoble. "He was a good-looking guy and was accompanied by an attractive girl," Marshall says. "They stayed to watch me perform both of my shows. This fellow was fascinated with magic. When I went over to talk with him after the last show, I asked him what he did for a living. He said he was a hypnotist."

By 1957, the nation was fascinated with hypnotism. Morey Bernstein's *The Search for Bridey Murphy*, a book about a housewife under hypnotic regression who revealed her previous incarnation, had become a bestseller. An LP record of the subject's alleged hypnotic trance sold tens of thousands, as public interest in hypnotism and reincarnation skyrocketed. Bridey Murphy parties, where guests "came as they were," were the rage. It had become fashionable to see a therapist who practiced clinical hypnosis. "Nightclub hypnotists who hadn't worked for years suddenly found themselves in great demand," wrote respected magician/philosopher Martin Gardner in his book, *Fads & Fallacies*.

Brodien told Knoble that his only encounter with a hypnotist had been a Professor Stevenson, and that was several years back when he worked at the Treasure Chest. Marshall admitted he had always been intrigued with hypnotism, asking if it was difficult to learn how to hypnotize people. Knoble said that it wasn't. Demonstrating how easy it was, he proceeded to hypnotize the girl who was with him.

"Not knowing much about the procedure," Marshall says, "I thought this stuff with 'the power of suggestion' was pretty cool. It just might be something I could use in a show. The next day, I invited this guy over to my house. I showed him some tricks and taught him how to do the ones he liked. In return, he explained how to put someone under a hypnotic spell."

The very next night, Marshall began experimenting with the simple induction method of hypnosis. He was surprised when it worked. He tried it on some people seated at the end of the bar, causing them to do some pretty amazing and entertaining things.

For Marshall's final night at the Beacon Inn, several magician friends felt it fitting to throw a going-off-to-the-army party. Senator Crandall was there, with his ever-present Chihuahua named Suzy, tending bar. Bobby Baer and Don Theobald from the Treasure Chest showed up. Don Alan stopped by on his way to the Don-Lee, a North Halsted Street magic bar he owned with Lee Le Roi. Jack Gwynne brought his wife Anne, daughter Peggy, his son Buddy, and Okito.

Abracadabra, You're Drafted

"I didn't want to go into the service," Marshall says. "But I had to."

On April 15, 1957, Marshall Everett Brodien (Caucasian male, 5 ft. 11 in., 150 lbs., blue eyes, blond hair, and single) was inducted into the U.S. Army. He was bussed to Fort Leonard, Missouri, where he underwent two weeks of processing, which meant waiting on papers that told where the next bus was waiting to take him. He waited in line to ask a clerk if there was anybody he could talk with about getting into Special Services. He was told to wait until he began basic training.

Marshall was stationed at Fort Carson, Colorado, just outside Colorado Springs. And it wasn't long before his magical presence was known. Wherever he went, be it the post-exchange store or the mess hall or the barracks, he was always performing magic. His card tricks were gaining him popularity with his fellow soldiers; however, his experiments with his newly acquired skills of hypnosis were giving him certain notoriety.

"I hadn't been at Fort Carson for more than a couple of weeks," Marshall remembers, "when I did a bit of hypnosis in the barracks that almost got me in trouble. I hypnotized a soldier by the name of Rodney Clay, who was from somewhere in Arkansas. I had given him a post-hypnotic suggestion that when he went to the bathroom, he would become stuck to the seat of the toilet."

A dozen soldiers clustered around the restroom stalls to watch. Sure enough, no matter how much Rodney tried, he couldn't get off the commode. The GIs' grins turned to chuckles, and the more times Rodney tried to stand, the louder the laughs got. Just as someone yelled, "Hey, Private Clay, it's time to shit or get off the pot!" a sergeant — one who'd been tagged with the code name of "Stonejaw" — walked in the bathroom.

Sergeant Stonejaw was clueless as to the nature of Private Brodien's experiment in mesmerism. "I don't know what's going on here," he shouted. "But I do know I want everybody out of here! Right now!" All smiles fell to the floor and, in pin-drop silence, the soldiers filed out. All except Rodney Clay, who told the sergeant, "Sir, I'm sorry, but I can't leave. I'm stuck to this toilet."

A buddy of Rodney's, also from Arkansas, stuck his head back in the bathroom and hollered, "He's stuck 'cause he is hip-no-tized by Bo'deen tha Great!" There were some snickers and giggles, and even Marshall had to smile at the soldier's assessment of the hypnotic stunt. But Stonejaw saw no humor whatsoever in the situation.

"The sergeant ordered me to 'Get that man off the pot right now!'" Marshall says. "So, I snapped my fingers and the soldier stood up. He pulled up his pants, saluted the sergeant, and walked out of the bathroom. The sergeant stared at me in disbelief, and I just stared back at him. He looked away for a few seconds, then he turned back and said, 'Brodien, don't mess with me, 'cause you're messing with the wrong people.'"

After that incident, anytime Stonejaw requested volunteers for a project, Marshall would look straight at him, staring. This inevitably caused the sergeant to look in other directions for helpers. Marshall says, "For some reason, he never messed with me and that suited me just fine."

• • •

On the very day that Private Brodien's eight weeks of basic training at Fort Carson were completed, he received a call from Colonel Lawrence A. Johnson, the director of Special Entertainment Services. Johnson asked Marshall to join the Fort Carson Little Theater and help with a variety show that was being staged for the Peak and Haven Clubs, the base's two officer's clubs. A review of the two-and-a-half-hour production appeared in the June 24, 1957 *Colorado Springs Gazette Telegraph*: "Brodien's magic proves the hand is quicker than the eye, he eats fire from torches then lights cigarettes with a personal flame from his mouth. However, he's currently learning 'the Army's magic' as a basic combat trainee with Company E of Fort Carson's 60th Infantry Regiment."

Accolades for the big show had barely subsided when Marshall was sent out on a two-week bivouac in the mountainous Colorado countryside. The recruits were trained how to pitch tents, forage for food, cook over an open fire, and basically survive in the wilderness.

"We'd just staked out our tents," Marshall says, "when I told the guys that, before it got dark, we needed to snake-proof the campsite." He started

First Class Brodien's performances at Fort Carson ranged from hypnotic shows to special events at the officer's club to birthday parties for families stationed at the base. *Marshall Brodien Collection*

stacking a line of pebbles and rocks around his tent, telling the soldiers, "Even though this little wall is only two or three inches high, those poisonous rattlesnakes and copperheads out there won't dare crawl over it."

It was an outrageous put on. The only reptiles Marshall had ever seen in his entire life were the lethargic alligator wrestled by the pink-haired Ada Ash, and Serpentina the Snake Lady of Blade Box fame at Riverview Park.

Yet, the soldiers believed every word of Brodien's who-do-voodoo. They shoveled rocks and rubble around the tents. Some even dug trenches, or "snake moats" as they called them, in front of the little stone walls.

A sergeant showed up for an unexpected field inspection the next morning. "What the hell's with the rocks and ditches around the tents?" he asked.

"It's snake-proofing, sir!" replied a soldier. "Protection against the rattlesnakes and copperheads. And it works, sir. There wasn't a single snakebite all night, sir!"

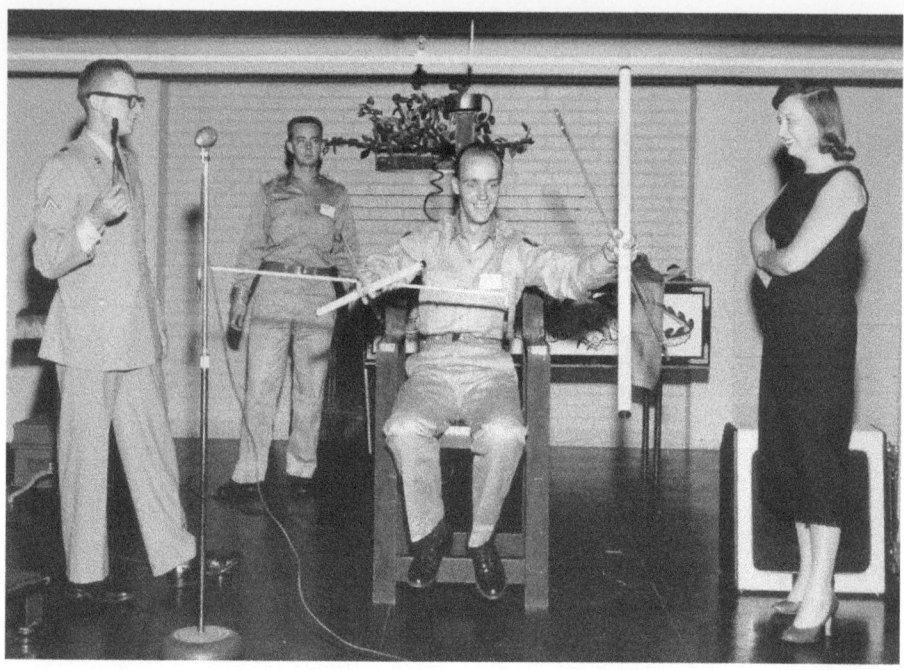

Only months after finishing basic training, Marshall had his mother ship his Electric Chair and Blade Box to Fort Carson and was soon performing them in his shows for the base's service clubs. *Marshall Brodien Collection*

"A very good idea," said the sergeant. "Have the men snake-proof the quartermaster's tent. Can't take any chances, since we're out here without medics."

"The bivouac was an adventure of sorts," Marshall says. "But it was dusty and hot and miserable and no fun. Then, on the second day, I had a stroke of luck. An officer showed up in a jeep to pick me up and take me back to the base. I was informed that a general needed me to entertain for a party at the Officer's Club.

"Fortunately, I'd already asked my mother to ship three or four boxes of my props to Fort Carson. So I was able to put on an elaborate one-hour magic show for the party. It went over really well. They asked me to stay the next night and do my hypnotic show. Afterwards, when I asked how long it would be before I had to return to the bivouac, I was told, 'You're not. You have been assigned to Special Entertainment Services.'"

Even though his foxhole-digging days were considered over, there was a catch. Whenever Special Services didn't have shows lined up, Marshall was assigned to guard duty — long, boring hours of standing watch. However, that little proviso wouldn't last long.

The following week, Special Services needed Brodien to travel to Fort Morgan, Colorado for a series of shows. "When I told my sergeant that I would be gone from the base for four or five days, he indicated I'd have to make up the guard duty after I returned. Well, as soon as the Chief of Staff found out about that, he telephoned and requested that I be put on ED, which meant 'Excused from all duties.'"

No war drums were beating. Marshall realized he was truly in the service of a peacetime Army. The brass at Fort Carson appreciated and recognized his talents and utilized them whenever and wherever possible. "And it sure did beat soldiering," Marshall says. "I made up my mind that amazing, amusing, and confusing the troops was going to be two years of great fun."

A Spell of Hypnosis

"Brodien Switches to Hypnotism" proclaimed a feature story in the July 27, 1957 *Colorado Springs Gazette*: "Brodien the professional magician from Chicago is a major part of the new soldier variety show at the Peak Service Club. Twelve men are hypnotized during his act. He has fellow soldiers picking up nonexistent pennies from the floor, brushing ants off their legs, singing, dancing, and putting their shoes on backwards. He has both the men and the women that are present imitating exotic dancers. He gave a soldier a lemon, telling him it was an orange, and the man tasted it and declared it sweet."

Marshall hadn't forsaken magic. He was simply enjoying the opportunity provided by the Army to hone his skills as a stage hypnotist. His show of hypnotism had become the talk of Fort Carson and Colorado Springs. When it played the Service Club on Saturday nights there was standing room only. The place was packed with enlisted men of all ranks, retirees, family members, and guests from the community.

At showtime, usually at nine or ten o'clock, the bandleader would introduce Brodien. Attired in an elegant black tuxedo, he walked out smiling, welcomed the crowd, and started recruiting volunteers from the audience.

"You people are the show and without your participation there would be no show. If you volunteer to be hypnotized tonight, be assured I am not going to embarrass you in any way. I'm not going to ask you to waddle around like a duck or bark like a dog. Instead, you will feel very relaxed throughout the show. When you return to your seat, you will feel as if you had eight wonderful hours of relaxing sleep."

Those few words were usually incentive enough for folks to start filling the 12 or 13 chairs that were lined up in front of the bandstand.

"There are probably some of you out there who would like to be hypnotized, but you do not want to come up onstage. You can be hypnotized right where you are sitting. Put your feet flat on the floor, hold your hands in your lap, relax, and listen. Just as the people onstage are doing, listen to the sound of my voice...."

His voice is smooth and pleasantly persuasive.

"Look at me and listen to the relaxing sound of my voice. Erase everything from your mind ... relax ... think of nothing ... relax and listen to the sound of my voice...."

It's a voice that is mellow and melodic.

"You are feeling nothing but your body relaxing. It is a very relaxing feeling ... listen to the sound of my voice ... the tone of my voice is relaxing you ... more ... and more...."

A voice that is hypnotic.

"Relax as I slowly count from one through ten ... on one, you will close your eyes ... let your head fall forward ... listen to my voice and close your eyes....

"One ... take a deep breath ... and relax....

"Two ... your eyes are closed and you're completely relaxed ... another deep breath ... you can feel your entire body relaxing....

"Three ... relaxing more and more ... each breath you take, you're relaxing more and more.... Four, you are feeling a heavy feeling over your entire body ... your arms, your legs are relaxed.... Five, you are so relaxed ... so relaxed....

"Your whole body feels completely relaxed.... Six, the sound of my voice relaxes you even more ... and more ... and....

"Seven, your entire body is now relaxed and asleep.... Eight, you're deeper ... and deeper asleep. Nine ... you are totally relaxed ... sleeping and ... ten, you are sound asleep."

Marshall says, "By watching the row of people I knew if they were already in a trance or if I needed to slow down the induction count. I'd walk by someone and gently push an arm from his or her lap, and when it slipped to their side I'd say, 'You're deep asleep. Nothing will awaken you.'"

He would walk down the line of chairs, lifting each person's arms up, asking them to hold them straight out in front of themselves.

"Your arms are rigid," he said. "So stiff that you cannot drop them down to your side. The harder you try, the more impossible it is for you to lower your arms. You simply cannot lower your arms." The audience started to laugh. It was apparent that none of the hypnotized subjects could bring their arms down. Some of them frowned as they strained to force their arms to their sides. No matter how hard they tried, they couldn't do it.

"At the count of three, your arms will become so heavy they will drop.

Listen as I count ... one ... two..." On three, all arms plunged downward. The audience applauded, but the subjects continued their slumber.

Brodien then asked them to rotate their hands and wrists in a circular motion. "Now, on my count of three, you hands will start rotating in the opposite direction. One ... two ... three ... reverse." The sight of a dozen pairs of hands frantically flailing around like puttering airplane propellers brought more laughs from the audience. And when Marshall told his subjects that they couldn't stop their hands from spinning around faster and faster and they were about to take off, the crowd screamed with laughter.

Thus began Marshall's hour-long roller-coaster ride of hypnotic highjinx. The subjects were transported to an imaginary movie theater. One moment watching the funniest film ever screened; the next, weeping at the saddest scene they'd ever seen. The temperature in the room was hypnotically adjusted from freezing cold, generating genuine shivers, to sweltering hot, causing some subjects to start shedding objects of clothing.

"In my hands, I am holding a X-ray napkin," Brodien would often explain to his line-up of hypnotized subjects. "In the center of this napkin is a hole that has remarkable properties. When you wake up and look through the hole in the X-ray napkin, you are able to see through fabric. Any kind of material — whether it's a piece of clothing made of cotton, wool, silk, or even nylon — you are able to see through it."

The cocktail napkin was dropped onto the lap of a thirtyish-looking lieutenant sitting in the centermost chair. When Marshall touched the gentleman's forehead, he opened his eyes and blinked a few times, then began unfolding the napkin. By the time the rest of the subjects were awakened, the officer was holding the X-ray napkin up his face, peering out at the front rows of the audience. Grinning.

An even bigger smile came over his face when he turned and gazed at the attractive redhead sitting to his left. There was pure lechery in the lieutenant's look.

"What the hell are you gawkin' at?" asked the lady, who as it turned out was a retired colonel's girlfriend. "Give me that thing, you pervert." She grabbed the napkin and fidgeted with it and hesitantly held it up to her face. Her eyes widened, as she screamed, "How disgusting!" She glanced through the napkin at the other soldiers to her right. "Why, this is absolutely gross! You're all naked." Then she looked down at her lap. "Oh, my God!" She threw the napkin back at the lieutenant, crossed her legs, and covered her chest with her purse.

At any point in the performance, Marshall was able to bring the subjects in and out of their hypnotic states with the greatest of ease. "Anytime I touch your forehead, or I say, 'Awake,' you will open your eyes. You will feel relaxed. Relaxed as if you had eight hours of restful sleep. Yet, when I touch you on the forehead again, or I say, 'Sleep,' you will return back to that restful sleep."

If and when he encountered an uncooperative subject — someone resisting hypnosis or perhaps a person who might have had a drink or two too many — the same method was used to get them off the stage. "I would touch them on the forehead and simply tell them to go back to their seat.

"On the other hand, if there was somebody in the audience who had 'gone under' during the induction, and I wanted to get him or her up on the stage, I would use a similar technique. I'd walk out to their table and touch them on the forehead, waking them up. Then I'd tell them, 'When I count to five you will wake up and come up on the stage and sit in one of the chairs.'

"As soon as that person would get on stage and sit in one of the chairs, I would say, 'Look at these hypnotized people sitting up here with you. Do you think something like that could ever happen to you?' Before he could answer, I said, 'Sleep!' and he would join the others in their relaxing hypnotic trances."

• • •

An aspiring stage hypnotist couldn't ask for better training grounds than those provided by the military. When Marshall arrived at Fort Carson, he was armed with only the basics — essentially what he'd learned in his crash course with the mysterious Mr. Knoble, the visitor at the Beacon Inn who exchanged his knowledge of hypnotism for a few secrets of Marshall's magic. Yet, within four short months, Marshall had attained a remarkable proficiency with rapid induction hypnosis.

"It was easy to hypnotize soldiers," Marshall says, "simply because they are accustomed to taking orders all the time — from reveille to lights out. Whenever I got a soldier onstage he did whatever I suggested."

Not only were Brodien's capabilities applauded during the hypnotic shows he staged at Fort Carson's Little Theatre, the Officers' Clubs, NCO Clubs, and service clubs around the base, his expertise with hypnosis was quickly being recognized and utilized by others on the base.

Captain Anthony F. Francavilla, with the Company 2D Battle Group of the 13th Infantry, called to see if Marshall's mastery of hypnosis could help with an amnesia victim. A young soldier was about to be assigned to a special project, but the officers needed to know more about his past. The young man could not remember details of his family or relatives or even where he lived.

"The Captain asked if I would like to try hypnosis to regress this kid back through the years and find out some things about his childhood. I'd never done anything like this, but, of course, I said yes. So, I went to the Captain's office where I met with the soldier. I talked with him, got him relaxed, and put him into a deep sleep.

"I suggested that he was eight years old, then seven, then six. He had his eyes closed, but nodded his head and said, 'Yes, I am six years old, and I am sitting at home....'

"That's when I asked him, 'Do you know where you live?' In a childlike voice, he said, 'I live in Chicago....'

"I asked him, 'Where in Chicago do you live?' And he said, 'I live on School Street.'"

Placing a pencil in his deep-asleep subject's hand, Marshall told him, "You are now sitting in your third-grade classroom.... Try to write down the number of your house on School Street." Sure enough, the soldier slowly printed out 672. And when requested, he was able to write out other information — his third-grade teacher's name, and the names of his parents and his brothers and sisters. The officers were now able to track down the soldier's birth record and other vital statistics that had been presumed to be lost.

"This was the first time I'd done this and, even though I knew it could be done," Marshall says, "quite frankly, at the time, I was amazed what could be accomplished with hypnotism."

On another occasion, after one of his hypnotic shows at the Officers' Club, Dr. Thomas Orban, an officer who was a dentist assigned to Fort Carson, approached Brodien. Orban's father was the famed research-minded dentist, Dr. Balint Orban, who strongly influenced the practice of periodontology in the 1930s through '50s by publishing over 150 scientific papers, as well as a number of widely used textbooks on oral surgery.

Dr. Thomas Orban's wife, Donna, had been one of Marshall's subjects and, while under his hypnotic spell, acted out the role of an exotic dancer. Though the doctor appreciated the onstage stunts with hypnotism were entertaining and amusing, he wondered if Marshall knew anything about using hypnosis in dentistry. Marshall told him about the session with Captain Francavilla and the soldier with amnesia, and indicated that he would be willing to experiment.

"Well, he called me up late one night and asked me to come over to his office to help with a soldier who needed a tooth removed. I put the kid asleep, and then I turned him over to the dentist. I said, 'The next voice you hear will be Dr. Orban, who you will obey.' The dentist told him that saliva would stop forming in his mouth, and he would feel no pain."

Dr. Orban proceeded to remove the tooth without Novocain or gas, and the soldier was completely unaware of what was going on. When Brodien awakened the patient, he asked him how he felt. He said he was fine, but he could still feel the tooth, and asked, "Why didn't the dentist pull it?"

Snapping his fingers and saying, "Look now," Dr. Orban held a mirror in front of the patient's face. The soldier grinned when he saw that his tooth was gone, and asked, "Dang! How'd you do that?" Orban replied, "We can't tell you. Between Private Brodien and me, it's a magic secret."

It was on that evening that Marshall realized the true secret of hypnosis? He says, "The person you are going to hypnotize must truly believe you can do it."

Straitjackets and Shenanigans

In the fall of 1957, when Colonel Johnson, the director of Special Services at Fort Carson, received a request to provide a halftime show at a basketball tournament, he called Private Brodien into his office to see if he had any ideas. "We've sent glee clubs, marching bands, and color guards in the past," the Colonel said, "but this year I want to give them something different. What about your magic or hypnotism?"

Marshall matter-of-factually asked, "How about I do a death-defying, upside-down straitjacket escape?"

"You mean like Houdini used to do? An escape stunt? Brodien, you're a genius! Pull that one off and we'll have 'em talking at the Pentagon."

Marshall had never done a straitjacket escape before; he had a week to learn how.

First off, he had to find one of those canvas-and-leather restraints that are normally associated with the criminally insane. Whipping out his trusty Abbott's Magic Novelty Company Catalog #13 (a one-inch thick spiral-bound book with artwork of dancing skeletons on the cover), he found a listing for a "Regulation Straitjacket Release" (Item #1063, $18 postpaid). Special Services had set up a fund for him to purchase new props for his magic shows, so it was a simple matter of requisitioning a check to be sent off with the order to Abbott's plant in Colon, Michigan.

While waiting for the straitjacket to arrive, he worked with engineers to re-rig the winch system that was used for the scoreboard at the gym. The length of heavy hemp rope was doubled up, which would allow Marshall to be lifted high above the basketball court. So high in fact, that he announced he would be performing the escape blindfolded. Colonel Johnson thought this was a brilliant move to garner more publicity. However, it was done because

Brodien had a fear of heights and didn't want to have to look down at the hardwood floor forty feet below.

A couple of days before the event, the Colonel upped the ante one more notch, by putting out a press release stating that Fitzsimmons Army Hospital in Denver had been contacted to send one of their straitjackets to Fort Carson. (Nothing was mentioned about the one from Abbott's arriving any day, and *it* would be used for the upcoming escape.)

"The game was a sellout, and there were even people who showed up just for the halftime stunt," Marshall says. "They strapped me into the straitjacket, put the blindfold on me, then cranked me up to the top of the gym. A strap between my ankles secured me to the rope line."

As Marshall started to squirm free of the straitjacket, each time he made a side-to-side twisting motion, he sensed what seemed like "a give" on the ankle strap. Actually, the windlass was slipping, and the rope was unwinding. The safety lock hadn't been engaged properly.

Because of his blindfold, Marshall couldn't see he was falling. A soldier sitting near the winch jumped and grabbed the rope lines. He was yanked upward and was thrown onto the floor; his dead weight stopped Marshall's fall — only five feet from the floor. Private Merl McIntire saved Marshall's life that evening. After McIntire was rushed to the hospital with severe rope burns on both hands, Brodien was lifted back up, the winch lock was double-checked, and he completed the straitjacket escape.

Brodien repeated the escape several more times over the next year. Ironically, every time he did it, Private McIntire was recruited to be his assistant. Dressed in an official looking white lab coat, he was introduced as "Dr. McIntire," whose job it was to verify that the straitjacket was authentic and the same as used in the wards of Fitzsimmons Army Hospital. The little showbiz ruse was never questioned. But when Marshall performed the stunt at a Fourth of July show in 1958, it would mark the retirement of the Good Doctor character. As a special feature of the Colorado Springs Kiwanis Fireworks Festival at Washburn Field, it was publicized that Brodien would attempt to break a world record with his straitjacket escape. At the time, Marshall admitted that he had no idea what the world-record time was; he only intended to beat his own time of two minutes by a few seconds.

That evening, the Colorado Springs' Fire Station No. 1 had parked their brand-new aerial ladder truck on the 50-yard line of the football field. The blindfolded Brodien was strapped into the authenticated (by Dr. McIntire, of course) straitjacket by a team of policemen and firemen. This time the ankle strap was tied to the top rung of the ladder, which was then extended 88 feet in the air.

Stopwatches clicked. Marshall started wiggling, getting the necessary

Brodien stuggling to escape from a straitjacket, seconds before his neardeath fall, when the lab-coated "Dr. McIntire" saved him. *Marshall Brodien Collection*

11. Straitjackets and Shenanigans

slack to affect his escape. The Army Band barely had time to play a second chorus of "Stars and Stripes Forever" when Fort Carson's greatest escape artist flung the straitjacket to the ground and waved to the crowd.

"I think I got out in a few seconds under two minutes," Marshall recalls with a smile. "I didn't break a world record, but I did beat my previous time by about five seconds."

Colonel Johnson was convinced that a world record had been broken. He paced about, shouting, "Goddamnit, Brodien! You beat it by five seconds! Five seconds is goddam good." The Colonel was on his walkie-talkie with someone up in the press box. In a matter of seconds, the stadium announcer was saying, "Ladies and gentlemen, may I have your attention please. It has just been confirmed that Private Marshall Brodien has broken the record for escaping from a regulation straitjacket." Applause. Marshall waved to the crowd again, chuckling to himself that the only record broken was *his* record.

As the crowd waited for the fireworks to begin, the fire chief and several of his crew came over and congratulated Marshall and Private McIntire. Suddenly, a second announcement came over the PA system: "Is there a doctor in attendance? If there is a medical doctor at the stadium, please report to the press box immediately."

Marshall froze when he heard the page for a physician. But by the time he looked over his shoulder for McIntire, he'd disappeared. The doc had dived underneath the fire truck, shed that lab coat, and crawled from the opposite side of the truck. Without his doctor's attire, Private McIntire blended in perfectly with the hundreds of other off-duty soldiers who'd turned out for the fireworks show.

Brodien's record-breaking stunt that evening was far from official. However, if the *Guinness Book of World Records* folks had been there that night they'd have to hand Private Merl McIntire the certificate for the 'World's Fastest Costume Change.'"

• • •

Private Brodien received word from Colonel Johnson of Special Services that General Joseph B. Crawford, the two-star Commanding General at Fort Carson was expecting an on-base visit from the Secretary of the Army, Wilber M. Brucker.

General Crawford was throwing a big party at the Officers' Club to honor Secretary Brucker. He specifically requested that Marshall be the featured entertainer at the gala event. Colonel Johnson called a strategic planning session to determine the scope of the celebration. After introductions and the prerequisite salutations, the multi-star team of lieutenants, colonels, and generals turned to Private Brodien to ask what he planned to do.

"I told them I'd do some comedy magic," Marshall recalls, "some illusions, maybe some hypnotism, and close with a demonstration of fire eating."

"That sounds spectacular," General Crawford said with a smile. "Gentlemen, what do you think?" He looked at the other officers who grinned and nodded their approval. "But as much as I enjoy Brodien's acts of fire eating," the General continued, "it might be … how should I say it? … sort of *vulgar* for the occasion. You know, the officers and their wives will be dining."

The General turned to the Colonel who, without a prompt, said, "Sir, I agree it would definitely be out of place." The other four officers at the table said, "I agree," with one saying, "Perhaps, *inappropriate* is the word…."

General Crawford asked Marshall, "With your experience, Private Brodien, do you think the fire eating would be inappropriate?" The heat was on. Responding matter-of-factually, he said, "Sir, the manipulation of fire and flames is an artistic thing. It's done with professionalism and, since the show is scheduled to take place *after* dinner is served, I feel it would be most appreciated."

Fifteen seconds of silence filled the room.

General Crawford reached inside his uniform jacket and withdrew an embossed silver cigarette case. From his pants pocket emerged a gold-plated Zippo lighter bearing the national symbol of the eagle. After a flint-snap and a lung-filling drag, General Crawford said, "I have to agree, Brodien. I think you should do the fire eating."

"Of course he should do it!" said one lieutenant colonel. There was a "Here, here!," a "Yes, sir!" and a "Certainly!" from the other officers. Colonel Johnson stood and said, "It's a damned good idea to do it. They'll go away talking about it."

At showtime, the officers at the head table paid as much attention to Secretary Brucker and General Crawford as they did to Private Brodien's performance. During his magical comedy, if the audience was amused *and* either the Secretary or the General laughed, the other officers roared. When the audience was genuinely astonished with Marshall's fire-eating finale, and the Secretary and Colonel applauded enthusiastically, the other officers boosted the ovation, adding whistles and shouts.

• • •

Special Services' Little Theatre at Fort Carson continued to book shows for Marshall at the officers' clubs, the NCO Club, and the post service clubs, as well as extra-pay "outside shows" at the nearby Air Force Academy and Ent Air Force Base, and benefits for the numerous hospitals and churches in the area." Bob Tillotson, a civilian hired by the Army as an entertainment director, organized these productions. Marshall was often joined by comedian Bob Kaliban, accordionist Gene Giuzio, and singing rope-spinner Lieutenant Montie Montana Jr. (son of the famed Hollywood rodeo star) for these touring shows.

One night when the troupe was playing a Thanksgiving benefit for the American National Red Cross at the Broadmoor Hotel, Marshall was "discovered" by local orchestra leader Bob McGraw. In addition to providing the house orchestra for the Broadmoor and other resorts around Colorado Springs, McGraw booked floorshows. He liked what Marshall did, and he started sending contracts his way.

They were all one-nighters, after-dinner shows for such clients as the Associate Grocers of Colorado, the National Farm Loan Association, the law firm of Bellinger & Faricy, Star Journal Publishing, the Colorado State Dental Association, and Preferred Risk Mutual Insurance. They paid a whopping $25 to $40, sometimes $50 per show. But for the times, it was great supplemental income and enough work that enabled Marshall to move off base. He rented a hotel room in town, bought a four-door Buick sedan to travel from gig to gig, and only reported to Colonel Johnson whenever he was needed for Special Services shows.

• • •

Lieutenant General W.H. Arnold, the Commanding General of Fifth United States Army, visited Fort Carson in the spring of 1958. "General Arnold and his wife saw my show at the Officers' Club. They really liked it, and insisted that I come to Chicago, where they lived. They wanted me to entertain at a big party they were throwing that weekend."

Orders were cut for Pvt. Brodien to accompany the General back to Chicago. He packed all his props and equipment, which were hauled to the airstrip to meet the plane. However, an hour before departure, the captain of the aircraft approached General Arnold and said, "We're overweight and there's no way the magician's stuff can go on this airplane."

After checking schedules and finding out there were no other flights to Chicago, not even the following day, General Arnold said, "It's imperative that we get this man's equipment on the plane. How do we do that?"

"Sir," said the pilot, "the only way to accomplish that is to take off fuel."

"Very well," the General said. "We'll wait while it's done." A salute and a phone call later, a tanker truck had sided the plane and pumped out enough fuel to equal the weight of Marshall and his magic show.

As they approached Chicago, one of the General's aides came to the back

Always entertaining the top brass, Brodien was flown to Fort Sheridan, Illinois, for a party at the home of General W. H. Arnold, the Commanding General of the Fifth U.S. Army. From left: Marshall, accordion player Gene Giuzio, General Arnold and his wife, and comedian Bob Kaliban. *Marshall Brodien Collection*

of the plane to talk with Marshall. He knew that Chicago was his hometown, and because it would be two nights before the party at the General's home, the captain wanted to know if Private Brodien would like to visit with his family until that time. When Marshall said yes, they radioed ahead, telling the ground crew that when they landed they would need additional transportation for the magician.

"When we stepped off the plane," Marshall recalls, "there was this shiny black Mercury with stars on it for General Arnold and his wife, and behind it was a brand-new staff car, driven by a sergeant who'd been given orders to take me to my house on North Avenue. Here I was a Private First Class, and they had a sergeant dropping me off at my house. I spent two days visiting with my mother and friends, then on the afternoon of the show, the staff car picked me up and took me out to the General's home at Fort Sheridan to set up."

Brodien's magic show was the hit of the party. The next morning he received a call: "We hope that you brought enough clothes to stay another two or three weeks. General Arnold has you lined up for a series of shows at not only Fort Sheridan, but at the Navy, Air Force, and Veterans Administration installations throughout the Chicago area."

Marshall ended up staying in Chicago for 23 days. He did shows at military hospitals and was shuttled around for performances at Nike missile sites and Army and Navy bases in the surrounding area. Just about all of these shows were during the day, allowing evenings free to pick up some private shows. It gave him a couple of weekends to book his hypnosis show at the Boston Nocturne Club, a venue where he'd eventually be headlining after being discharged from the Army.

"When it was time to return to Fort Carson, I was booked on a commercial airline flight. Because it was the weekend, I delayed my flight and did a couple more nights at the Boston Club," Marshall recalls. On the following Monday morning, when he finally did report to Fort Carson, his sergeant informed him, "The Captain wants to see you, now."

"Brodien, you are three days AWOL!" the Captain barked. "Where in gawd's name have you been for the past three days ... and nights?"

Marshall said, "Didn't General Arnold call you?"

"No, he didn't!"

"Well, sir, he kept me for a few more shows. You can call him and he'll verify that."

"I'm not about to call him," the Captain said. "You're dismissed." Then he turned to the sergeant and said, "Make sure Brodien gets paid expenses for the extra three days they kept him in Chicago."

• • •

Brodien had become Fort Carson's unofficial ambassador of good times for the top brass. So impressed was General Arnold with Marshall's talents and capabilities that he dispatched him to entertain at military ceremonies everywhere.

When General Willard G. Wyman, the Commanding General of the United States Continental Army was retiring, General Arnold invited Brodien to board a plane and fly to Fort Monroe, Virginia to entertain for the four-star General's retirement party. Marshall was told, "You an entertainer. Have fun. Don't worry about being a soldier tonight."

"After the big show," Marshall says, "I kept on doing more tricks for the admirals and commanding officers who'd gathered at the bar. They were all having a good time and didn't want the party to end."

However, most of the Army Air Force brass had to be in Florida the next day for the launching of Explorer 1, which would carry the first successful United

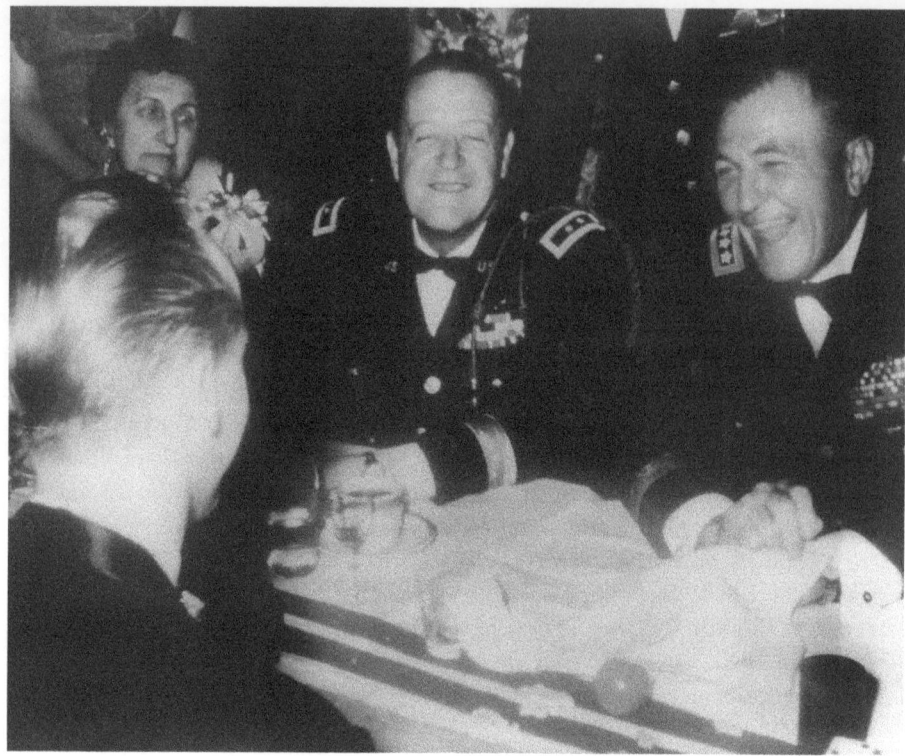

Private Brodien entertains General Buchanan (left) and retiring General Willard G. Wyman (right) at Fort Monroe, Virginia, in 1958. *Marshall Brodien Collection*

States satellite. They couldn't take him with them, so the General decided, "Let's keep the magician here on the post. We'll be back in a couple of days."

He remained at Fort Monroe three more days. "The captain, who was the aide to General Wyman, gave me his car to drive around while he was gone. It had all the official stickers, so when I'd drive off post and do as I pleased, the guards would salute me, not knowing I was a PFC just taking a joy ride."

Meanwhile, General Crawford was calling from Fort Carson: "Brodien, why in the hell are you still there? That show was supposed to be over days ago. Hell, you even missed your bartender friend Carmie Manno's wedding. He married mob boss Sam Giancana's daughter — think her name's Antoinette — last Saturday. A telegram arrived the day you left, inviting you to the wedding. But more important than that, I need you for a goddammed party tomorrow night, a big shindig honoring the commanding general of the U.S. Air Defense Command."

11. Straitjackets and Shenanigans

"I told General Crawford that General Wyman wanted me to stay at Fort Monroe while they were at the missile launch. I said that orders were issued for me to wait there and do some more shows when his party returned."

In a voice loud enough to negate the need for a long-distance phone connection, General Crawford roared, "Brodien, you may be a goddamned in-demand celebrity over on the East Coast, but just remember you are stationed at Fort Carson, which is under my command over here in beautiful Colorado Springs, Colorado! I order you to be back on post by noon tomorrow! The show is at nineteen-hundred hours, sharp!"

Eventually, enough aides made calls to reach General Wyman's party in Florida, and permission was granted to release Marshall to fly back to Fort Carson. At the party he was introduced as "the entertainer who has brought much prestige and recognition to Fort Carson."

"Again, after my show, I did close-up magic for all the officers and politicians who'd gathered at the bar. I walked up to the three-star Commanding General of the Army Air Defense Command and told him I wanted to show him a trick with a pencil on a string. I unbuttoned his coat, which raised the eyebrows of the other officers. I fastened this pencil to his coat, telling him it was a puzzle to see if he could get it off. He was laughing and after a few minutes said, 'I can't get the goddamned thing off.'"

A captain volunteered to help, hoping to avoid any embarrassment. But Marshall stopped him saying that all it takes a little magic. He snapped his fingers and pulled the pencil free of the buttonhole. The General said, "That's pretty good..." But the rest of the brass were obviously nervous about the trick.

The next morning, when Marshall showed up at the Little Theatre, where Colonel Johnson's office was, the head of Special Services yelled out, "Brodien, come in my office you sonovabitch! What the hell happened with you at the party last night? You had the nerve to walk up to a general and mess with the buttons on his coat. Your ass is going to Cheyenne Mountain!"—a place in the nearby Colorado mountains that was apparently akin to the tundra of Russia.

An hour later, the phone rang at the Colonel's office. It was the aide to the General. "That trick that the magician did last night with the pencil ... the General wants to know how he can get a few more of those."

After lunch, Marshall was called back into Johnson's office. This time, the Colonel was laughing, and said, "Brodien, I'm sure I scared the shit out of you this morning, didn't I?"

Marshall looked puzzled, and said, "Well, I wasn't exactly expecting..."

Johnson interrupted. "I was just kidding around with you. That magic pencil thing you did with the General was really amazing. Uh, by the way ... how long would it take to get a few more of those sent in?"

"Should be no problem," Marshall said, placing a call to the magic shop in Denver.

An orderly was dispatched to pick up a dozen of the then patent-applied-for Magic Holetite Pencils. As soon as the trick pencils arrived, Colonel Johnson personally delivered them to the visiting general's quarters.

More than one ass was saved from going to Cheyenne Mountain.

• • •

One Saturday morning that fall, three or four of Marshall's soldier friends were looking for something fun to do on their weekend leave. So, they all piled in his big Buick and headed down the highway. They passed a billboard advertising the Colorado State Fair in Pueblo, about 30 miles south of Colorado Springs. It took no arm-twisting whatsoever to get Marshall to head for the fairgrounds. "I told my friends I might even know some of the showpeople working there. There was always the possibility that Al Szasz or Dick Best could have traveling shows there."

Once inside the front gate, the quartet of soldiers whizzed past the tents with the livestock, baked and canned goods, mining machinery, and institutional exhibits and headed straight for the fun and games of the midway. As they strolled toward the carnival rides, Marshall spotted a sideshow tent. The ten-in-one attraction was called *The World of Wonders* and was operated by an old carney from South Florida. As Marshall perused the banners out front, he didn't recognize a single act.

"The guys wanted to go in anyway. But when I looked over to the opposite side of the midway, I saw another show tent — something I knew they'd much rather see." Leading the way across the crowded midway, Marshall advised, "Hey, I'm going to treat you men to a real show." There, playing the midway of the Colorado State Fair, in all its tantalizing and titillating glory, was *Hedy Jo Star's French Follies*. A scratchy needle-drop, sultry saxophone solo blared over the loudspeakers. Seven of the gorgeous show creatures were lined up on the platform. They were about to start the ballyhoo.

"It was an eerie feeling when Hedy Jo came out on the stage," Marshall recalls. "I didn't say anything to the guys that might clue them to the fact that I knew her." It'd been a long time since the experience in East St. Louis, and he thought maybe she wouldn't recognize him. But when Marshall smiled at Hedy Jo and she winked and grinned back, the troops grew suspicious. The moment Hedy Jo finished the bally, she motioned Marshall over to the side of the ticket box.

"If it isn't the magician," Hedy Jo said. "I knew I'd be seeing you again. I still can't believe you just left me there, wherever the hell we were, in the middle of the night without a goodbye..." The soldiers were dumbfounded and looked at Marshall with mouths agape. Hedy Jo winked again and said, "Well, as they say in gay Pariee, *C'est la vive!* Let's hurry and get you and your friends into this next show!"

Hedy Jo hustled the guys into the tent, patting a couple of them on the butt. She escorted them to front row seats and said, "Boys, when the show's over don't run off. I want you all to come backstage and meet the gals."

"This is wild!" said one of the soldiers, after Hedy Jo had gone backstage. "Yeah, Marsh, we can't believe it," said another. "You're the man!"

The bump-'n'-grind soundtrack cranked up, the houselights dimmed, and Brodien did not know what to expect when the curtain parted. He only remembered the warning he'd been given at the diner in East St. Louis, when the carnival owner cautioned, "That whole damned show is full of them boy-girl types." Now, two years later and only two minutes into the show, Marshall knew it was true. But the costumes were lavish, and whatever the young men had done to alter their bodies was amazing. Just about everybody in the audience, including Marshall's buddies, was whistling and hooting and hollering. They had no idea that *Hedy Jo Star's French Follies* was a full-bloom drag queen revue.

"After the show, I wanted to get out of there quick, but out came Hedy Jo to give us the backstage tour." Marshall's soldier friends were obviously still fooled and apparently awestruck when they were introduced to the ladies who really weren't. "I was nervous and really felt uncomfortable when Hedy Jo put her arm around me and told the cast, 'Marshall and I go back a long way.' And even though the guys wanted to stick around for the next show, I finally got them out on the midway, telling Hedy Jo we were going to get something to eat before we watched another show."

As they ordered hot dogs and hamburgers, Marshall told them the story of meeting Hedy Jo at the carnival and how he was suspicious of her gender, but didn't know until today that the whole cast was comprised of female impersonators. At first, the soldiers refused to believe him. But the more they thought about the manly sounding voices and the mountains of make up and mascara that the "ladies" wore, the more they realized something was fishy at the *French Follies*.

"Thankfully, by the time we finished our food, my friends were convinced the girls were not girls. But now, the crazy thing was they wanted to see the show again, more than ever!

"I said, 'You guys can go back, but I'm not. I'll meet you at the car.'"

• • •

During his two-year tenure in the United States Army Reserve, Specialist 4th Class Marshall E. Brodien gave an estimated 575 performances of his magic and hypnotism.

Several months before he was to be discharged, he received a call from Lieutenant General Arnold, the man who'd been a staunch supporter of his talents since the day he first saw him perform. The General tried to talk him into staying in the service. "Make a respectable career of it," he advised. There wasn't a war going on, yet Marshall got the old "Uncle Sam Needs You!" pitch. General Arnold offered to commission him as a lieutenant and put him in charge of Special Services at 5th Army Headquarters in Chicago. Marshall graciously declined the offer and told the General that he had aspirations to pursue the life of a professional entertainer.

As Marshall's discharge date neared, the question arose as to how much of the magic equipment accumulated over the two years actually belonged to the Army. "I had a $150, sometimes $200 per month, expense account from which I could purchase props and order new tricks whenever I needed them. Some of the things I had brought with me when I enlisted, but I did go through quite a few dollars worth of magic apparatus."

The chief of staff at Fort Carson called a meeting to decide what they were going to do with the equipment. One officer said, "Well, when we get another magician drafted in, he will certainly be able to use most of that stuff we bought." Another said, "The problem is we bought a lot of this equipment to replace items that Brodien brought with him when he enlisted." One colonel suggested, "How about if we compensate Brodien for all the props and things of his that were expended, then we keep the rest of the equipment to use in Special Services shows?"

All heads turned when Brigadier General Crawford stood and said, "You know, Brodien did a lot of shows for us. A lot of very good shows. And these shows were not just for our post and the community. Remember when he represented Fort Carson for an entire month, doing all those shows for General Arnold at the veterans' hospitals in Chicago? Maybe we should entertain the idea of selling this equipment to Brodien. Don't you think he deserves to have it? Besides, who else knows how to make it work? Maybe we could just sell it to him for $75 or something like that, a figure that would look good for the records."

"Well, once the General suggested that plan," says Marshall, "and even though some of the officers were against it, they all had to agree. A week later, I went out and rented a U-Haul trailer and started packing up everything to take back home."

No sooner had he started loading the trailer when he received a call from Brigadier General R.A. Risden. The post was planning a recognition dinner for a group of key defense contractors and they desperately needed Brodien to entertain. However, the party was scheduled for April 17, 1959, three days *after* Marshall's discharge date of April 14.

11. Straitjackets and Shenanigans

He told the general that he was booked to open that weekend at a nightclub in Chicago. He didn't see how he could do it. A friend was on the way to Colorado to help him pack up and drive back home. The general couldn't order him to perform, so he pleaded, adding that if there was ever one time in his life he could do his country a favor it would be now.

Marshall mulled it over, and being the true Special Services trouper that he was, said that he would call and arrange for the nightclub to delay his opening. He would hang around the base and do the show ... providing his commanding officer could arrange a reciprocal favor.

His friend from Chicago had never flown in an airplane. Marshall requested that after the show, they go up for a day of aerial sightseeing around the great State of Colorado. A deal was struck and a plane was dispatched from the Air Academy to Fort Carson. The plane was to be at the service of civilian Brodien for the entire day. "The pilot had orders to take us anywhere we wanted to be flown. We went up and over Cheyenne Mountain and flew over the Rockies all morning. For some reason, I couldn't talk that pilot into flying under the Royal Gorge Bridge."

12

Nightclub Necromancer

MARSHALL BRODIEN! AMERICA'S MOST ENTERTAINING HYPNOTIST! MAGICIAN EXTRAORDINARY! The 12-foot wide, 3-foot high, red lettered canvas banner in front of the Boston Nocturne Club at 4224 West North Avenue heralded the return of the neighborhood's favorite son. His smiling countenance graced the cover of *Chicago Welcome, The Complete Guide for Chicagoans and Tourists.* On the inside pages, Jimmy Karris and Joe Sciortino, proprietors of the Boston Nocturne — which was advertised as the "West Side's Smart New Club" — proudly pitted their headliner, young Marshall Brodien, against the likes of Johnny Mathis at the Chez Paree, the Pepper Pots at the Town Casino, Jerry Murad and his Harmonicats at the Chase, and comedian Jack E. Leonard at Mister Kelly's.

Brodien wasn't exactly a new face at the Boston Nocturne. He'd already been booked there three times, between those Special Services performances at Fort Sheridan. The owners loved his act and he was promised a job when he got out of the Army. And because the club was just across the street from his three-story apartment building at 4211 West North Avenue, where he lived with his mother, he could walk to work.

Settling into the two-a-night show schedule, Marshall quickly discovered that the fun-seeking civilian-folks of the Windy City perceived his show of stage hypnotism a little differently than the troops had. Whereas Marshall could usually anticipate the actions and reactions of his soldier subjects, the high-spirited nightclubbers taught him to expect the unexpected.

"I had this bit where I told the five or six hypnotized people who were onstage, 'When you wake up there will be a gorilla standing out there, and the gorilla will just be looking at you.' I told them that the gorilla wouldn't bother them or hurt anybody because he was stuck to the floor."

Despite the hypnotic suggestion that the jungle beast was harmless, when the subjects were told to wake up most were startled or frightened. Some screamed the second they opened their eyes. Others bolted from the stage to escape from the gorilla.

Then one night, there was a man who, when awakened, just sat in his chair and stared. When Marshall asked, "Sir, do you see the gorilla standing there?" the man nodded, as he slowly reached into his jacket, and pulled out a .38-caliber pistol.

Patrons seated in the front row ducked beneath their tables and scattered to the floor. Marshall immediately said, "Sleep!" The command was obeyed. The gentleman's head fell forward, the gun dropped into his lap.

Marshall grabbed the weapon and stuck it in his pocket. He told the man, "There was no such thing as a gorilla. It was only something you imagined. When you wake up, you will not remember a gorilla or anything." Marshall then slowly counted from one to four, reminding him that on "four" he would open his eyes and not remember a thing.

"I asked the guy how he felt, and he said, 'Fine.' I said, 'What would you do if a gorilla walked into the Boston Club?' He said, 'I'd probably shoot him.' When I asked him what he did for a living he told me he was a police detective. 'Does that mean you carry a gun?' I asked. 'Of course,' he said, 'right here inside my coat.' When the cop patted the front of his jacket, then looked inside at his empty holster, he said, 'Hey, what's goin' on here? Where's my piece?'

"I said to him, 'Does this look familiar?'" When Brodien casually produced the pistol from his pocket and asked the detective if the safety was on or off, the place went ballistic. "It's a loaded gun!" yelled a lady in the back. People scattered again and ducked beneath their tables. "After that incident," Marshall says, "I took the gorilla bit out of the act."

• • •

Hypnosis was the focus of Brodien's first five months at the Boston Nocturne. However, by summer's end, he had convinced the owners to build out the stage at the center of the club so he could perform more magic and illusions. Eddie Kosmer, a regular patron at the club and the owner of Dun Rite Cabinets in Chicago, was contracted to do the improvements.

While Kosmer and his crew were at work, Marshall booked himself into Caesar Marconi's Sunset Arms Hotel on Grand Avenue for a two-week engagement. He did some club dates for the Samuels Agency, including a big-budget banquet show for New England Mutual Life. Then he took off to do a private party for "Tex" Moncrief, wealthy owner of Moncrief Oil in Fort Worth.

For the trip to Texas, Marshall went out and bought a shiny black Coupe de Ville. It was a second-hand model, but if you're driving to the land of oil wells and millionaires, why not drive a Cadillac? His buddy Al Szasz wasn't busy so he went along for the ride. The show at Moncrief's sprawling ranch-style estate in Fort Worth was such a hit, the oilman had Marshall stay over the weekend and do another show at the Richland Hills Country Club, for about 200 of Moncrief's employees.

Before they returned home, Marshall and Al pointed the big Cadillac south and drove to Houston, where they met up with Bill Siros, a carnival and sideshow magician who was also in the outdoor advertising business. Siros used his billboard and sign shop to construct props and illusions for magicians, and he had just fabricated a Broomstick Suspension — an effect where a lady floats in the air with her only visible means of support being the straws of a broom placed under her arm. The illusion dates back to 1847, when Robert-Houdin, the "Father of Modern Conjuring," performed it as the Ethereal Suspension. But for this century, Marshall thought a Broomstick Suspension would the perfect addition to his show at the Boston Nocturne. Siros usually charged $175 for building the apparatus, but because Marshall was a fellow carnival worker he got it for $125. After the preemptory hour-and-a-half of cutting up jackpots (gab sessions among carnies), Marshall and Al loaded up the custom-machined broomsticks and were on their way back to Chicago for the big November 7th re-opening of the club.

The new stage at the Boston Nocturne, with rich red velvet curtains and plush carpeting, was spectacular. Eddie Kosmer had done a first-class job with the construction and the decoration. After several intense rehearsals with Evelyn Vogt, a girlfriend that Marshall had given the job as the new "floatee," the Broomstick Suspension was performance ready. Always conscious of the fine art of promotion and ballyhoo, Marshall invited the press to a special showing. One TV station sent a reporter and cameraman to film the festivities. As backup coverage, Eddie was on hand to shoot 8mm movies of the show.

The *Chicago American* of November 11, 1959 carried a photo feature in its "Dusk 'till Dawn" column: "Marshall Brodien, magician and hypnotist at the Boston Nocturne Club on the northwest side, performs one of the most amazing illusions ever done by any magician. He hypnotizes his lovely assistant, Evelyn, so that she is stiff and rigid and then places her atop the sweeping-end of a broom, where she remains suspended in space. It's a real fooler, and when we asked Brodien how it's done, he said, 'Tell your readers to come see me and *maybe* I'll explain it.'"

In addition to hypnosis, Marshall performed comedy magic and illusions at the Boston Nocturne Club. *Marshall Brodien Collection*

• • •

On Monday, June 6, 1960, Marshall's father Arthur Olaf Brodien died at age 57. He was buried at Irving Park Cemetery. "Art," as his friends called him, married Mildred "Millie" Genevieve Erickson on July 26, 1927. A first son, Charles Arthur, was born on February 5, 1930. It would be over four years later before the birth of their second son, Marshall Everett, on July 10, 1934. Marshall's earliest memory of family life was from age five to eight, when he lived with his parents at his grandfather and grandmother's house on Diming Place, near Columbus Hospital. Millie Brodien and her sons later moved into an apartment on North Avenue. "My father was in the painting and decorating business with my grandfather," Marshall says. "Before that he worked as a store manager for National Tea Company. I saw him in the morning before he left the house and in the evening for supper. He belonged to a Swedish club, where he sang in the choir, and he was there every night."

In 1951, the year that young Marshall started working as a magician at Riverview Park, his father pulled a disappearing act. He left home. "My mother just accepted it," Marshall recalls. "She was married to him and remained married to him, even though he'd decided not to stay with her."

Art Brodien didn't return until six years later, when Marshall got out of the Army and started working at the Boston Nocturne Club. "When my father came back, he moved in with me and my mother and my grandfather at the building on North Avenue. But he was uncomfortable staying there, and he would not come into the club to see me performing." Art continued to hang around the neighborhood. Then one afternoon, while shoveling snow in front of the apartments, he met a man who worked with a church around the corner who gave him the opportunity to get back into the decorating business. However, while painting at the church, he had the misfortune to fall from a ladder. The accident put Art in the hospital, where he died two weeks later.

Not long after the burial of his father, Marshall, along with his grandfather Carl August Erikson, bought an apartment building on Talman Avenue. "My grandfather worked at the Sunshine Gospel Mission on Clark Street. He was always helping people out, giving them jobs, and he and his buddies remodeled the building." Marshall's mother moved into the apartment above and realized a substantial income from renting the rest of the building.

• • •

Brodien continued to headline at the Boston Nocturne until July 1960. That's when it became evident that the operating partners, Jimmy Karris and Joe Sciortino, had serious business problems. They hadn't reported sales taxes for the last 11 months, causing authorities to put a padlock on the front door. The landlord was looking for a new tenant.

Marshall was determined to reopen the nightclub. He'd been packing the place every Wednesday, Thursday, Friday, Saturday, and Sunday night for the past year. And though all the cash may not have been part of the former owner's nightly deposits, he knew that food and beverage sales were decent. After talking over the situation with Eddie Kosmer, Marshall decided he wanted to take over. He'd change the name to the Mystic Club and become a nightclub impresario.

"Eddie said he'd let me borrow $5,000 to get the place back up and running. I told him I would make him a partner. But he said he just wanted to make the loan as a friend. He loved magic and he liked the idea of being part of a place where he could bring his friends anytime." Eddie and Marshall became even faster friends that summer, boating and water skiing with friends

Opposite: **Fresh out of the Army, Brodien signs for a run at the Boston Nocturne Club that is so successful he ends up buying the place and changing the name to the Mystic Club.** *Marshall Brodien Collection*

12. Nightclub Necromancer

BOSTON NOCTURNE CLUB
4224 W. NORTH AVENUE

proudly presents

MARSHALL BRODIEN
AMERICA'S MOST ENTERTAINING HYPNOTIST
AND MAGICIAN EXTRAORDINARY

at Fox Lake, an idyllic lakeside community, 42 miles north of Chicago. Marshall would soon be buying a new home there that Eddie was building.

Marshall negotiated a lease with the nightclub's landlord for $500 a month. The first thing he did was change the sign to the Mystic Club, and that was fairly easy because B-O-S-T-O-N had the same vertical letter spacing as M-Y-S-T-I-C. Because he wanted as little down time as possible, a contractor was hired to make the necessary electrical and mechanical repairs, Marshall set out to acquire the licenses and permits that had expired. It was a three-day-long task that taught the real meaning of greasing palms, juicing the joint.

"The first inspector to show up," Marshall remembers, "was one from the health department. He walked into the kitchen, looked at the grease on the grill and in the sink, and then noticed a vent hood that wasn't fixed yet."

Taking a half-smoked cigar from his mouth, the inspector spat into the mop sink and said, "You know you gotta score 90 points on this inspection or they ain't givin' you a license."

"We just need a little time. We can't clean up the greasy mess in the kitchen until they finish the repair on that vent," Marshall said, as he laid a $20 bill on the edge of the sink.

"I understand," the inspector said, putting his cigar back in his mouth, freeing up his left hand to slide ol' Andy Jackson underneath the corner of his clipboard. "Yeah, I do understand. So, I'll put down here that you just got this dirty sink, something I'm sure you're gonna get cleaned up before I get back to the office."

That afternoon, it was the same song, second verse, when the building inspector stopped by to check out the wiring. He found an exhaust fan in the ladies room that wasn't working, and said, "You know I can't okay this job till next time I'm in the neighborhood, which might be a while." Marshall assured him that an electrician had ordered a new fan motor, as he peeled off another $20 bill, which elicited the stock reply of "I understand, I *do* understand."

• • •

Only hours before the Mystic Club's grand opening, a uniformed cop walked in the front door, looked around, and took a seat at the otherwise empty bar. Marshall approached the policeman, who said, "In checking out your place from the outside, I notice that you can't see the lounge through a front window. It's a city ordinance — you gotta be able to see the bar from the street."

Marshall argued that the large glass front doors were windows. "You can look right into the lounge through those doors. And besides," he said, "the other owners ran this place for years without a window."

"Sorry, but you have to take care of it," the cop said, starting to stand.

"How about if I take care of you?" Marshall asked. The officer looked down, noticing that Marshall was holding a folded twenty spot.

"I'm going to the washroom, but I'll leave my hat here on bar."

When the cop returned, he picked up his hat and Old Andrew, too. He nonchalantly strolled outside and, after the door closed behind him, he turned and looked through the glass. He smiled and tipped his hat toward Marshall, whom he could clearly see, standing there in the lounge.

• • •

Until Marshall took over the lease, he had little occasion to go down to the basement. It served as the bar's liquor storage area, had a 100-cubic-foot walk-in cooler, and was the location of Karl the Bomber's workshop. Former club owner Jimmy Karris let his friend Karl Ferarro keep a corner workbench where he made bombs for his fishermen friends. While not exactly sanctioned by the game warden, Karl's explosive charges were used to stun fish, making them easy to collect with a net.

As soon as Marshall saw the small dynamite sticks, fuses, and pyrotechnic paraphernalia stashed about the area, he called Karl and told him that, as the new club owner, he did not want those explosives in his basement.

Karl showed up the next morning to remove his arsenal. He'd spent about an hour hauling everything up to the trunk of his car. He had the place pretty much cleaned up, with the exception of a metal tool chest, when he called Marshall to come downstairs and take a look at something.

"This one's my pride-'n'-joy," Karl said, holding up a piece of lead pipe. "This foot-long baby, with an inside diameter of an inch-and-a-half, is filled with enough gunpowder to…" he hesitated, stepped closer to Marshall, lowered his voice and continued. "If I threw this sucker into the sewer, every manhole cover for a mile would blow sky high."

"I believe you," Marshall said. "So please get it out of here."

"Can't do that. Not till I disarm it," Karl said. "Unless it's dismantled, it has the potential blow this building to smithereens." He started unscrewing the two end caps. "You gotta be careful. Do it slow and easy. You don't want friction to cause a spark."

Suddenly, a shrill whistling noise filled the basement. Karl flinched. The compressor motor of the walk-in cooler had kicked in. Karl tossed the pipe into the air. It fell to the concrete floor with a dull *thud*.

"That's it!" Marshall shouted. "Get your stuff out of here now."

It took Karl one more trip up and down the stairs to vacate the basement and be on his way. Then five minutes later, after Marshall had gone back to his office to do some paperwork, there was a tremendous explosion in the back parking lot. "I looked out the window and saw smoke pouring out of a huge hole in one of the garbage cans. I was heading for the door to see what the damage was when the phone rang."

It was Karl, and he was laughing so hard he could barely talk. "How 'bout that one, Marsh? Just a parting shot for you. And, hey, that's one of Karl the Bomber's little ones!"

• • •

One night a young man came into the club, sat at the bar, and ordered a drink. It sounds like the first line of one of those a-man-walks-into-a-bar jokes, but it's actually the start of a true tale of the woes of owning a place that sells liquor. "No sooner had the guy been served," Marshall says, "when two plain-clothes policemen approached me. One asked, 'Do you know that kid at the bar?' When I said no, the other said, 'He's 19 years old, and he's drinking in your place.'"

When the teenager spotted the two detectives talking with Brodien, he darted into the restroom to flush the fake ID he'd flashed to the bartender. The cops could care less. The law that had been violated was serving a minor.

"When they told me that," Marshall says, "I said they ought to corner the kid and arrest him, acting like I was just the owner who didn't know the rules. But the detectives weren't buying that. They told me, 'We're taking you down to the station. This could cost you your license.'"

When Marshall arrived at the precinct station, he asked if he could make a phone call. He told the sergeant at the desk that he needed to phone his friend Eddie Kosmer. The call was allowed. Eddie talked with the sergeant on duty, assuring him that first thing in the morning the chief of police would receive an important call.

"Because of what Eddie told them, they kept me off the books that night. At eight A.M., the chief of police called me in and said: 'I got a call from a good friend of mine, who assured me you're a nice person, a pretty good magician, too... Since you are really the main entertainment at the club, there will be no charges pressed.'" As it turned out, the detectives were trailing the teenager because he was wanted for some misdemeanors, and he just happened to pop into the Mystic Club.

• • •

A year later, Marshall was ready to get out of the nightclub business. "My dream was to *perform only*. I wanted go into the Cairo Supper Club, because that's where all the classy hypnotists headlined. It's where Dante, Ted Boyer, and Dr. Michael Dean worked."

That summer he sold the Mystic Club to Eddie Balzac, a friend who loved magic and hypnotism. Balzac struggled to keep the place alive, booking magicians and even trying his hand at doing an act, but without Brodien's name out front, the place was destined to go under in less than a year.

13

The Cairo

Bill Anastos, the owner of the Cairo Supper Club at 4015 North Sheridan Road, just off Irving Park, had come into the Mystic Club more than once to see Brodien's act. And on more than one occasion, Marshall had suggested to Bill that his hypnotic show could be a big draw at his posh nightclub.

"I don't know," Anastos said, "The Cairo has such a mature clientele, and you're so young looking. I'm not too sure it'd work. But I'll consider it." Marshall, using the same tactic he'd employed when Dick Best told him he was too young to be the sideshow magician at Riverview Park, put forth the old just-try-me-for-a-week, it's-free-if-you-don't-like-it offer. Anastos had the urge to take him up on it then and there, but said, "That's interesting. I'll give it some consideration."

In early July of 1961, an opening did come up at the Cairo. Their stage hypnotist of the last two years, Dr. Michael Dean — his name was Dr. Stanford I. Berman, and he held a master's degree from Columbia University and a doctorate in communications from Northwestern University — had received invitations to serve on the faculties of both Northwestern and the University of Chicago. Performing nightly at the Cairo no longer had a place in Dr. Dean's new schedule, and he gave notice that his hypnotic pursuits would be more academic.

Anastos needed a hypnotist, and rather than wasting time trying out Brodien for a free week as he'd offered, he phoned him and booked him for a month.

"The Cairo Supper Club was like a Vegas showroom," Marshall says. The décor was elegant with linen on the tables, candle lighting, plush booth seating, and at showtime the bar moved forward making way for the extended thrust stage. Anastos prided himself on the fine dining, music for dancing and, in addition to a headline hypnotist, there was always a top musical-comedy group — favorites such as the Dyna-Tones, the Flaim Brothers, the Million-Aires, Frankie Mayo and his New Yorkers. Brodien opened on July 7, 1961, with the popular group, the Pepper Pots.

During the first week, at the insistence of Anastos, Marshall performed some magic and the Broomstick Suspension as part of his show. However, as much as the patrons were entertained by the illusions, they had come to the nightspot to see hypnotism. Showtime at the Cairo Supper Club had become synonymous with hypnotic shows. So, in the tradition of pioneer nightclub hypnotist Ted Boyer, the flamboyant Ronald Dante (who married actress Lana Turner), and Dr. Michael Dean, the professor who had just bowed out, Marshall's show at the Cairo became all hypnosis.

Brodien worked at a much faster pace than most nightclub hypnotists, and his high-energy show more than pleased Anastos' "mature clientele." But of greater importance were the new faces showing up in the audiences every night. Word was out that the young hypnotist at the Cairo was hip and doing hilarious things that you had to see to believe.

One hypnotic stunt that was getting favorable press was something Marshall called his "One Hundred Dollar Test." He would inform his hypnotized subjects that for being such good sports tonight, he had a gift for them — $100. "I would show them a $100 bill, but tell them that no matter how hard they tried to pick it up, they wouldn't be able to. I'd place the bill on a chair and say, 'Okay, pick it up and it's yours.'"

The subjects tried, one at a time, to pick up the bill, but no one could. Each person grew even more frustrated when given a second chance and couldn't budge the flimsy piece of paper. Sometimes, two or three men teamed up and tried to pick it up. It was as if the $100 bill was engraved on the leather upholstery of the chair.

"I finally told one fellow that when I woke everybody up, he'd be able to walk over to the chair and pick up the $100. However, I warned him that the bill would be extremely hot, burning hot. When everybody was awakened, this guy looked over at the chair and said, 'Hey, that's my $100!' But as soon as he grabbed it, he yelled, 'Hot damn!' and dropped it. I would walk over and pick it up, put it in my pocket, and say, 'Well, if you don't want it, I'll take it.'"

Marshall's experiment with the $100 bill made the columns of the entertainment writers, but when he upped the ante and started performing it with a $1,000 bill, he received the attention of the news reporters. "Want to pick up $1,000 tonight?" asked the headline of a *Chicago News* story about the show at the Cairo. One UPI-wire story carried the bannerline: "Brodien's hypno-stunt with $1,000 is simply grand."

Marshall was known for the speed with which he put his subjects under a hypnotic spell, sometimes with a mere snap of his fingers. *Marshall Brodien Collection*

• • •

About 95 percent of the fun of participating in a hypnotic show, being one of the onstage subjects, takes place *after* the show — when your friends who were sitting out in the audience tell you of the totally unbelievable things that you did onstage.

However, there was one bit Brodien did that was nearly impossible for people to explain to their hypnotized friends. It was the "ABC Speaker." Marshall would tell a subject, "You are the world's greatest public speaker. You have achieved fame and fortune with your ability to excel in persuasive speaking using only the 26 letters of the alphabet." He then turned toward the audience and introduced "a prominent politician who would like to speak to us on some important issues."

Upon hearing the snap of Marshall's fingers, the subject awakened and stepped up to an imaginary podium: "A, b, n, c, y, d? K, p, e, r, i, t, t, e, g, o, u, t!" The audience would applaud, encouraging the speaker to make even more profound statements. "R, u, n, d? F, e, a, i, o, u...." More applause. "U,

Subjects under Marshall's hypnotic spell were completely oblivious to the audience's screams of laughter. *Marshall Brodien Collection*

k, k, e, a, t, t, y! W, h, i, m, k! J, l, o, n, o, t!" The hypnotized speaker rambled off random letters of the alphabet with such conviction that people in the audience believed they were hearing sentences that made sense. The crowd howled with laughter, and to their collective chagrin, usually couldn't remember the nonsensical strings of letters or what made the ABC Speaker so funny.

The finale of the hypnotic show became the talk of the town. It was something he'd done occasionally while in the Army, and then for almost two years at his own club on North Avenue. But it wasn't until he started working at the Cairo Club that he used it as his dramatic closer.

"At the end of my show I selected a lady who was still in a hypnotic trance and placed her in a *rigid state*. I would tell her, "Your body is totally rigid ... just like a piece of solid steel ... so stiff that you cannot bend it.' She was lifted and balanced between two chairs. Her neck rested on the back of one chair; her ankles were across the top of the other chair."

The mesmerized lady was indeed stiff as a board, stretched out 180-degrees flat, supine and perfectly parallel with the stage floor. Brodien removed his patent leather shoes and stood on the seat of a third chair that had been scooted near the woman's waist. With a helping hand from one of the band members, he gently placed his right foot on the lady's upper thigh. Carefully lifting his other foot and stepping onto her midriff, the entire weight of his 165-pound body shifted to the middle of her body. There wasn't the slightest sway. As Brodien stood atop his sleeping subject and raised his arms, there was an enthusiastic ovation, and cries of "No way!"

When the applause subsided, Marshall quickly stepped down and took a seat directly beneath his unbendable assistant. He said, "When I count to four, your body will become limp and completely relaxed. You will not remember anything that has happened. Any tension you might have had will disappear. In fact, you will feel as if you had eight wonderful hours of relaxing sleep." On "four," the lady opened her eyes, obviously surprised to find herself resting in the hypnotist's arms.

Marshall would say to the audience, "How about a big round of applause for the star of our show?" As the woman was shown back to her seat, she would invariably ask Marshall, "What did I just do up there?" This brought the standard reply, "Just ask your friends...."

Not too long after beginning the engagement at the Cairo Club, Brodien's rigid-lady stunt experienced what might be called an unexpected curtain call. "It really started *after* my first show. I'd done the rigid bit and sent the lady back to where she was sitting; this time it happened to be at the bar. She started talking with a gentleman sitting next to her, and it wasn't long before they left together. I later learned from the bartender that the guy invited her to go have a drink somewhere else." In other words, she got picked up.

Ten minutes before showtime for the midnight show, Marshall was

Brodien stands on the rigid body of a young lady in a deeop hypnotic trance, as she's suspended on chair backs only by her ankles and neck. *Marshall Brodien Collection*

13. The Cairo

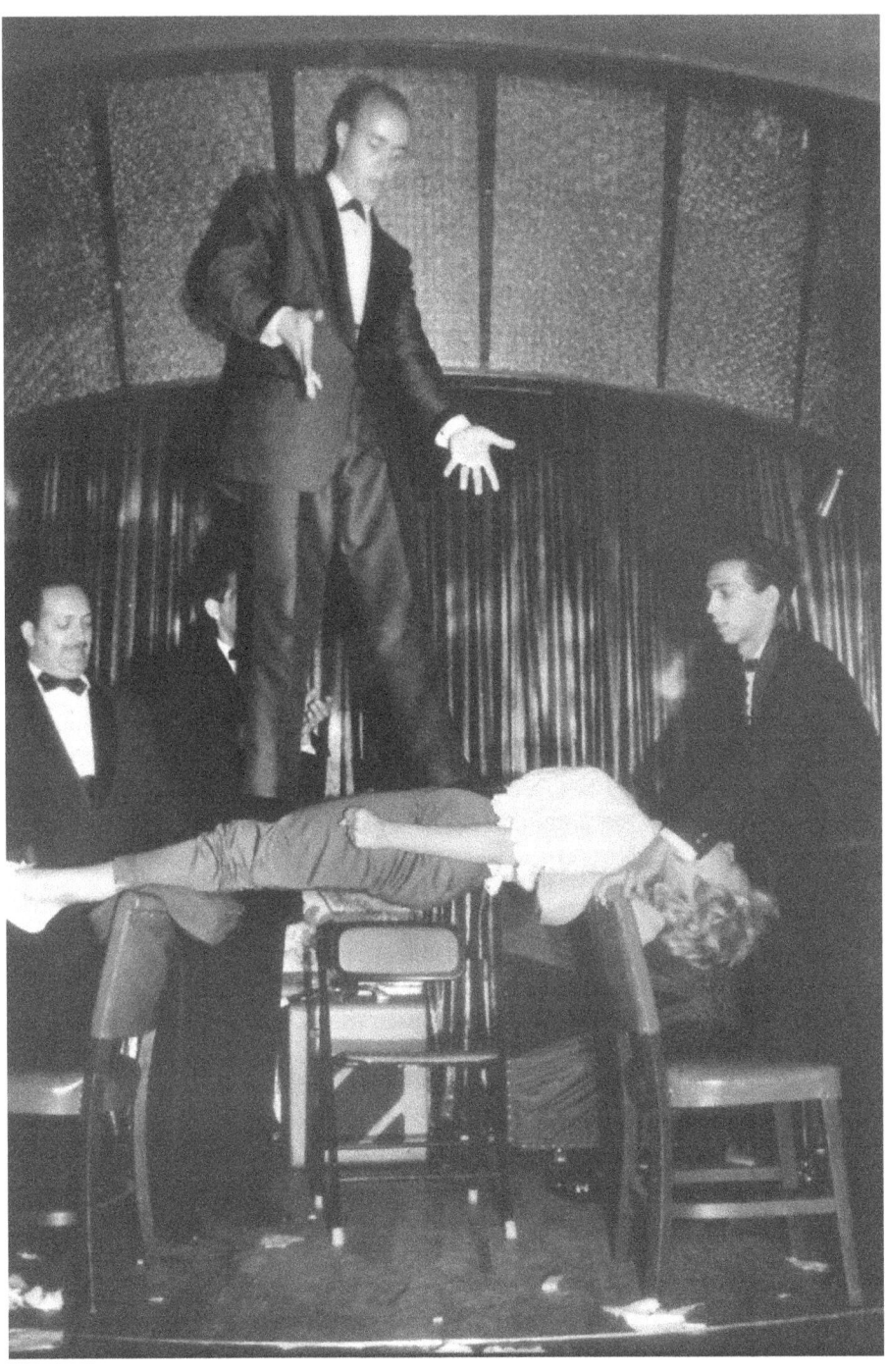

informed he had a telephone call at the front desk. When he picked up, a panicky voice said, "Excuse me, Mr. Brodien, but, this is Jack, uh, Jack Crow. I was just at your place about an hour ago and, uh, anyway, do you remember that girl you hypnotized? You put her between chairs and stood on her?"

"Yes, I do," Marshall said. "A tall, attractive young lady, brown hair, brown eyes, wearing a red dress."

"Uh, yeah, red dress, that's her. Well, we came here to this other club to do some dancing, if you get my drift. You know, just have another drink. Well, as soon as the music started she went stiff on me."

Apparently, when the band began playing it caused the woman to regress to her rigid state. She was lying on the dance floor, flat on her back, unyielding as a slab of Italian marble. Marshall advised, "Just let her stay there for a couple of minutes. She will probably come out of it."

Exactly three minutes later, the phone rang. "She's still stiff! Just like she was when you hypnotized her. Whatta I do? Should I take her to a hospital somewhere? God-a-mighty, I don't even know her name!"

Because it was less than a minute till showtime, Marshall said, "Talk to her and tell her she was part of the show at the Cairo Club. Remind her she was hypnotized. Maybe that will be enough to get her out of the trance."

Marshall started his midnight show, but he didn't finish it. He had about ten minutes to go and was beginning the rigid-lady finale, when a big commotion broke out at the front door. Jack Crow was back. "I brought her here!" he yelled. "Tell Mr. Brodien I have returned the girl in the red dress! And it's not rigor mortis 'cause she's still breathing! She's out in the car." Marshall apologized to the audience and told them the performance would be cut a little short due to an emergency situation.

Marshall went out to the parking lot to discover that Jack was driving a Volkswagen. And the girl wasn't sitting in the front seat of the bug. Instead, she was lying rigid across the tops of the car seats. Her feet were stuck over the backseat, up against the rear window; her shoulders hung over the front seat, with her head almost touching the front windshield. She had been *loaded* into the compact vehicle.

"When I woke her up," Marshall remembers, "she looked around and asked, 'What are we doing out in the parking lot? Whose car is this? Can't we go back inside?' The woman didn't remember being hypnotized or leaving the club."

By the end of August, Bill Anastos changed the marquee sign out front of his building to read: MARSHALL BRODIEN — AMERICA'S MOST ENTERTAINING HYPNOTIST. The offer to fill in for three weeks had turned into the bigtime. He was headlining without the hassles of running a restaurant. And he would end up staying at the Cairo as long as the club stayed in business.

13. The Cairo

• • •

Before the woman-on-the-chairs stunt, there was "Bubbles La Rue." It was a laugh-filled closing piece employing post-hypnotic suggestion. However, because the rigid-lady had become such a strong finale at the Cairo — placing audiences in a true state of awe and often mute with amazement — Marshall decided to move the Bubbles bit to his encore or callback piece. It was a surefire piece that left 'em laughing.

"I started doing it in the Army, in my first hypnosis shows at the officers' club. Toward the end of the act, I would tell one my subjects, usually a soldier or an officer's wife, that when the band played 'Night Train' they were going to jump up and do a crazy, sexy dance. I said, 'As soon as you hear that music, you will become the famous exotic dancer, Bubbles La Rue.'"

Immediately following Marshall's performance, as soon as his deep-sleeping subjects were awakened, thanked, and sent back to their seats, the band returned to the stage and went into to the raunchy rhythms of "Night Train." Drums and cymbals crashed. Saxophones honked. It was Bubbles' cue to boogaloo.

Upon hearing the music, the person harboring the post-hypnotic suggestion stood up, sometimes on a chair, often on the tabletop, and commenced to bump and grind. Brodien would grab the microphone: "Ladies and gentlemen, please give a rousing welcome to the internationally known dancing star, Bubbles La Rue!" There were cheers, whistles, and screams of laughter as the hypnotically transmuted exotic dancer gyrated and sashayed toward the stage. And no matter whether Bubbles was male or female, there were the inevitable cries of "Take it off!" and "Yeah, baby, take it *all* off!"

More provocative males were allowed to strip off their shirts and start unbuckling belts to drop their trousers. Naughty women unbuttoned blouses down to revealing a bra. At that point, to avoid post-hypnotic embarrassment, Marshall gave the "Sleep!" command. The payoff came in the surprised look on the subject's face when he or she was awakened and discovered they were partially undressed.

One night at the Cairo, when it was time to invite people onstage to be hypnotized, there were two extremely attractive young women sitting at the bar. One of them, a redhead, was more than eager to volunteer. Marshall already had eight or nine people onstage, but he quickly pointed to her, saying, "And how about this lady sitting at the bar?"

"You'll be sorry!" shouted her companion, laughing loudly.

At the time, Marshall had no clue why the friend said that. "Before I knew it she was standing beside me," he recalls. "She was about five-foot-ten, had a terrific figure, and looked like a movie star. During the induction, she went under like a charm. I'd already decided I was going to use her for the Bubbles bit at the end of the show."

When the time came, the redhead was given the usual hypnotic suggestion to be the famous exotic dancer, Bubbles La Rue. However, when the band played "Night Train," her response was a little more usual than unusual.

"She was up there dancing like a real pro," Marshall recalls. "Then, all of a sudden, without any warning whatsoever, she pulled her dress up and over her head. She wasn't wearing underwear. Dancing totally nude!" It was a strip without the tease. Brodien snapped his fingers and told her to "Sleep!" He grabbed the dress she'd thrown on the floor and attempted to cover her naked body as he hustled her offstage to a dressing room, where the hypnotic spell was finally broken.

When Marshall escorted the woman back to her seat at the bar, her friend was laughing even louder and said, "What did I tell you, honey!" She told Marshall that her friend's name was Scarlett O'Hair and they both worked at the Back Stage, a burlesque club at 935 Wilson Avenue, about half a mile from the Cairo. She was simply a stripper, it was her night off, and she was just doing what came *au natural*.

"Night Train" wasn't the only song that worked to induce hypnotic dancing. Often, Marshall would tell a subject, "After I awaken you, when you hear music, music of *any* kind, you will start dancing."

One evening, a gentleman onstage who'd been given the post-hypnotic suggestion to dance had to go to the bathroom. The very second Marshall gave him the wake-up command, and even before he went back to his seat in the audience, the fellow made a beeline for the men's room. The audience was applauding as Marshall took his bows, thanked the audience, and announced that the band would be playing for dancing. Naturally, the music was the cue for the subject to start dancing. But the man was nowhere to be seen.

"I was standing on the edge of the stage, looking all over the room for him," Marshall says, "when all of the sudden he hopped up on the stage and started dancing. The audience was laughing like crazy, but I noticed that this guy had all these wet stains on his pants and even on his jacket. It looked like he'd spilled his drink all over himself."

Marshall later found out exactly what happened from another gentleman who'd been in the restroom at the same time. As the hypnotized subject approached the urinal, the band started to play "Night Train." He heard the music and threw up his hands, spun around and started shaking, dancing, and peeing all over the place. "So, what I thought was his drink wasn't," Marshall says.

On another occasion, the post-hypnotic suggestion induced a bit of street dancing. At the end of the show, before the band even had the chance to return to the bandstand, the subject walked straight out the door, got in his car, and headed home. But it wasn't more than twenty minutes later before two policemen brought him back to the club.

He'd driven five or six blocks down Irving Park, when he decided to turn on his car radio. The second he heard music playing, he slammed on the brakes, came to a screeching stop, jumped out of his car, and started bumpin' and grinding. Unfortunately, he was at an intersection where a black-and-white patrol car was parked.

"The two coppers later told me they had to grab him and shake him back to his senses. He told them that he had no idea why he was dancing in the middle of the street, but he did tell them that he'd volunteered to be hypnotized at a nightclub over on North Sheridan. The policemen stopped by the Cairo to verify he'd been part of the show."

• • •

That autumn, Bruce Elliott, the executive editor of *Rogue*, a monthly magazine *Designed for Men*, visited the Cairo Supper Club to watch Brodien's show. Elliott was also the editor of *The Phoenix*, an insightful magicians' journal of the 1940s and '50s, as well as the author of several popular books on magic, among them *Classic Secrets of Magic* (1953) and *Magic as a Hobby* (1958). Accompanying Bruce was none other than professional magician Jay Marshall. The duo was on a research mission for a magazine article they had slated as "A thaumaturgic tour through the bars and bistros where the black art — and a dram of enchantment — is served up with every drink." In addition to witnessing Marshall's show at the Cairo, Bruce Elliott and Jay went to the Gay 90s Bar of the LaSalle Hotel to see Johnny Platt; the Ivanhoe on North Clark Street to experience the brash and baffling bar magic of Frank Everhart; and to Duberville's Central Inn, a neighborhood saloon where the inimitable Senator Crandall was working.

The pictorial story titled "Chicago: Magic City," was photographed by Elliott and penned by Jay Marshall, and it appeared in the December 1961 issue of *Rogue*. The article opened with a two-page spread of the highlights of Marshall's show, and Jay wrote how "Cairo Club audiences are stunned at the incredible speed of hypnotist Marshall Brodien — the seemingly instantaneous response of his subjects."

Bozo's Circus

Chicago's WGN-TV broadcast the first episode of *Bozo's Circus* on September 11, 1961. Television personality Bob Bell portrayed the character of Bozo, and Ned Locke, an announcer who also sold advertising time for the station, was the ringmaster. The live show aired at noon, Monday through Friday, and featured comedy sketches with clowns, fun and games with a studio audience of 240, music from the 13-piece Big Top Band, and performances by guest variety artists, usually circus acts.

While WGN-TV's Bozo program attracted tens of thousands of viewers almost overnight, who would ever dream that the program would become a Chicagoland television institution and was destined to draw millions and stay on the airwaves for four decades?

• • •

The original character of Bozo the Clown was created shortly after World War II, when Alan W. Livingston, an enterprising producer at Capitol Records in Hollywood, came up with the concept of story-telling records to accompany a set of children's books he'd written. *Bozo at the Circus* was the title of the first album produced, and Pinto Colvig, a former circus clown, portrayed Bozo. Colvig was hired to make promotional appearances at libraries and schools for Capitol, thus establishing the image of Bozo across the nation.

In 1949, through a license arrangement offered to television stations, KTTV in Los Angeles became the first station to produce a Bozo show. *Bozo's Circus*, a half-hour program starring Pinto Colvig as Bozo, was broadcast live every week. The following year, when Capitol Records cranked up a television division, 13 30-minute programs — starring Sid Saylor as Bozo, Alan Livingston as the ringmaster, and acrobats from Jimmy Woods' All-American Circus — were filmed and syndicated to local stations. By 1953, Livingston had become the V.P. of Creative Productions of Capitol (having achieved fame and fortune by signing Frank Sinatra), but he was still big on Bozo and commissioned Hal Roach to produce a 30-minute *Bozo the Clown* pilot with Gil Lamb as Bozo. A network never picked it up and Capitol closed its television division. However, the format of mixing cartoons with a live clown host inspired the creation of *Bozo and His Friends*, a weekly program produced in 1955 at WHBQ-TV in Memphis, Tennessee. The show lasted one season.

Larry Harmon, one of the actors that Livingston hired to play Bozo at various promotions, bought the licensing rights to the Bozo the Clown character. In 1958, he provided the voice for and produced a series of 20 limited-animation Bozo cartoons. Harmon started distributing these cartoons to TV stations, along with the rights to hire a live Bozo host. Another 84 cartoons were produced and Bozos started popping up on stations everywhere.

Although Harmon's franchised cartoons had run on WGN-TV since 1959 as part of the weeknight *Bugs Bunny and Friends*, it wasn't until 1960 that the station considered someone to become a Bozo host. Robert Lewis "Bob" Bell, who'd already established himself as a WGN-TV personality, was chosen to portray Bozo the Clown. A live *Bozo the Clown* show was broadcast weekdays at noon until January of 1961, when the program was put on hold to facilitate WGN's move from downtown Chicago to its newly constructed studios on the city's Northwest side. That fall, with WGN-TV's state-of-the-art Studio One as its new home, the live, one-hour *Bozo's Circus* made its debut.

• • •

Bozo's Circus quickly became a showcase for circus performers, variety acts, and magicians. Magician De Yip Loo was booked for the second week of *Bozo's Circus*. Other magicians who made guest appearances that first fall season were Don Alan, Billy Bishop, and Ron Urban. Marshall Brodien probably would have been asked to be on the show had Howard Schultz, the theatrical agent who booked the acts, known of him.

Marshall met Schultz through his animal-trainer friend Al Szasz. "Al was going downtown to talk with his agent about some upcoming fair engagements," Marshall recalls. "And he asked if I wanted to go along and meet Schultz. I did."

When he was introduced as being "a magician," the agent said, "Yeah, you magicians are a dime a dozen." Hearing that quip, Marshall had to let Schultz know that he wasn't there looking for work, and when he told him that he was always performing magic or hypnotism somewhere and was rarely out of a job, the agent said, "That's hard to believe." So Marshall invited him to come out to the Cairo Supper Club and see him work. "Be my guest any night," he said. "I have just signed for another six months."

As they were leaving the office, Schultz asked Brodien if he'd be interested in appearing on the *Bozo's Circus* show on WGN-TV. He said that it did pay scale, and the station would be willing to let him plug his show at the Cairo. Marshall told him he would like to watch the show first, then let him know.

The next day at noon, Marshall tuned in the Bozo show. Of course, it was a children's program, but he was impressed with the production values of the show. He says, "As soon as I realized they had this big orchestra to play for the acts, and that all the acts were professional — be they jugglers, magicians, or circus acts — I wanted to do it." He called Howard Schultz and told him he was available. Marshall was booked to do his first *Bozo's Circus* guest appearance on January 5, 1962.

"I watched the program several times to determine what I was going to do when I went on. I decided I should perform tricks or effect that required the assistance of the show's clowns." Those characters, at the time, were Bozo (Bob Bell), Oliver O. Oliver (portrayed by Ray Rayner), and Sandy the Tramp (who was Don Sandburg, the show's writer and producer). For that first appearance, Marshall performed the "Mystery of the Arrows through the Head" — a funny illusion where a box was placed over Sandy the Tramp's head, and when the box was pierced with a dozen or so arrows, his head disappeared. The kids and the parents in the studio audience loved it. Don Sandburg liked it because he saw the potential in doing more interactive skits with magic; he called Schultz and said he wanted Brodien back soon.

When contracts were issued for the *Bozo's Circus* show, there was a clause that specified an act could only work the show twice within the period of one year. Because Marshall appeared on the January 5th show, it meant he would have to wait until June to be booked again. That policy was sort of shot out of the cannon when Sandburg called Schultz and said that he needed to make an exception in the talent policy. He wanted Marshall back for the February 28th show.

Along with the help of ringmaster Ned Locke, Marshall performed a comical, yet confounding, levitation of Bozo. Sandy and Oliver suspected there were "invisible wires" holding Bozo afloat, and they sneaked around Marshall's back to cut them down. But to no avail. Bozo continued to float in midair. Al Hall enjoyed directing Brodien's magical appearances: "Shooting Marshall's skits was always a creative challenge, and a heck of a lot more fun than pointing a camera at a circus act and letting it run till the band went tah-dah."

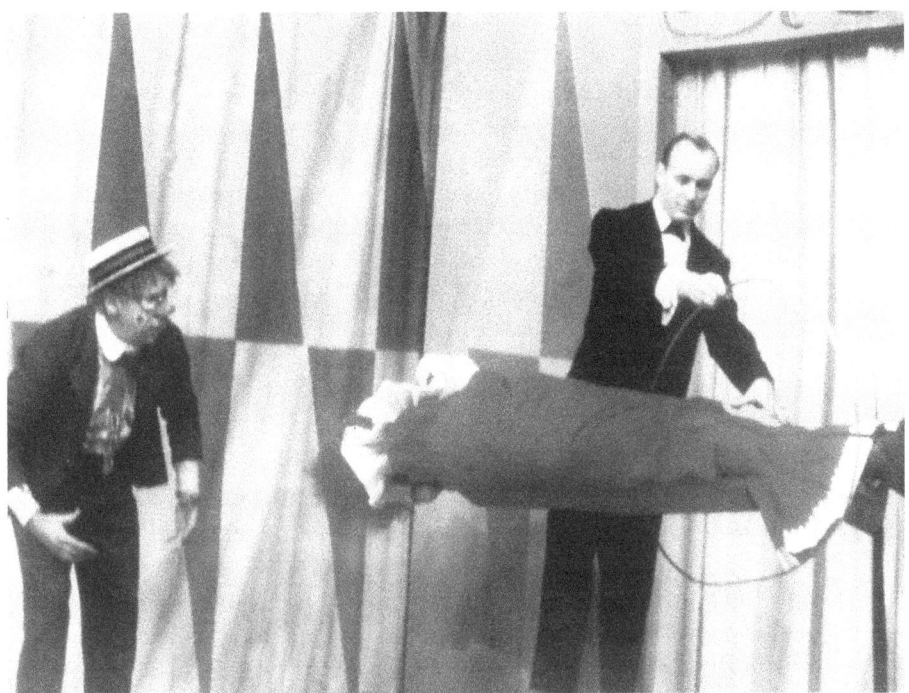

Marshall's early successes on *Bozo's Circus* depended on his willingness to perform his magical feats with the clowns. Here he levitates Bozo, as Oliver O. Oliver (Ray Rayner), looks mystified. *Marshall Brodien Collection*

Now that the twice-yearly booking policy had been completely blown away, since Marshall appeared two times in two months, it was considered okay to contract him for two shows in one month. At the request of Don Sandburg, he was booked for the March 13 and 22 shows. On April 11, he went on the show and did his six-minute sideshow magic act — exactly as he'd performed it ten years ago at Riverview Park — involving Bozo, Sandy, and Ringmaster Ned Locke as the suckers for the Egg Bag, Chinese Sticks, and Hippity-Hop Rabbits. After his invites back on May 2 and 28, and a June 21 appearance, one might be so presumptuous to say that Marshall Brodien had become a *Bozo's Circus* regular.

• • •

When Marshall showed up for a July 19, 1962, appearance, he brought along his trusty straitjacket, a prop that hadn't seen service since his time in the service. WGN's Studio One had a 21-foot-high ceiling, so Marshall suggested they do the old upside-down straitjacket escape. Sandburg had his stagehands rig a rope pulley and block-and-tackle system that would hoist Marshall high above the lighting grid.

When it came time for the big escape, Bozo and Ringmaster Ned recruited a couple of longshoreman-looking dads from the studio audience to strap and buckle Brodien into the straitjacket. Sandy cranked him upward as Ned, in true ringmaster style, warned of the perils of this feat. From the control room, Al Hall called for an extremely low-angle camera shot that made it appear that Marshall was hanging twice as high.

It had been nearly four years since Marshall had attempted to extricate himself from a straitjacket. After the first minute-and-a-half of twisting, bending, and wriggling, it was apparent he wasn't going for a record breaker on the Bozo show. The Big Top Band went into a second chorus of "Stars and Stripes Forever." Hanging heels over head drained blood to the brain, and the heat generated by the 22,000 watts of studio lighting was unbearable. Ned didn't tell the kiddies, but it was torture. After three full minutes of toil and travail, Brodien hurled the spent straitjacket to the studio floor. The Big Top Band sounded a big brassy tah-dah. The audience stomped and cheered. Marshall managed a smile of victory.

Don Sandburg stopped by the dressing room to congratulate Marshall. "That stunt looked dangerous enough to never try again," he said with a grin. "You really were struggling up there. I swear it was the first time I've ever seen a face turn red on black-and-white TV."

15

New Girlfriend and a Prize Fight

July is traditionally and, according to the climatological records of the *Chicago Sun-Times*, predictably the warmest month of the year in Chicagoland. But who would have ever predicted that the sweltering month of July of 1962 would see an ice show at the Cairo Supper Club?

Marshall was still performing his two-a-night hypnotic shows. However, sandwiched in-between, at ten o'clock sharp, was Robin Nelson's *Jamboree on Ice*. The mini ice revue was staged on a 12-by-12 rink of real ice, and it spotlighted the fancy figure-skating talents of Robin Nelson and a quartet of gorgeously costumed ice skaters.

Nightclub ice revues had been a popular attraction since the late 1940s, with the lavish ice show staged in the Boulevard Room of Chicago's Conrad Hilton being the granddaddy of them all. From time to time, the ever-changing theme productions featured magicians. Jack Kodell, Marvyn Roy, Freddie Fah, and Ron Urban were among those who enjoyed long runs in that prestigious showroom. Realizing magic's appeal to ice show aficionados, Robin Nelson began choreographing sequences with magic and adding illusions to some of his ice shows.

Although Nelson was not doing magic in his *Jamboree on Ice* show at the Cairo, Marshall drove over to the club to meet him and take a look at rehearsals. After watching a run-through, Marshall talked with Robin about what kind of stuff he performed when his revues included magic.

When Robin had a ten-month run at the Gaslight Club on Rush Street, he had choreographed a sequence that centered on a classic illusion, the Temple of Benares. A tiny model of an East Indian temple glided onstage, and a skater crawled inside. A dozen sharp swords were thrust into all four sides and through the roof of the temple. Then, the front doors

113

were opened, showing the girl had disappeared. The doors were closed and, as the tempo of "Song of India" accelerated, the ice-chorines skated around the temple while Robin quickly removed the swords. A crescendo from the band, and the girl majestically popped through the roof doors of the temple.

"Where did you get your Temple illusion?" Marshall asked. "Did you order it from Abbott's?"

"No, I bought it from Jack Gwynne back in '55 or '56. Haven't used it since. It's stored away somewhere in my warehouse over on South Rhodes Avenue."

Marshall couldn't believe what he just heard. He remembered hearing that Jack sold his famous one-of-a-kind Temple of Angee because bad health was forcing his retirement, but he had no idea that it was hidden away in a warehouse on the south side of Chicago. When Marshall asked Robin if he was interested in selling it, Robin said, "Yeah, but you might want to look at it first. There are quite a few scratches and ice-skate nicks inside. The dancers were pretty careless going in and out of the thing."

The "Temple of Angee," as it was called when Gwynne conceived and constructed it in 1935, was without doubt the most famous — and most pirated — stage effect the master illusionist ever invented. (In the early 1940s, it was ripped-off, fabricated, and marketed without permission by Abbott's Magic Manufacturing Company as the Temple of Benares.) Jack presented his Temple of Angee in theaters and nightclubs around the world for over 25 years, always assisted by his wife, Anne. He had taken the principle of an illusion called the Doll's House — performed by magicians to make a person appear — and reversed the methodology to vanish a girl. The Doll's House principle was combined with the Sword Box — a sideshow adaptation of the Indian Sword Basket — and the cabinet was fashioned to represent a miniature of the Taj Mahal. The illusion was affectionately named after his wife, Anne G.

It would be the ideal illusion for one of the many *Bozo's Circus* shows Marshall was called upon to do. Sure, he could a buy knock-off made by Abbott's. But why not have the original? After all, Jack was Marshall's idol and magical mentor. Numerous were the times in the 1940s when Marshall sat in a front row or balcony seat of the Oriental Theatre to admire and study the dramatic style of the world famous Gwynne & Company. So wasn't it only logical that he should be performing Gwynne's Temple of Angee on television? When Robin Nelson said he wanted a $100 for the illusion, Marshall said, "It's a done deal."

That vintage illusion wasn't the only thing he acquired by the time the ice show left the Cairo that August. He had a new girlfriend. Judith Skarda was a young, perky blonde ice skater who'd gone out with Marshall a few times during the summer. They enjoyed each other's company and were having so much fun together that when the ice revue moved on to an engagement in Detroit, Judy decided to stay in Chicago. She took a part-time secretarial job downtown. But that didn't mean she was getting out of show business. Marshall was starting to do more and more club dates using his magic and illusions. So, whenever he needed an assistant, Judy was the one recruited to pop in and out of the Temple of Angee.

• • •

Because Judy worked in the offices of boxing promoter Cus D'Amato, she became privy to some goings-on concerning the Illinois State Athletic Commission and the upcoming Floyd Patterson/Sonny Liston world championship fight. Judy told Marshall that the word "hypnotism" had come up countless times in meetings and conversations she overheard. The September 25, 1962, heavyweight match at Comiskey Park was two weeks away, and Cus D'Amato, Floyd Patterson's manager, was complaining to the Commission, claiming he had reason to suspect that Liston would be fighting the bout while under a hypnotic spell.

It seemed that D'Amato had come by a letter intended for Liston, even though it was plainly addressed to Patterson's camp. It was from fight promoter/trainer/magician/hypnotist Jimmy Grippo. In his misguided missive, which began "Dear Sonny," he offered Liston the benefit of his hypnotic powers, "to give him the indomitable will to win, more strength than even he now possesses, and complete immunity from any distress that the opponent might inflict."

When Marshall heard about the Grippo letter and the fray that Cus D'Amato had gotten himself into, he told Judy to let Mr. D'Amato know that he would be interested in talking with him. "Cus already knew of my hypnotism," Marshall says, "because some people in his office had been out to the Cairo Supper Club to see me work. The next day, he called and invited me to come down to his office on Michigan Avenue. He told me he had been granted a formal hearing before the Athletic Commission and needed my help."

Basically, D'Amato wanted to convince the commissioners that if Grippo hypnotized Liston and he was truly impervious to pain, Sonny would have an unfair psychological advantage over Floyd. As Cus told Marshall, "It would be the ultimate frustration to my man Patterson, who will be trying to pound a lesson into Liston's hypnotized head."

At the September 10 proceedings in the Athletic Commission's 17th-floor

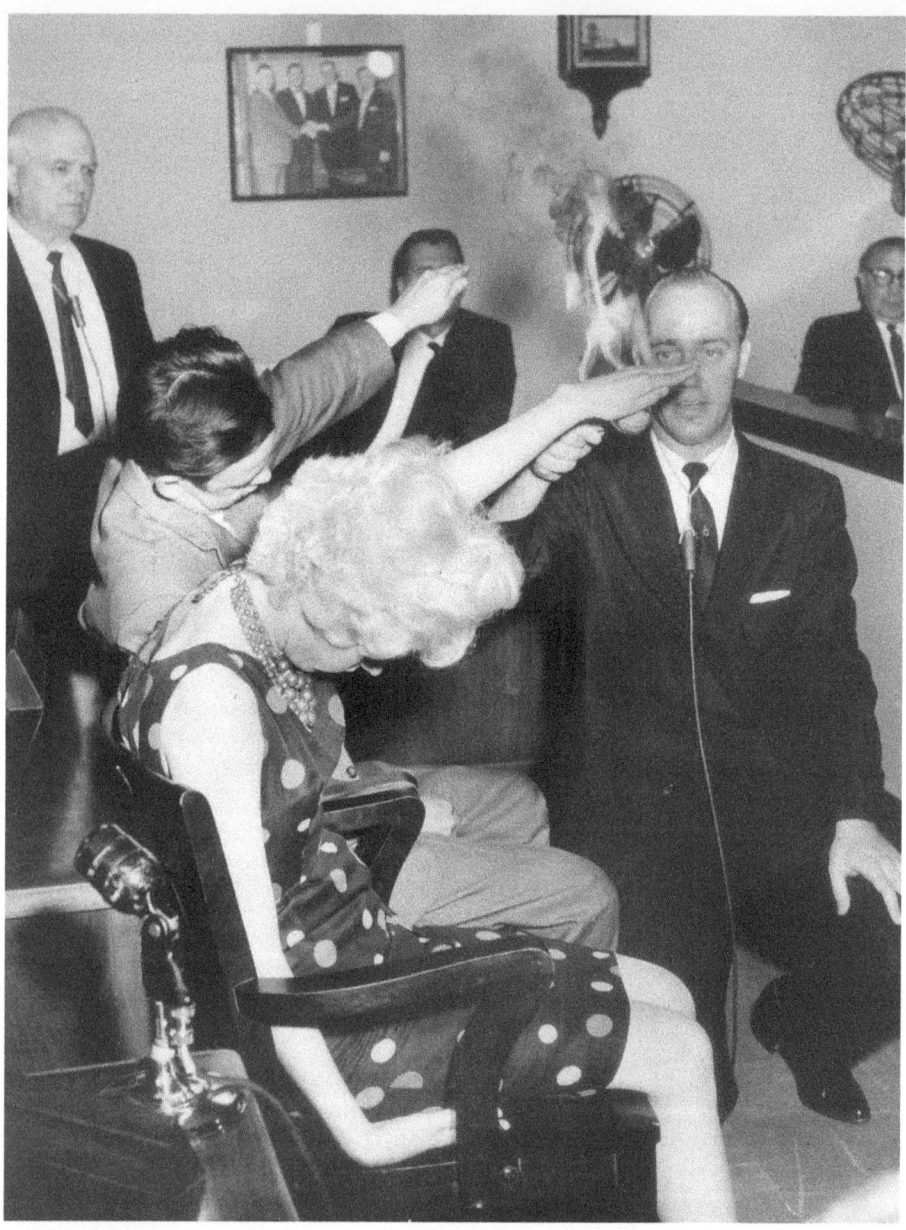

Marshall appears before at a hearing of the Illinois State Athletic Commission to demonstrate the powers of hypnosis for overcoming feelings of pain. Boxing promoter Cus D' Amato (standing, at left), manager of Floyd Patterson, looks on. *Marshall Brodien Collection*

chambers at 160 North LaSalle, D'Amato submitted the Grippo letter as evidence. He added, "I feel the Commission should take steps to ground Jimmy Grippo. If Mr. Liston were to fight while hypnotized, Mr. Patterson might break any number of his bones and Sonny would not feel it." Cus further speculated that Liston could go on fighting with a broken jaw or a broken hand, or even a broken heart, completely oblivious to his handicap. "Fortunately, I have secured the services of one of the best-known hypnotists in the country, who will enlighten the Commission as to the potential dangers of utilizing hypnotism in boxing." Marshall was called to the stand, and at D'Amato's request, Commission Chairman Joe Triner put him under oath as he was questioned.

Marshall says, "I looked at this whole thing as a stunt to get PR for the fight, so I answered their questions then proceeded to put on a little show ... a demonstration of hypnotism for them."

A volunteer by the name of John Lane was asked to step forward. "I had already conditioned this guy and was able to put him to sleep real fast. When I slapped him across the face, he just swayed and didn't flinch, proving there was no pain." Cus laced a glove onto the left hand of Frankie Mastro, a boxing writer who used to fight professionally. With a cigar stub clenched between his teeth, the former pugilist threw two solid hooks to Lane's midsection. "Those are liver punches!" Cus announced. "They can inflict excruciating pain." Yet, when Lane was awakened, he said, "I feel fine. Has anyone hit me yet?"

Brodien introduced Brenda Green, a 22-year-old receptionist who weighed in at exactly 100 pounds. After a rapid hypnotic induction, he lit a torch and held it beneath her outstretched palm. There was no wincing whatsoever. "She feels nothing and, because of that, she'd probably sit there and let her hand burn off," Marshall explained as he extinguished the flame. For the finale of his courtroom drama, Brodien summoned Brenda to serve as the subject of the rigid-lady stunt — the tried-and-true test of no suffering while under the influence of hypnotism. As Marshall stood atop her body suspended straight across the backs of two chairs, a UPI sports writer uttered, "The only time I saw a babe that stiff was when she fell off a bar stool."

ABC's 16mm news cameras documented the proceedings for the evening news. Flashbulbs popped and shutters snapped, freezing images that would travel via the wire services to accompany tomorrow's headline stories. "A spellbound solution for boxing board," declared Cleveland's *Plain Dealer*. "Hypnotist cool and judicial," wrote the *New York Herald Tribune*. The *Chicago Sun-Times* headlined it a "Vaudeville show at the boxing meeting."

As Cus D' Amato (standing, at left) and reporters look on, Marshall hypnotizes volunteer John Lane in preparation for a boxer's punch that will prove to be painless. Marshall Brodien Collection

    Brodien received no compensation from either the Illinois State Athletic Commission or Patterson's organization, but he garnered untold dollars worth of publicity from the event. He and Judy were given ringside tickets and special VIP passes for the fight. A crowd of 18,894 flocked to Comiskey Park on Chicago's South Side that night. The traffic was tremendous. The new 14-lane Dan Ryan Expressway hadn't opened yet, and their chartered bus went through blocks and blocks of detours. By the time they got to the parking lot, the fight was over.

    The match ended in round one. Sonny landed the first punch of the fight, a right to the head. Floyd threw a wild left but missed. Liston retaliated with a left of his own, which landed on Floyd's right jaw. Another right and a left and Patterson went to the canvas, shaking his head as the ref gave him the ten-count after exactly 126 seconds. When the press asked Liston if the fallen champ had hurt him, he replied, "Yeah, he hurt me when it looked like he was gonna get up on the nine count ... but he didn't."

    The fight was the richest one-time sporting event to date. Floyd Patterson's take was $1.7 million, and Sonny Liston went home with $400,000 and the heavyweight crown. Patterson, in a state of utter embarrassment, exited his locker room via the usher's dressing room. He wore a cheap-looking fake beard and mustache, a disguise that looked like something sold at the costume counter of the Treasure Chest.

16

Pass on the Playboy

Hugh Hefner paid a visit to the Cairo Supper Club in December 1962, expressly to see Brodien's hypnotic show. Hefner's *Playboy* magazine was approaching its ninth year of publication and boasted a circulation of over three million. In addition to the flourishing Chicago Playboy Club at 116 East Walton—where "members only" ogled cocktail waitresses clad in skimpy bunny costumes with rabbit ears and cottontails—other clubs had popped up in New York, Los Angeles, Miami, Detroit, St. Louis, Phoenix, and New Orleans.

That evening, Hef was accompanied by a voluptuous doe-eyed blonde, who was introduced around the Cairo as Susanna, the "executive assistant" at the Playboy Mansion. After the show, Marshall was invited over to their booth. With a shy, yet, confidential smile, Hugh told Marshall that he enjoyed the show and complimented him on his energetic performance. He said that he was especially keen on watching nightclub hypnotists because his brother Keith had studied hypnotism and was interested in pursuing it professionally. At the time, Keith Hefner hosted *Time for Fun*, a children's show on WABC-TV in New York City, but would later go on to be a stockbroker.

The following evening, Susanna returned to the Cairo Club, sans Hef. She told Marshall that her boss had sent her to invite him to the Playboy Mansion that weekend. Hefner was throwing a party for Margaret Whiting. It was the popular jazz vocalist's birthday, and Susanna made it clear that Marshall would not be asked or expected to do any entertaining. "Just come and have a good time," she said.

The 48-room pleasure palace on North State Street, in the heart of Chicago's affluent Gold Coast area, had actually become a home/office for

Hefner. He had recently moved his desk out of the Playboy headquarters building on Michigan Avenue and now operated his publishing empire from the famed circular bedroom of his mansion. On the massive oak front door, a brass plate was engraved with *Si non oscillas, noli tintinnare*, which roughly translates from the Latin as "If you don't swing, don't ring."

"When I walked into the mansion," Marshall remembers, "Hef was standing in the foyer, smoking his pipe, and greeting everyone. He shook my hand and said he was glad I could come." Hefner was surrounded by the usual complement of five or six stunning Playmates. A pair of amply endowed bunnies approached Marshall with trays of drinks and appetizers, prompting Hefner to smile and say, "Marshall, we might have too many women here tonight ... I might have to order up a few more guys."

Benny Dunn, Hefner's public relations man, was also welcoming the guests. Marshall knew him from his days as a popular entertainer and went over to say hello. When Marshall was 12, he'd appeared on a variety show with Benny at the RKO Palace in Chicago. Dunn was billed as "The Cheyenne Kid" and young Brodien performed as "A Western Magic Act."

Benny and Marshall were swapping show-biz stories when Hefner interrupted to tell Benny of his recent visit to the Cairo Supper Club. Hef elaborated on how much he enjoyed the show, insisting that Benny go see it. Then he asked Marshall, "Do you think you might be interested in working the Playboy Club circuit with your hypnotic act?"

"I definitely would," Marshall said. "But I have a slight problem. I'm engaged to get married in a few months, and I'm not too sure how my fiancée would feel about me being out on the road, working night after night with all those beautiful bunnies around."

Hef laughed and said, "I understand. But if you get cold feet, let us know. We're opening three more clubs this spring. We could keep you more than busy. In the meantime, make yourself at home."

• • •

Marshall married Judith Skarda on February 10, 1963. After a one-week honeymoon in Southern California, they moved into the house on Fox Lake that Marshall had bought from his friend and boating pal, Eddie Kosmer. Looking forward to a leisurely lifestyle on the lake, Marshall had acquired all sorts of water-ski gear and a speedboat with enough horsepower to tow the entire Big Top Band of the Bozo show. But those recreational activities would have to be put on hold for a couple of months. The lake was frozen over.

Judy, however, took advantage of the icy winter, practicing and polishing her figure-skating talents. She even lured Marshall onto the frozen-over channel in back of their yard and taught him a few basics of ice-skating — something he'd be grateful for when, later that year, a job offer would come up for a magical emcee who could skate.

17

Presto! Less Hypno

In June 1963, WGN-TV asked Marshall to join the *Bozo's Circus* cast as for a 45-minute show for the 34th annual Chicagoland Music Festival at Soldier Field. A record 68,135 people attended the event. It probably had nothing to do with the fact that Marshall's magic fared well in the great outdoors, but all of a sudden he found his calendar filling up with state and county fair dates. From July 2nd through 6th, the grand illusions act of Marshall Brodien & Company (Judy plus two other assistants) was featured, along with the Osmond Brothers and Grand Ole Opry star Minnie Pearl, at the South Dakota State Fair in Brookings.

Marshall and Judy then traveled to Montana for a week at the Great Falls State Fair. This was a big show starring Jimmy Dean, Bobby & Barbara (from *The Lawrence Welk Show*), the Elkins Sisters, Victor Julian & His Pets, and Paul Lennon. Of bigger significance to Brodien was the fact that he'd been hired to replace the great Richiardi Jr., the Peruvian illusionist who, in time, would hold the distinction of having 28 appearances, the most ever by a magician, on *The Ed Sullivan Show*. However, since Richiardi was having difficulties getting the proper work permits to appear in the United States, he was forced to cancel. To publicize Marshall's appearance on opening day, the *Great Falls Tribune* carried a front-page photo of him floating Judy on the wing of a F89 Scorpion that was parked at the National Guard airbase.

From August 5th through 10th, Brodien played the Midland Empire State Fair and Rodeo in Billings, Montana. He again replaced Richiardi Jr. and also on the bill were the Willis Brothers, Minnie Pearl, the Elkins Sisters, the Four Debuntes, the Goestchi Brothers, and the Flying Marilees. Marshall and Judy would finish out the month of August, playing three smaller county fairs in Missoula, Kalispel, and Plains, Montana.

Publicizing his appearance at the Great Falls State Fair, Marshall levitates wife Judy on the wing of a jet fighter at the nearby National Guard airbase. *Marshall Brodien Collection*

When the Brodiens returned home, there was a letter from an ice-show producer inquiring if Judy was interested in skating that fall in *Ice Royals*, a touring show that played arenas and civic centers under the auspices of local sponsors. Tickets were sold via phone promotions, with the proceeds benefiting such organizations as the police or firefighters, Veterans of Foreign Wars, or civic clubs like the Kiwanis or Lions.

The offer became a contract deal when he the producer learned that Judy's husband was an entertainer and had "experience" on ice. She was hired to skate; he was to master the ceremonies. Marshall was also given a featured spot to perform a magic act. Judy's backyard pond skating lessons paid off quicker than he ever expected.

The tour began in Wisconsin with an engagement at the Madison Civic Center. On opening night, after the overture, there was an orchestral fanfare and the booming voice of an offstage announcer proudly introduced "The Mystery Man on Ice." Immaculately attired in white tie and tails, Mr. Bro-

When the Brodiens played ice shows and fairs in the 1960s, they presented the Temple the Temple of Angee as the illusion's creator Jack Gwynne had performed it. *Marshall Brodien Collection*

dien gracefully glided toward the microphone. To avoid slicing an exposed cable, he slightly lifted his left skate, causing him to fall flat on his butt. "After that, my skating was limited to hitting the center-stage mark, where I stood and produced some doves, did a few more tricks, and finished with the Temple of Angee illusion."

That November, *Ice Royals* went on to play arena dates in Nebraska, Kansas, and finally Texas. On November 22, while Marshall and Judy were resting in their hotel room in Fort Worth, they heard on TV that President John F. Kennedy had been assassinated in Dallas. That evening's performance of *Ice Royals* at Will Rogers Coliseum was canceled. The tour was no more. Marshall felt numbed. Judy, who was six months' pregnant, cried. They packed their suitcases and made reservations for the return to Chicago.

• • •

After completing the long summer streak of fairs and the brief autumn run of ice shows as Marshall "the illusionist," Brodien "the hypnotist" returned to the Cairo Supper Club. The first week of 1964 marked the beginning of his third extended engagement at the club, sharing the billing with Tony Smith and his Aristocrats.

On February 19, Marshall and Judy became the parents of their first child, a daughter they named Anita Leah. Suddenly, their cozy home in Fox Lake wasn't large enough. They decided to add two rooms. "I hired a couple of local carpenters to do the construction and really didn't think I needed to get a building permit. Well, two days later, my doorbell rings, and there's the building inspector and the chief of police. They stopped the job, arrested me, took me downtown, and booked me."

"Luckily, I knew a businessman there, who was good friends with Joe Armando, the mayor of Fox Lake. My friend convinced the mayor that I was a decent guy, a good citizen not out to break any laws. He explained that we'd just had a baby. He told how I was working in Chicago past midnight every night, not getting home to Fox Lake until two or three in the morning. He told about my having to drive back into town three times a week to do the Bozo show. My friend made it sound like I was so overworked that I just didn't have time to get the necessary paperwork to add a room to my house."

The next day, about noon, the mayor and the building inspector showed up at the Brodien's house and advised that the charges had been dropped. All Marshall had to do was write a check for the $62 building permit. That done, the inspector started to leave when the mayor said, "Mr. Brodien, we just wanted you to know that we watch the Bozo show whenever you're on doing your magic."

Then, much to the delight of the construction workers and the two city officials, Brodien put on an impromptu 45-minute magic show, right there in his basement turned bar and rec room. He told Mayor Armando that anytime he wanted to bring his family and friends to see the Bozo show, just give him a call.

The phone rang the following week. It was the mayor. But it wasn't a call for Bozo tickets. His Honor wanted to know what it'd cost for Marshall to put on a show for the Lion's Club. Naturally, Marshall did it for nothing. The show was a hit, and all of Fox Lake was abuzz about the magician in their midst. A few months later, there was a call from the Fox Lake Chief of Police. This time, Marshall volunteered to stage a magic show at the high school auditorium for a big community fundraiser.

By now, his good deeds had more than paid back the favor of the building permit. But Marshall didn't stop there. When he found out that Mayor Armando was in charge of training the Fox Lake Junior Police's youth choir, he threw in another favor. "I told Joe that Don Sanburg, the producer of the Bozo show at WGN-TV, had agreed to my request to have his Junior Police choir do a guest spot on *Bozo's Circus*." Mayor Armando couldn't believe it. He was thrilled that his choir got to sing a song on live television. To cap it off, Bozo introduced Joe as the mayor of Fox Lake, the man doing all these great things for the kids.

Mayor Armando was truly indebted to Marshall. Every time he'd see him, he would stop and say, "Marsh, I owe you one. Just let me know if there's something I can do for you."

Marshall said, "You know, I've been thinking about your Junior Police program and how the kids serve as patrolmen. It's really an honor. I was just wondering if you could sign me up as a patrolman for Fox Lake."

"No problem," Joe said. "Come down to town hall and we'll swear you in, give you a badge, make you a patrolman."

The City of Fox Lake, Illinois Police Department Badge No. 20 was officially assigned to Marshall E. Brodien. He would end up carrying the identification for eight years, and numerous were the occasions when the badge proved worthy of its weight in gold. A memorable incident occurred shortly after he acquired a new car.

"I'd just bought a Lincoln Mark III. The dealer was getting the license plates for me, and he told me it was okay to take it home and drive it until the tags came in. So, the next day, I was traveling down the expressway toward Schaumburg, and no sooner had I pulled off the exit than I saw flashing red lights behind me."

A uniformed officer sauntered up to the automatically rolled-down window. He cautiously leaned in and sniffed the factory-fresh leather interior.

"Sir, I noticed you don't have license plates on this automobile. Are you the owner?"

"I just bought it," Brodien said, handing him his driver's license. "The dealer is getting the plates for me. By the way, I'm a patrolman in Fox Lake," he said and proudly produced his laminated identification card as evidence.

The officer warily studied both sides of the ID, matching it up to the name on the driver's license, then stepped back to have another look at the shiny new Mark III. "So, this really is your car?" he asked.

"Yes, sir."

"And you really are a patrolman in Fox Lake?"

"That's right."

The cop handed back the license and ID card and asked, "Do they have any openings out there?"

• • •

Things were rolling along rather routinely with the two-a-night schedule of hypnotic shows at the Cairo Supper Club, until the evening of May 11, 1964. It was a Monday night, the only night of the week that the club was closed. Marshall was relaxing at home, watching the ten o'clock news, when a bulletin was handed to the on-camera newscaster: *"We've just received word that a fire bomb was thrown into a front window of the Cairo Supper Club at 4017 North Sheridan tonight. The explosion, which gutted the lounge area of the popular restaurant and nightclub, happened around 9:15. A witness has reported that a well-dressed man stepped from a 1964 white hardtop automobile and hurled the explosive into the building, then quickly fled the scene. There were no injuries, as no one was inside the nightclub. When Cairo owner, William Anastos, was contacted at his home at 3720 Racine, he had no explanation for the bombing, saying that business has been good at the nightclub. In the past nine months, incendiary fires or bombs have damaged or destroyed nearly 30 restaurants and taverns in Chicago. The Cairo Supper Club will remain closed while the incident is investigated. In other local news...."* Marshall clicked off the television, turned to Judy, and said, "I guess I'm out of a job."

The closing of the Cairo affected the direction of Marshall's career as an entertainer. He appreciated the steady work as a hypnotist that the supper club had afforded, but he really enjoyed the engagements as a magician that agent Howard Schultz had been sending his way. Marshall also liked the recognition he was receiving as the "regular magician" on *Bozo's Circus*. He came to the conclusion that it was the right time to get back to doing more magic.

He called Howard and told him that it wasn't going to happen overnight, but he would soon be dropping the hypnotism. It actually took several months to break the spell. "I continued to do hypnotic shows on weekends at the Top of the Mark, a club in the Sunset Arms Hotel in Franklin Park," Marshall says. "I had a six-week run at the Prime Steak House on Harlem Avenue. After that, I went into a place called the Cat and the Fiddle on Cicero Avenue, for two weeks. But these places were nothing like the Cairo Supper Club."

• • •

Fortunately, the decision to put hypnotism on the back burner of his show-biz priorities coincided with an important move being made by the Chicago Park District. City Council had voted to support entertainment — specifically, magic shows — at the summer day-camp programs in recreational centers throughout the city.

Because of Marshall's previous experience with the Dan Rostenkowski Youth Council setting up Easter programs at various city parks for underprivileged children, Brodien was the Park District's magician of choice. Producing the annual Easter magic shows for five years allowed Marshall the opportunity to become well acquainted with Daniel Rostenkowski, who was then a U.S. Representative from Illinois. In the years that followed, Marshall became more involved with the Youth Council and was always invited to Rostenkowski's fund-raising parties.

Every weekday during the summer of 1964 found Marshall entertaining the thousands of children enrolled in the day-camp programs. "I'd do a morning show at one park, say Chase Park or Marquette Park, then I'd drive to another, like Pulaski or River Park, for an afternoon show." He would go on the Bozo show regularly to announce where he'd be appearing that week.

The day-camp programs were over by Labor Day weekend, allowing Marshall to join up with Army buddy Montie Montana Jr. for a four-day run at the Ravalli County Fair in Hamilton, Montana. The grandstand revue featured a band called the Four Young Men from Montana, Montie's rope spinning and trick riding skills, a sheep dog act, a cowboy comedy team, and the magic and illusions of Marshall Brodien & Company.

Those very same tricks and illusions were also an important part of *Bozo's Holiday Circus*, a 90-minute show taped at WGN-TV just before Thanksgiving. A complete ice rink was built on the Bozo set and Marshall performed the act he'd done on the *Ice Royals* tour. When the show aired during the Christmas holidays, it established him as one of the first to perform magic on ice on primetime television.

18

Taking on Trade Shows

In late 1964, agent Howard Schultz dispatched Marshall and Chinese magician Dee Yip Loo to the offices of Kitzing Incorporated, a trade-show producer requesting a magician. Kitzing specialized in the design, manufacture, and installation of convention and trade-show exhibits. One of their clients at the upcoming National Association of Home Builders Show, Owens-Corning Fiberglas, thought it might be unusual to use magic to provide a little entertainment on the sales floor.

Brodien and Loo worked a day apiece at the Owens-Corning booth, however, because Marshall was available for the run of the show at McCormick Place, he got the job. Never having seen a magician perform at a trade show he didn't know what was expected. Three other magicians working different booths there — close-up wizards Eddie Tullock, Dick Ryan, and Bud Dietrich — all performed solo, wore business suits, and did mostly card tricks while talking about their sponsors. Therefore, when he reported to the exhibit space wearing white tie and tails and armed with a trunk full of magical props and an attractive female assistant, Brodien was clearly "out of the ordinary."

Without realizing it, Marshall was taking the traditional trade-show presentation up a notch. Kitzing had supplied a script full of sales points that had to be made, but Marshall had come up with some routines with highly visible magic props that enhanced the Owens-Corning marketing message. His innate skills as a magical pitchman transformed what might have been a ho-hum product demonstration into show-stopping entertainment, drawing large crowds in front of the booth. And the Owens-Corning sales reps loved it — each performance delivered a clipboard full of sales leads.

Marshall also received some leads of a different sort. Marketing execs with other companies watched his magical presentations and liked what they saw. They envisioned him working for their company. Many asked for his business card. And Marshall was handing them out, not knowing this was a no-no. After his first show on the second day, a gentleman handed him a business card. It was Fred Kitzing himself, the president of the company that had hired him to do the trade show.

"I admire the way you've taken our script and customized it with your tricks," Kitzing said. "I'm interested in working with you on a regular basis." He realized Marshall's approach to communicating a sales message with a magic theme was something his company could market. The two had several discussions about how to structure an agreement, and by April 1965 they had negotiated a retainer deal.

"Kitzing paid me $2,000 a month to be exclusive," Marshall says. "That meant if an exhibitor or a prospective client for a trade show approached me and wanted to hire me, I had to tell them to go see Kitzing, because they booked me for all my trade shows." Kitzing would be building new clients for his exhibit-fabrication business; in return, Marshall received a fee every time his talents were used. He was paid $500 to $600 per day for a three-to-four-day trade show, in addition to the retainer.

Bethlehem Steel was one of the first big trade show clients they collaborated on. "The company was introducing a new galvanized sheet-steel called Galvalume at automobile shows across the country," Marshall remembers. "Bethlehem was out to convince car-makers that this new steel was the ideal material for fabricating mufflers." Bethlehem's marketing staff met with Marshall and asked what he had up his sleeve for their exhibit space. He asked if he could borrow a seven-inch-long model of a muffler that Bethlehem's engineers had constructed. Marshall advised that he'd take the miniature and come up with a trick that would work with Kitzing's script.

Bethlehem Steel had committed to a 20-foot-long booth space at the SAE Auto Show, and Marshall requested they construct a six-foot wide, 18-inch high platform at the center of the space. At showtime he stepped onto the stage and started building a crowd by recruiting an assistant from the audience to help with a card trick: "So, what's new from Bethlehem Steel? We have a full deck of new ideas and products. Let's get started with this perfectly normal deck with 52 cards to choose from — just like the variety of choice you get with Bethlehem's selection of carbon and alloy bars...."

The card routine had the backs of the deck magically turning blank, then the faces of the cards were blank with the exception of the card selected by the volunteer. And because the magic-and-message-mixed presentation was getting lots of laughs, it didn't take long before the aisle was packed five or six deep with customers and prospects. Marshall thanked his volunteer from

Bethlehem Steel became one of Marshall's first trade show clients in 1965 and the company continued to use his services into the mid 1980s.

the audience, saying, "You have a real talent for this sort of thing, sir! If I ever need another assistant, I'll give you a call."

"What about me?" asked a beautiful model standing over by the Bethlehem logo-sign.

"Are you this year's model or last year's model?"

"I come equipped with a body style that's designed for the ages," she purred.

"That's apparent," said Brodien. "But not now. I'm busy."

"Oh, Marshall, don't give me the cold shoulder."

"Go buy a muffler. That'll keep you warm... Wait!" Marshall said, reaching behind her back. "I think there's one hiding there, just behind your transmission." He handed her the miniature muffler.

"Why, that muffler's made of Bethlehem's new Galvalume," she said with a wink, going right into her product pitch. "Galvalume is the sheet steel with an aluminum and zinc alloy coating that makes it ideal for muffler applications. It's just the thing for corrosion and heat-oxidation resistance."

"I can't resist testing it," Marshall said, disassembling the muffler piece by piece as he launched into his magical demonstration. "We'll punish it. Smack it, bang it, and beat it up real good!"

"Marshall, I can't bear to look ... even though I know Galvalume is tough!"

He dropped the various muffler pieces into a pan. "A muffler has to go though a lot," he told the audience. Lighter fluid was squirted into the pan and ignited. "Such as extreme heat in the summer ... and it has to go through rain year round." A small pitcher of water was poured over the flaming muffler parts. "And has to go through snow and ice...."

The lovely assistant tossed pieces of dry ice into the pan. "During the winter it has to withstand all that salt thrown on the road." The top of a saltshaker was removed and its contents dumped into the pan. By now, a nasty sounding chemical reaction was at work. A frying, whistling, screeching noise emanated from the pan. As Marshall placed a lid on the pan, he said, "Listen to that muffler suffering in there."

At this point, the assistant stepped forward and enumerated on the strengths and astonishing weather- and corrosion-resistant properties of Bethlehem's Galvalume, ending with the statement, "There's no way that my precious little muffler could be suffering — it's made of Galvalume!"

Marshall nodded in agreement, lifted the lid, and there sitting on a regal-looking, red velvet pillow was a shiny, absolutely brand-new-looking muffler. "As if by magic!" Brodien said. "Nothing happened to the muffler. After all, it's made of Bethlehem Steel's Galvalume!"

• • •

"The first time I used a stage illusion at a trade show was when I performed the Blade Box for Bethlehem Steel at the Packaging Show in 1965." All 12 blades of Brodien's Blade Box had been customized to represent 12 different steels produced by Bethlehem. The assistant gracefully crawled inside the box and carefully positioned herself. Marshall plunged down the first blade and said, "This one is made of Alphatized Steel." The girl inside had a microphone and launched into a spiel about Alphatized Steel, expounding upon its amazing properties of formability. Marshall would interrupt, slamming down a blade of Galvalume steel, allowing her to talk about this sheet steel's toughness and weldability. A blade of Chromatized Steel prompted a lengthy discourse on Chromatized Steel. And so it went with blades of Stainless Steel, Industrialized Steel, Beta Steel, Aluminized Steel, Ultra-Form-80 Steel, et cetera.

The final blade, one forged of Velvetized Steel, was only inserted halfway into the box when there was a cry of "Ouch!" from inside. Marshall halted, looked down, then gently slipped the blade into its slot. The girl said, "Wow, that was almost too close for comfort. That must have been the blade of Behtlehem's Velvetized Steel, the remarkable all-weather alloy used in com ... mercial and resi ... tal ... constru ... projects around the..." Suddenly, her microphone went dead. There was no more dialogue from the box. However, as per the script, Marshall finished the presentation, removed the blades, and helped the young lady out of the box. "Now you've done it," she said, holding up a pair of severed and frayed microphone cables. "You cut me off before I could finish."

"That's because I prefer to work alone," Marshall said, taking the two loose wires. With a wave of his hand he magically mended them together. Using the restored microphone, he said, "How about a round of applause for my lovely assistant? She's going to take a well-deserved break. In the meantime, our Bethlehem Steel representatives will be more than happy to answer any questions you have about Bethlehem Steel's magical products."

Were there secret methods behind Marshall Brodien's instantaneous entry into the trade-show industry? "Yes," Marshall says. "I always insisted on having a stage, I always had a female assistant up there who kept the pitch going with the props, and I always had something visual and entertaining going on during the pitch."

The formula was working. In addition to the repeat shows for Bethlehem and Owens-Corning, Kitzing kept Brodien busy with new shows for Reynolds Metals, Westinghouse Electric Corporation, Nalco Chemical, and Lennox Industries.

• • •

The years of experience as the sideshow talker at Riverview Park made Marshall a natural for working trade shows. Pitching products on the crowded trade-show floor was akin to building the tip on the busy midway of a fairground or amusement park. Instead of hawking tickets to see the strange and otherworldly ten-in-one show inside the tent, Marshall was now hyping an array of all–American products and luring prospects into the carpeted exhibit area where high-powered sales reps took over.

One particular trade show that made Marshall feel like he was back on the grounds of Riverview Park was the Iowa Farm Show. "Everyone had their exhibits outdoors and some of them were in tents," Marshall says. "And like the sideshow it was a challenge get people inside to see the product demonstrations. So, when Kitzing produced a show for Keystone Wire & Steel, whose product was Red Brand Fencing, I suggested that they construct a stage in front of the exhibit tent and I would do magic to get the people inside."

He used the Pillory Escape illusion as his traffic stopper. An attractive woman assistant was bound to a wooden post. Three lengths of rope were wrapped and tied around her neck, arms, waist, legs, and ankles, as Marshall expounded upon the mysterious manner of escape she would be attempting. "But first, ladies and gentlemen," he would say, "let me tell you about Keystone Wire & Steel's even more amazing demonstration located inside our tent. The very young lady who's secured to this post will be presenting that demon-

No matter who the corporate client was, Marshall's large illusions and highly visible magic presentations stopped record crowds on trade show floors across the country. *Marshall Brodien Collection*

stration. And, folks, what she does out here is nothing compared to what she does inside!" As soon as there was a crowd of 50 or 60, Brodien would say, "Watch! The escape happens quicker than you can say Red Brand Fencing!" On those words, the ropes fell to the floor and the lady stepped away, miraculously loose. Marshall would say, "That means it's showtime!" and the crowd would follow her and Marshall inside the tent.

Marshall recalls that trade-show veterans Karrell Fox and Dick Ryan were working the Iowa Farm Show that year. "At the time, very few, if any, trade-show magicians were performing illusions, so they came over and watched my show several times. Afterwards, we'd go have coffee and they were always complimentary about my use of the Pillory Escape illusion to build a crowd."

The next year, both Karrell Fox and Dick Ryan showed up with attractive assistants and were doing illusions in front of their exhibits.

19

The Mike Douglas Show

Amidst of the flurry of trade-show work, Brodien received a call from the talent coordinator of *The Mike Douglas Show*, a daytime talk-and-variety program televised from Philadelphia. Marshall's animal-trainer friend Al Szasz had just done the show and told Larry Rosen, the associate producer of the program, that Marshall would be an ideal guest act for the show. Mike Douglas' longtime producer, Woody Frasier, who knew of Marshall from his appearances on WGN-TV, told Rosen to book Marshall.

The Mike Douglas Show was first broadcast in 1961 from the studios of KYW-TV in Cleveland, Ohio. Douglas' formula of featuring a mix of celebrities and rising young entertainers paid off as the program quickly attained note for its exposure and introduction of singers such as Barbra Streisand and Aretha Franklin. The show went into national syndication in 1963, and by the time Marshall got the call in December 1964, operations had moved to a 142-seat basement studio at 1619 Walnut Street in Philadelphia, the headquarters of Group W Productions. *The Mike Douglas Show* aired in all five of the Westinghouse Broadcasting Company's major markets and claimed a daytime viewership of more than six million.

Marshall and Judy drove to Philadelphia. They packed all sorts of magical props and illusions, including the Substitution Trunk, the Temple of Benares, and the Broomstick Suspension — not having any idea what they would be expected to perform. Upon arrival at the studio, Marshall met with Larry Rosen and learned that popular standup comic Bill Cosby was Mike's co-host for the week, and they wanted Cosby to be involved in some of the magic. Marshall was agreeable, and it was decided if he could have a half-hour rehearsal with Cosby, they would be able to perform some illusions with him. The rehearsal ended up being a five-minute talk-through with the director, but Marshall felt confident they could pull it off.

19. The Mike Douglas Show

Rosen also told Marshall that actor Robert Culp was a "surprise guest" on the show that day. Culp and Cosby were involved in the production of *I Spy*, an upcoming action series scheduled to debut on NBC the next fall. They had secretly flown Culp from Los Angeles, sequestered him at a nearby hotel, and the plan was to sneak him into the studio after they'd gone on air.

Cosby was surprised when ten minutes into the taping of the program an on-camera telephone rang. Mike Douglas picked it up and said matter-of-factly, "Yes, he's sitting right next to me." When Cosby was handed the receiver, he was shocked to hear Robert Culp's voice. And when Cosby was told to look around the corner of the set, where there was a prop phone booth, he was absolutely flummoxed to find his *I Spy*-cohort standing there talking to him.

Midway into the 90-minute program, Mike introduced Marshall, who opened with a series of dove productions and vanishes. Mike and Robert Culp assisted Marshall with a cut-and-restored rope routine, which gave Judy the necessary backstage time to get Cosby into costume and ready for the next illusion.

After a commercial break, Marshall dramatically informed Mike that he was fortunate to have an assistant that had traveled all the way from the Far East for the next trick. Cosby entered wearing in a colorful karate jacket and bowed ceremoniously. There were quite a few snickers, from the audience as well as Mike, as Brodien went through the motions of getting Cosby into a hypnotic trance for the Broomstick Suspension. Despite the dreamy music played by the Ellie Frankel Quintet, and Marshall's suggestions, "You're getting sleepy ... very sleepy," Cosby's left eye kept popping wide open and peeking about. His exaggerated yawns and smacking lips had the studio audience laughing. But Mike was suddenly in awe when he looked over and saw the six-foot two-inch-tall comedian floating in midair with the greatest of ease.

For the big finale of the 15-minute magic spot, Mike and Robert Culp helped Marshall handcuff Cosby and lock him up in the Substitution Trunk. Marshall then stood next to the secured trunk as a curtain was raised around him. With the band playing lively music, Marshall said, "Watch what happens when I count to three." He counted, "One ... two," then ducked below the curtain on "three." Both Culp and Douglas were amazed when the cloth fell to the floor and there was Cosby, standing nonchalantly beside the trunk. Brodien was nowhere to be seen. When the trunk was unlocked and opened, out popped Marshall, wearing Cosby's handcuffs.

The production staff loved Marshall and his magic. He attributes the favorable reception to his willingness to work with the other guests. He says, "It was exactly like it was when I went on the Bozo show for the first time and involved the clowns with the magic tricks." Larry Rosen wanted Brodien

For one of Marshall's appearances on the *Mike Douglas Show* in the 1960s, he performed the Broomstick Suspension with comedian Bill Cosby. *Used with permission of King World Productions.*

back right away. However, it would be a full year before he could do the show again — his calendar was filled with trade show dates.

• • •

Brodien's second appearance on *The Mike Douglas Show* was on December 9, 1965. Louis Nye was the co-host, and guests were Tony Bennett and trumpeter Bobby Hackett. Marshall was introduced at the midpoint of the program, and for his first sequence — some close-up tricks with cards, ropes, a ring, and a magic wand — Tony assisted. Mike then volunteered to be the victim for the Arrows Through the Head mystery and the Guillotine illusion.

Marshall asked for a little Arabian music as he introduced his enchanting lady assistant, Lewnyà Salami. It was, of course, Louis Nye in a harem outfit, complete with a frumpy wig, false eyelashes, and a sheer veil. Lewnyà used her flute-playing talents to cajole a comical snake in a basket into finding a playing card that Tony had selected.

19. The Mike Douglas Show

Coming back from a commercial break, the Ellie Frankel Quintet was playing "In a Persian Marketplace" as Brodien solemnly announced that for his next illusion, Lewnyà would be playing the role of the Egyptian Torture Girl. The studio audience screamed with laughter as Lewnyà bellydanced her way over to where Marshall, Tony, and Mike were standing.

"Before I can place Lewnyà on the tips of the sacred sabers of Egypt," Marshall said, "I must put her through a test of pain."

"Oh, yes, baby," growled Lewnyà, with eyelashes aflutter.

Mike and Tony helped secure a wooden stock around the Egyptian Torture Girl's neck. Marshall removed a slender, 29-inch-long sword from a scabbard, and said to Lewnyà, "We must run the entire length of this sword through your neck."

She crossed her eyes and said, "I vant you to." Louis Nye's facial expressions wavered between pain and pleasure and kept the studio audience in stitches.

Marshall then pretended to hypnotize Lewnyà, commanding her to become "as rigid as a mummy of antiquity." She leaned backward and Tony and Mike picked her up by the shoulders and ankles to place her on the points of two upright swords. There was quite a bit of bumbling in their attempts to get Lewnyà to balance. Actually, Marshall was having trouble locating the secret attachment on the back of the costume. Louis Nye started giggling, trying to sneak a peek from beneath the veil to see what was wrong. The audience was roaring with laughter.

Tony smiled and said, "Folks, it wasn't this way in rehearsal."

"Yeah," Mike said. "That's because there wasn't one." He turned his back to the audience and in a stage whisper asked, "Marshall, what's the matter?"

"I can't find the hole," he said.

Tony couldn't hear over the screams of laughter and asked, "He can't find what?"

"Marshall can't find the *hole*," Mike said in a loud voice, causing Tony to break up and let go of Louis, who was also in tears. A stagehand ran out to help, as all four grown men — one in drag with mascara running everywhere — were doubled over with laughter. The director had the presence of mind to cue the band to play them out for a commercial.

As soon as the director shouted, "We're clear," Marshall started apologizing. "I can't believe this happened. I'm sorry...."

"Are you kidding?" Mike said, wiping tears from his eyes. "Listen to that audience. They love it! This is great. Can we get Louis on the sword by the time we come back? It's a one-minute commercial." When they returned from the break, Lewnyà was floating serenely on the tip of the sacred saber of Egypt. Mike picked up one of the swords and passed it over her body, proving there were no visible means of support.

When Lewnyà's feet finally touched the floor and Marshall commanded her to awaken from the hypnotic spell, she uttered, "Oh, gracious gods of amuck, we must do this rigid experiment again when it is 'Tony Bennett Week' in my native country."

• • •

Within a month of the second appearance on *The Mike Douglas Show*, Marshall was invited back for a third time. Totie Fields was the guest host for the week and, again, they wanted her to be part of the magic. The portly comedienne was up for anything for a laugh, so they decided to teach her how to do the Broom Suspension and the Electric Chair. However, during rehearsal, things didn't go too smoothly with the broom trick.

"When I lifted Totie Fields into the floating position," Marshall remembers, "there was this metallic creaking sound, which was not normal. Her husband was sitting in the front row of the theater, and he jumped up, yelling, 'Oh, no, no, no! She's gonna fall. Don't do it!'" Even though Totie was willing to try it again, the director said no and made the decision to instead do the Electric Chair illusion that Brodien had brought along. All Totie had to do for this one was take a seat as the electricity was turned on. Marshall introduced her as *"Totie Electro, the Human Dynamo ... struck by lightning at the age of five, she could not speak or hear for three years ... doctors and scientists examined Totie Electro and claimed her body is immune to electricity. She could light up this entire television studio with the tips of her fingers if she wanted to."*

The studio audience chuckled throughout the Totie Electro ballyhoo, but when Marshall finally threw the switch for the power, and Totie ignited a torch with a spark that shot from her fingers, they applauded with astonishment. "Pretty shocking, huh!" she exclaimed. A pair of fluorescent and neon tubes glowed brightly when Totie held them in her hands. And when two torch sticks were touched to the ends of the tubes they burst into flames, giving Marshall the opportunity to do some carnival-style fire eating.

When the Electric Chair bit was over, Totie, who always made fun of her own generous portions, stood and asked, "Hey, do you have any openings for the Fat Lady?" She laughed and said, "I'll knock off a few pounds if that's what it takes to get the job!"—which gave her the opportunity to deliver her famous line: "I've been on a diet for two weeks ... and all I've lost is two weeks."

A Movie and a Trip to the Moon

When Brodien worked for Kraft Foods at the National Restaurant Show at McCormick Place in 1966, his presentation involved the introduction of a new line of Kraft products. His slick use of magic to make products appear caught the eyes of a team of Pillsbury marketing executives. They had an idea for using Marshall's talents in a film they were producing. In the '60s, it was not uncommon for companies to produce 16mm movies that were distributed among employees for training purposes. Film was also an effective way to roll out new products without incurring the expense of flying 1,400 salespeople to headquarters in Minneapolis.

In early 1976, he filmed a 13-minute, black-and-white film introducing Pillsbury Sweet Cream Pancake & Waffle Mix, featuring Marshall Brodien as "a hard-working, God-fearing, run-of-the-mill Pillsbury salesman." It opens in a grocery store where Marshall is found stocking the shelves with Pillsbury products. An attractive homemaker whisks by, picking up a package of Aunt Jemima Pancake Mix. Marshall stops her and magically transforms the competitor's product into a box of Sweet Cream Pancake Mix. When Marshall offers the Pillsbury product to her as a gift to try out in her kitchen, he gets an invite to her kitchen — which just happens to be a convertible ride away to the test kitchen at the Pillsbury Building in downtown Minneapolis. As it turns out, the lady is a Pillsbury home economist (she was grabbing the Aunt Jemima box in the store for market research), and she knows all the statistics that prove why Sweet Cream is going to sell better than the competitors. As she reels off the vital marketing information for the salespeople watching this kitchen caper, Marshall magically produces the essential ingredients that go into a box of Sweet Cream Pancake Mix. These feats of hocus pocus are easily accomplished because the Pillsbury test kitchen is miraculously equipped with all sorts of magician's props — an appearing bouquet of feather flowers (for flour), an Egg Bag, a Vanishing Milk Pitcher, and a Jack Gwynne Flip-Over Box for making the Pillsbury Sweet Cream Pancake Mix package appear.

Marshall finished up the cinematic shenanigans for Pillsbury on March 31. The following day, when he was scheduled to fly off to do a show for U.S. Plywood at the Pacific Coast Builders trade show, his son Marshall Walter was born on April 1st. He delayed the trip a day so he could celebrate the joyous event.

• • •

In the summer of 1967 — two full years before astronaut Neil Armstrong would step on the surface of the moon and take that "one small step for man, one giant leap for mankind" — Don Sandburg and Brodien were making some steps toward launching a new pilot for a show called *Moon Magic*.

Don had written a script about a pseudoscientific venture that took place in a laboratory within a huge glass dome located on the moon. He cast himself as Doctor Dimly, a scientist with a clipboard full of questions about the possibilities of lunar life. Marshall played Professor Marshall, a sort of science-magic guy whose experiments provided more mysteries than solutions for Doc Dimly's questions. Artistic puppeteer Roy Brown fabricated and operated a chubby little creature that kept questioning the Doc and the Professor's inhabitation of the moon.

Professor Marshall arrived at Doc Dimly's glass-domed lab via the Teleportation Chamber. He performed the off-the-magic-shop-shelf Chen Lee Water Suspension trick to prove that, despite the fact that there was very little gravity on the moon's surface, water did exist in a state of suspension. A sponge ball routine performed for the moon-man puppet, demonstrated that lunar morsels are where you least suspect them. A moon rock became lighter than air and floated when covered with the Professor's magic cloth. Doc Dimly was invited to sit in the high-tech Electron Throne (plywood cutouts applied to Marshall's old Electric Chair from the sideshow), and when Professor Marshall summoned "the force," Doc was able to light up a fluorescent light bulb with his fingertips. For the finale, when Doc Dimly stepped into the Teleportation Chamber, lights flashed and there was a puff of smoke and he transformed into the beautiful Star Maiden, a blond creature portrayed by Marshall's wife, Judy.

"Trouble hounded the project from the beginning," according to Sandburg, who'd taken it upon himself to get the 25-minute pilot episode filmed. Sears had an option to sponsor the program, so Don took the liberty of scheduling a camera crew, even though WGN-TV's program director was on vacation and unable to okay the use of the studio. Because there was no time to memorize lines, the night before the shoot, Don and Roy Brown taped script pages to the backs of set pieces. After an afternoon of adlibbing and improvising, they had enough footage to edit together an episode.

However, Don was in deep trouble when the program director returned. Because he hadn't authorized the production, he refused to screen the pilot for Sears. It stayed in the can — forever.

• • •

The 1967 season at "The World's Largest Amusement Park" ended rather uneventfully that Labor Day. Twelve years had passed since Marshall began working as the magician and sideshow talker at Riverview Park. A news blurb in *Amusement Business*, reported that the park grossed in excess of $2.6-million that season. So it came as a shock to many when, on October 3, George Schmidt, the grandson of Riverview's original owner, announced that the property had been sold. On December 1, there was an auction and 27 of the 121 rides were dismantled and sold. The other rides, attractions, and structures — including the freak-show building where Marshall had waxed eloquent for five years with his sideshow spiel — were totally demolished.

Doody, Doody, Do

For the first half of 1968, Brodien was so busy working with Kitzing, Inc., traveling across the country doing trade show after trade show that he had no time for appearances on *Bozo's Circus*. The constant calls from Howard Schultz, who continued to book the show, were usually answered, "Can't do it this month, but keep me on the list." Schultz's records reflect that the first time Marshall was available was on July 31.

The week before doing that show, Marshall was wrapping up a trade show at McCormick Place. It was for the American Gas Association and the theme of the exhibit was "The Magic of Gas." Kitzing had constructed an elaborate Arabian Nights set, a costume designer from the Goodman Theatre made harem outfits for the four beautiful girls who assisted and, for the levitation that was the talk of the trade-show floor, Marshall wore a sultan's costume. As they were breaking down and packing up the exhibit, Marshall was told that if he wanted the costumes he could have them.

"I told Don Sandburg about this really nice sultan's outfit when I went in to do the Bozo show," Marshall says. "It looked like something a wizard would wear, and I asked if he would be interested in having a mystical character come on every now and then and do some bits with the clowns."

Don liked the idea, and a week later he called Schultz and said, "Book Brodien for next Wednesday and tell him to bring in that new costume." Don had dusted off an old script from a Bozo show in 1962, where Marshall, Bozo, and Sandy performed some funny tricks with eggs. He crossed out the name "Marshall the Magician" and penciled in the name "The Wizard."

If there's truth in the saying "Clothes make the man," it was *the costume* that created Brodien's character. A rajah's tunic of metallic gold fabric was encrusted with spangles and faux jewels. Pajama-like maroon trousers were fastened with a satin waist sash. A turban with feathers and stones was worn atop a frumpy wig of jet-black frizzy hair. Marshall added a mustache and a goatee, making his character a little more mysterious and strange.

This weird wizard arrived on the scene about the same time Roy Brown joined *Bozo's Circus* as Cooky the Clown. Roy Brown was the puppeteer for WGN-TV's *Garfield Goose and Friends* and created the character of Cuddly Dudley on *Ray Rayner & His Friends*. At Don Sandburg's insistence, Roy developed the character of Cooky, a circus cook who carried on running gags with Bozo, Sandy, Oliver, and Ringmaster Ned concerning the quality of food at the circus. And since the circus that Cooky referred to was *Bozo's Circus*, it became a never-ending inside gag about the questionable culinary offerings of the WGN employee cafeteria.

It wasn't long before "Wizzo," as the cast starting calling Brodien's wizard character, caught on and he was making weekly appearances. By the fourth week, it was learned that Wizzo the Wizard hailed from the faraway land of Arobia — a place that just popped into Brodien's mind when Bozo asked, "Hey, Wizzo, where you from, anyway?"

• • •

Marshall claims that most of the character bits that comprised the wacky persona of Wizzo the Wizard came about by accident. "One time, after I rolled my eyes, which always made the audience laugh, I just happened to say, 'Doody, doody, do...' and it made the people laugh harder. Rolling my eyes and saying, 'Doody, doody, do' at the same time made them laugh twice as hard." When the eye-rolling was combined with hand waving and finger wiggling, "Doody, doody, do" meant something magical was about to happen.

Marshall found a costume-jewelry pendant with a gaudy stone glued to it, and he started wearing it on a chain around his neck as part of Wizzo's wardrobe. Whenever asked what it was for, Wizzo just rolled his eyes and explained it was an amulet from the land of Arobia and it had magical powers for protection from evil and injuries. The first time Wizzo used its powers was when he performed the Stocks of Zanzibar illusion with Cooky and Bozo. Cooky's head was chained and locked in the torturous-looking headstocks. Wizzo paused and announced, "I will now magically transpose myself into the locked stocks, and the magic will happen when..." The amulet suddenly swung down and whacked Cooky on the head. Wizzo continued, "...Yes, the magic will happen because the Stone of Zanzibar ever so lightly touched Cooky." Wizzo mysteriously raised a foulard in front of Cooky's head, and Doody, doody, do! When the cloth fell to the floor, Cooky was free, and Wizzo was locked in the stocks.

The Character of Wizzo the Wizard became a regular on *Bozo's Circus* in 1968. On this program, ringmaster Ned Locke and Cooky (Roy Brown) schemed to cut the wires suspending Galli the Gorilla, but were completely mystified when the creature continued to float in mid-air. *Courtesy WGN-TV Chicago*

From that show on, things magical happened whenever Wizzo touched something with the Stone of Zanzibar. A coin would not disappear from a child's hand unless the hand was gently tapped with the Stone of Zanzibar. A rabbit couldn't be coaxed from a hat until stroked with the Stone of Zanzibar. Yet one time, when Wizzo was trying to get rid of Bozo, the amulet had little effect.

"I told the audience that we'd make Bozo disappear by touching him with the Stone of Zanzibar. So, I touched Bob Bell with the Stone of Zanzibar. Bob didn't move. I said, 'Bozo, I touched you with the Stone of Zanzibar.' He just stood there, looked at me and said, 'Yeah, Wiz. I remember the time you got stoned at the Zanzi Bar.'"

Practically *everything* about Wizzo was magic, not just his utterances of Doody, doody, do or his Stone of Zanzibar, but every part of his wizardly body. The magic would happen when Wizzo touched things with his "magic finger," stepped on things with his "magic foot," blew on things with his "magic breath." Marshall tells, "One time I was doing this trick where I borrowed a dollar bill. After Bozo wrote down the serial number, I sealed it in an envelope. After the envelope was burned, the bill would end up inside a lemon or an orange. Well, when I put the dollar bill in the envelope, I said, 'Before the magic begins, I must lick the envelope with my magic tongue.' Bozo turned to me and said, 'Wizzo, the mommies like your magic tongue.' Everybody was about to bust out laughing, but held back. Cooky couldn't. He had to walk off the set."

As Bozo, Bob Bell was the perfect foil for Marshall's Wizzo, Roy's Cooky, and Don's Sandy. Bob would sling more than his share of straight lines for his fellow clowns, but it was usually Bozo who got the last laugh. Bob had an innate ability to come back with razor-sharp ad-libs. His off-the-cuff jokes broke up the crew as well as the parents in the studio audience. Bob Bell was one of those rare children's show performers who appealed as much to the adults as he did to the kids. Grownups could tell that beneath the makeup was a guy having as much fun as they were.

• • •

In October 1968, Bob Bell suffered a brain aneurysm. He underwent surgery and was hospitalized for two months. All of a sudden, Marshall found himself doing five shows a week, as the faithful four — Ringmaster Ned, Sandy, Cooky, and Wizzo — kept the show alive for the next six months while Bob recovered.

Marshall enjoyed the challenges that came with creating new skits and different magic bits, but it meant he had to down the trade-show work on his calendar. He was forced to cancel his exclusivity contract with Kitzing, and referred all his trade-show jobs that fall and winter to magician friend Johnny Thompson. Marshall admits that it was actually a relief, getting away from the endless hours of standing on concrete floors, the incessant gladhanding with clients, and wearing the superficial corporate smile all day long.

Performing on the Bozo show as Wizzo was an escape — sort of like a kid running off with the circus. "When I put on that bizarre wizard's costume and the mysterious makeup," he says, "I could act crazy, do and say all kind of crazy things."

• • •

A blizzard whitened the Midwest the first week of January 1969. The Bozo show was canceled because of the weather, which was good for Marshall. He was stranded in Detroit, where he had been working the Auto Tech-

In the 1970s, the National Association of Broadcasters stopped children's show hosts from promoting their own products on the same program. But it didn't stop Brodien. He had Wizzo pitch Marshall Brodien Magic Company products. *Courtesy WGN-TV Chicago. Bozo the Clown® & ©Larry Harmon Pictures Corporation. All rights reserved.*

nology Show for Bethlehem Steel. On January 7, his wife Judy called. She had just given birth to the Brodiens' third child, a second daughter they named Christine.

Don Sandburg left WGN-TV in February. He had joined *Bozo's Circus* as the main writer only a week after its September 11, 1961, debut. Within two weeks Sandburg was the producer, and shortly after that was appearing twice a week as Sandy the Tramp. Throughout his seven year tenure at WGN, Don had written and participated in many a clown skit that ended with an "unexpected" shaving-cream-custard pie in the face. So, true to form, on his last day, he turned the tables on his unsuspecting coworkers. During the live broadcast, armed with three-dozen pies Don raided the studio, attacking the cast, the band, the entire production crew, and the audience as well — an unforgettable last stand of custard pies.

Sandburg moved to the West Coast, hoping to hook up with the Disney organization. It would be only a matter of two years before he and Marshall would join forces again and work on some mutually rewarding projects.

• • •

On Saint Patrick's Day 1962, Cooky and Wizzo were in the middle of a sketch in Cooky's kitchen when Ringmaster Ned wheeled in a dolly with a big box labeled SURPRISE. They started arguing over what the surprise could be, who it was from, and who would have the honors of opening the box when — Surprise!— the lid flew off and it was Bozo. Bob Bell's doctors had said he could return to the show. A few cream pies flew through the air and things were back to normal at *Bozo's Circus*.

TV Magic Cards

Marshall Brodien had peddled trick decks since he was a teenager. The shelves behind the Treasure Chest's magic counter were stocked with at least 20 different gaffed-and-gimmicked packs of playing cards, each bearing an easily discarded wrapper that advised the decks were sold FOR ENTERTAINMENT PURPOSES ONLY. And Brodien had an entertaining and persuasive pitch for each and every one of the trick decks he demonstrated.

There were marked cards known as Readers, with codes printed on the backs, secretly identifying the faces of all the cards in the deck. There were Strippers, with the sides of the pack shaved and tapered, facilitating the finding and "stripping out" of any card or cards (such as the four Aces). The Force Deck provided a foolproof method for knowing which card a spectator would select — all 52 cards were the same. More specialized trick decks included the Menetekel Pack, X-Ray Cards, Ultra-Mental Deck, Simplex Rising Cards, the Haunted Pack, and the Brain Wave Deck.

And, there was the ever-popular Svengali Deck, a gaffed deck so magical it creates an optical illusion best described as eye-popping. A pack of cards is shown to consist of all different cards. A single card is picked — say, the Queen of Hearts — and returned to the middle of the deck. With a mere riffle of the cards, the Queen of Hearts is on top of the pack. A cut and another riffle and every single card of the deck is shown to be a Queen of Hearts. Yet, with another cut, the deck is back to its original condition of all different cards.

The Svengali Deck was invented in 1909 by magician Burling Hull, and it was magic dealer W.D. Le Roy who named the mechanical deck after Svengali, the fictitious evil hypnotist in George du Maurier's 1894 novel *Trilby*.

The Svengali Deck sold for a buck, and during his tenure at the Treasure Chest, Marshall sold hundreds of them. Yet his hundreds came nowhere near the thousands of Svengalis he saw being peddled on midways and fairgrounds in 1953 and '54, when he traveled with Dick Best's sideshow.

"I'd watch those pitchmen stop a crowd of at least 100 people," Marshall says. "After the pitch they would unload at least 50 decks. At the time, I asked myself, 'If a magician went on television and reached a million people with a good pitch, I wonder if he could sell a half-million decks of cards?' I would think about that for years."

Marshall thought about it some more in 1963 and '64, when he was playing fairs in Montana and South Dakota. Svengali pitchmen were on the carnival midways, at the fairground entrances, and even in the parking lots. "But this time," Marshall recalls, "the decks were selling like hotcakes for $2 a pop."

But because he became so busy with trade shows across the country, it would be another five years before he'd have the chance to seriously consider pitching Svengali Decks on TV. That opportunity finally arose in 1969, when Marshall found himself in need of, of all things, a fence.

He had called a contractor to come out to his house in Fox Lake and give a bid on installing a fence between his yard and his next-door neighbor's driveway. The fencing company was owned by the town's chief of police, Frank Meyer, and the salesman they sent was Rick Carey, a friend Marshall hadn't seen in ten years.

"I first met Rick Carey in 1959, not long after I got out of the Army, while I was appearing at the Boston Nocturne. He was only 19 and was booking bands into the nightclub on Sundays, my usual night off. As we got to know each other, I told him about my idea of going on TV to sell Svengali Decks. Rick was interested in any sort of scheme to make money, and he offered to be a partner. He was forever reminding me, 'Anytime you want to do the deck deal, I'll be your partner.'" After the nightclub closed, they went their separate ways. Rick was aware that Marshall had become a regular on the *Bozo's Circus* show, but had no idea he had married, moved to Fox Lake, and was living in the same community.

"After the fence was installed, Rick continued to stop by the house. And, of course, he kept bugging me about when we were going to do that 'deck deal.' I suggested that we go down to WGN-TV and investigate the cost of shooting a commercial. Ned Locke, the ringmaster on the Bozo show, was also an advertising salesman for the station, and I knew he could advise us on how much it would cost."

Locke said that producing the spot would cost them nothing — as long as they contracted for the airtime. He said, "We'll go into the studio after a Bozo show is over. We'll hold the camera crew long enough to shoot a one-minute spot. I'll do the voiceover. All you guys have to do is run the commercial several times a day for a period of three weeks. It needs to air that long to realize any results. The package will cost you $5,000."

Rick was insistent they do it. Marshall was hesitant. Running one commercial on one station for three weeks seemed like overkill.

Ned said, "Here's the reason you guys need to repeat the spot over and over. The first time somebody sees a commercial, they might be impressed with the product, but they forget or don't have the time to order it. The next time they see it they'll say, 'That's really interesting, maybe something I should have.' The third or fourth time they see it, they'll say, 'I've got to get that deck of cards,' and they'll buy it. So, boys, it's about six weeks till Christmas, which means it's time to do it or get off the proverbial pot."

Putting up $2,500 apiece, Brodien and Carey signed a contract with WGN-TV, and made the decision that their product would hit the airwaves as "Magic Cards." The 60-second black-and-white commercial opened with a close-up shot of a grotesque-looking hand that had five jumbo thumbs. Ned's voiceover made the statement: *"Even if you're all thumbs, you can do fantastic card tricks with Magic Cards, the foolproof deck that works amazing card tricks all by itself!"* The extra thumbs were tossed aside as the camera pulled back to reveal Marshall's deft fingers going through the razzle-dazzle demo of the deck, as the announcer said: *"Ask a friend to pick a card."* The Ace of Spades was pulled aside. *"Place it back into the deck. Tap the deck and it's back on top."* The Ace was turned over. *"Make three piles. Whatever pile he points to the card is there."* The Ace appeared to jump to the top of all three piles. *"But the fun's just begun. Take the top card..."* It was a face card. *"Tap it and it changes back to his card. Place it on the bottom of the deck and they all change into his card."* The cards were were all Aces of Spades. *"Tap the deck, and they're all different again ... Magic Cards, the foolproof deck that works card tricks by itself is available at Treasure Chest, 19 West Randolph Street, across from the Oriental Theatre in Chicago."* A graphic with another address for ordering the cards remained on the screen, as Ned's voice informed viewers, *"For immediate delivery send two dollars in cash, check, or money order to MAGIC CARDS, Box 11, Fox Lake, Illinois. A fantastic gift for anyone from six to sixty. Magic Cards! A good deal!"*

The first Magic Cards commercial aired on November 18, 1969. On the third day of the three-week ad campaign, Box 11 at the Fox Lake branch of the U.S. Post Office was empty. By the morning of day four, Rick had made two trips to check the mail. Not a single piece of mail until the fifth day, when there was a bill from a printer *and* five orders that totaled $12. One customer had ordered two decks.

"The next day, I had to go out of town to do a week-long trade show

22. TV Magic Cards

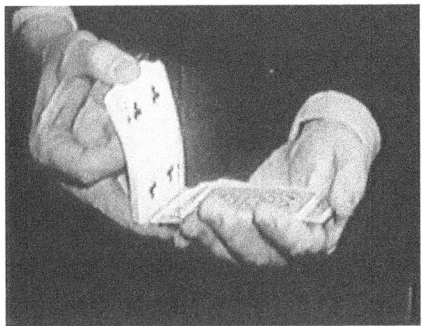
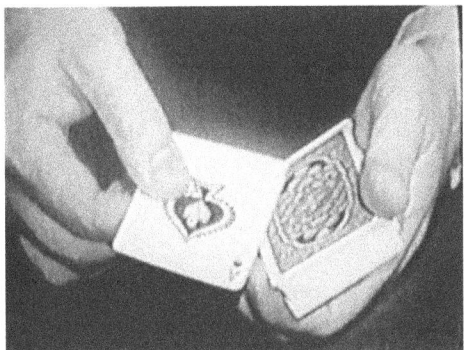
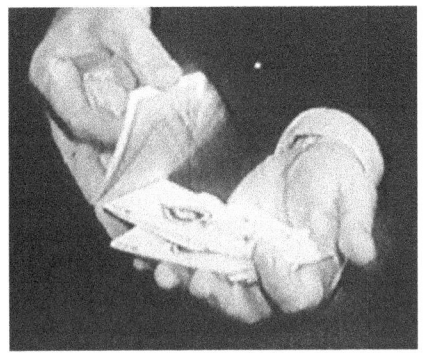

Frame captures from the original 60-second TV Magic Cards commercial that was produced at WGN-TV studios in 1970.

for Bethlehem Steel," Marshall remembers. "After the first day of the show, I called Rick to ask how many orders we had received. He said that about 20 had come in. When I called the next day, he was pretty excited. We had over 80 orders. By the second week, we were getting 200 orders a day, 500 by midweek, then it shot up to over 800. When the Post Office called to let us know they ordered more mail sacks sent out to the Fox Lake branch just to hold our mail, we knew we had a hit on our hands.

"By the start of the third week of the TV commercials, Bobby Baer called from the Treasure Chest and said, 'I need at least 2,000, maybe 3,000 more decks.' Bobby was buying them directly from us and had already gone through his initial stock of three thousand decks." Marshall had their supplier drop-ship two thousand more decks to the Treasure Chest.

Bobby later told Marshall, "We were practically selling them off the pallet. Nobody needed a demonstration. I'd never seen anything like it. As soon as they walked in, they'd get in line to buy them."

Even though the mail orders continued to pour in for two weeks after the commercials stopped running, the over-the-counter sales at the Treasure Chest came close to topping the mail orders. It dawned on the partners that without the expense of packaging and mailing they could be making a quicker profit if they were selling Magic Cards in more stores.

• • •

The decades-old Svengali Deck — a trick-store product that was arcane and not readily available to the general public — was essentially re-invented when it was pitched on television. New generations of Chicagoans looked at it as something novel. Suddenly there was a demand for the trick deck — "As seen on TV" — and thus was born the everlasting name of "TV Magic Cards."

In March, when a new commercial was shot, this time at WGN-TV's Continental Broadcasting Company Studios, a TV MAGIC CARDS ©1970 label was affixed to the card box, giving the stock Svengali Deck a distinctive identity. The "all thumbs" intro was eliminated, and instead of Ned Locke delivering the pitch, it was Marshall. "Hi, I'm magician Marshall Brodien. Most magic tricks are easy, once you know the secret," he said, going into the 50-second deck demonstration that was the same as before, except for the ten-second tagline at the end. Instead of informing that TV Magic Cards were available only at the Treasure Chest, a voiceover announcement and graphic was inserted, giving the name of local retailers, such as True Value Hardware or Walgreens.

Another block of airtime was purchased from WGN-TV and although decks could still be ordered from Box 11, in Fox Lake, Illinois, Marshall and Rick were banking on consumers buying from retail outlets. Also, the TV Magic Cards were now accompanied by an instruction sheet that on its backside advertised other trick decks that could be ordered: X-Ray Cards, the Wizard Stripper Deck, Simplex Rising Cards, and the Wonder Deck (marked cards). They were $2 each or all four for $6 postpaid.

The partners in pasteboards had outgrown TV Magic Cards' original Fox Lake mail-order headquarters — Rick's double-car garage — where a next-door neighbor and several friends were hired part-time to fill the first 10,000 or so orders. A 600-square-foot office space on Grand Avenue was rented to house

TV Magic Cards as they appeared on racks of drug stores and retail outlets in the early 1970s. *Photograph from Marshall Brodien Collection*

the expanding business and its inventory. Marshall and Rick rented a van and were delivering decks to all sorts of retail outlets within the broadcast radius of WGN-TV. Marshall recalls, "We went to drug stores, tobacco shops, hardware stores, five-'n'-dimes, and frankly, any other local merchant who would let us place a WE HAVE TV MAGIC CARDS sign in their window.

• • •

In late summer of 1970, Marshall and Rick decided to venture beyond the Chicago market. They placed the decks in several stores in Peoria, Illinois, and bought airtime on a station there.

"Will it play in Peoria?" was a famous question that originated during the days of vaudeville, when the mid-sized Midwest town was considered a barometer of show-biz success. New acts or shows were booked into a Peoria theater and if they did not receive strong approval, they were canceled. It was believed that if a performer or production scored with the Peoria audience, it'd be successful anywhere else in the country. Only a year before Brodien and Carey hit Peoria with TV Magic Cards, President Richard Nixon's administration had rekindled a public awareness of the old "Will it play in Peoria?" query. While campaigning in 1969, Nixon viewed Peoria as his model of the American norm. To this day, polls and surveys taken in Peoria are still used as a measure for predicting political views and marketing trends.

Planning and projecting sales far beyond Peoria, in October 1970, Marshall contacted his friend Don Sandburg, who was now living on the West Coast, to see if he had any interest in getting on the TV Magic Cards bandwagon. Marshall mailed him a 16mm print of the most recent commercial, told him of the sales successes he'd had with retail stores in the Midwest, and asked Don if he had any interest in becoming a part-time sales representative. Since leaving the Bozo show, Don had been writing and producing various shows in Hollywood and Los Angeles and was currently involved with the production of a syndicated daytime talk program, *The Virginia Graham Show*. But because he was on the verge of leaving Virginia and about to make a deal with Hanna-Barbera Productions to produce a new kid's show, *The Banana Splits*, Don said he had some spare time and would like to give it a try.

"It was a Friday the thirteenth," Don recalls, "when I made my first sales call. It was to the Thrifty Drug Company, which owned a chain of over 200 discount stores in Southern California." The appointment was for seven o'clock in the morning, and when Don walked in the doors of Thrifty's headquarters at least an hour early, the receptionist's area was overflowing with salesmen waiting to see the buyers. "When I sat down to wait my turn, the gentleman next to me asked how long I had been calling on Thrifty Drugs. I asked him what time it was. He told me, and I answered, 'I've been calling on them about two minutes.' I was so new in the business, I didn't even have a business card. All I had was a deck of TV Magic Cards and my old 16mm movie projector with Marshall's one-minute TV spot threaded and ready to show the buyer."

22. TV Magic Cards

When he was finally ushered into the buyer's office, Don found himself in a tiny cubicle surrounded by glass panels that went from near the ceiling to the floor. There wasn't a single solid wall or even a door on which to project the film. Yet he forged ahead with his pitch, setting up the projector at an angle on a desktop, focusing the moving image onto the floor. "It was a distorted picture, but the guy watched it intently. He liked it and believed the commercial would sell the product." Sandburg told the buyer that he was prepared to run 200 spots during the upcoming Christmas season and tag each one with the message: AVAILABLE AT ALL THRIFTY DISCOUNT DRUGS.

"Without taking a breath the buyer ordered 200 gross," Don says, "and he added that that was just for starters." Sandburg was asked to write up the order — for what he'd mentally calculated was almost 30,000 decks — on his company invoice. "I didn't have a company, much less an invoice. I didn't even have a pen. A secretary had to type out a letter of confirmation on Thrifty Drug stationery."

Don triumphantly exited the buying office and headed straight for Metromedia Television's sales department to talk about purchasing airtime on KTTV. But first he thought it might be wise to phone Marshall, and make sure the 28,800 decks of TV Magic Cards he'd just sold could be shipped out.

When Marshall and Rick heard of Don's sale they were in shock and awe. The Thrifty Drug order was for twice as many decks as were sold last Christmas. They were ecstatic but had no idea how they were going to get that many decks of cards that quickly from their suppliers.

• • •

In the beginning, Brodien and Carey bought Svengali Decks from the Ed Drane Company, a magic-and-novelty supplier that was assembling them from card stock printed by the Arrco Playing Card Company in Chicago. After the second commercial was made and they started selling tens of thousands more decks at selected retail stores, Arrco couldn't print the cards fast enough to fill the orders. Marshall and Rick augmented their inventory with Svengali Decks purchased from Haines House of Cards, a company that assembled trick decks from cards printed by the U.S. Playing Card Company in Cincinnati, Ohio.

The day after the jubilant Mr. Sandburg called with the news of the Thrifty Drug order, Marshall went to the Drane Company to talk about the possibility of scheduling a special print run of cards. They needed 40,000 Svengali decks.

The Drane Company had just been acquired and a Mr. Robinson, the new owner, told Marshall that the 40,000 decks could be delivered in the timeframe required, but he said, "If you're buying decks in numbers like that the price is going to be higher."

"I had a hard time understanding that," Marshall says. "When they sold us decks in quantities of 4,000, they charged 50¢ apiece. Now, when we wanted 40,000, they wanted 70¢ a deck."

When Brodien asked about the price increase, Mr. Robinson shrugged his shoulders, and said, "That's our price. You're making more money, we want more money."

Marshall phoned his friend Jay Marshall, who ran Magic, Inc., a wholesale/retail operation on Lincoln Avenue. Marshall said, "This new guy at Drane is trying to stick it to us. What can I do?" Jay suggested he call the Stancraft Playing Card Company in St. Paul, Minnesota. He said the company could not only put together the decks, but they could print the cards with the TV Magic Cards logo on the backs of the cards and on the boxes.

"I phoned Stancraft," Marshall says. "They said they had printed runs of Svengali Decks for magic shops, but an order for 40,000 decks was unheard of. When I told them we were marketing them on television, they said they would send an account executive to Chicago to talk with Rick and me."

Since Marshall and Rick really didn't have an office, they arranged to meet the Stancraft salesman at United Airline's Red Carpet Room at O'Hare Airport. He was impressed with the partners' track record selling Svengali Decks on TV. As he listened to the plan to sell more decks via key outlet marketing, he figured the printing costs for 40,000 decks of custom-printed trick cards. Handing them a quote for $20,000, he said, "A signature is all that's necessary. I assume you are listed with Dun & Bradstreet."

Almost in unison, Marshall and Rick said, "No, not yet."

"What other credit references do you have?"

They looked at each other and said, "None."

"Well, we cannot print that many decks of specialty cards without some kind of credit references."

"I told him I understood," Marshall says, "And even though I knew we only had about $8,000 in our business bank account, I turned to Rick and said, 'Write the man a check for $20,000, if that's what it's going to take to get this order in the works.' Rick looked at me, wondering what kind of craziness I was up to. But he reached down, picked up the checkbook and opened it."

"Wait," said the salesman. "Before you do that, let me go back and talk with my boss. A down payment might be all we need. Besides, an order like this could lead to more business for us in the future."

Marshall agreed and said, "You are right, the future could mean another order for 100,000 decks. Next? A half-million or more. So, you'd better take our check so your boss will know we're serious."

The Stancraft account exec said a check wasn't necessary. He shook their hands and hurried to catch his plane back to St. Paul, probably calculating what his commission would be on the sale of a million decks.

"Rick stood there shaking his head," Marshall remembers. "He asked me 'Are you out of your mind? What if we'd written that check and his boss tried to put it in the bank?' I just explained we'd have tell them it was a mistake and we didn't have that much in the bank."

The following day, the president of Stancraft called and told Marshall that they would print the cards for immediate shipment if he and Rick could send them a down payment of $5,000. They would have 60 days to pay the balance.

Meanwhile, Don Sandburg had been given the green light to schedule 100 "run of the station" television spots with KTTV in Los Angeles. This meant the station was entitled to insert the one-minute TV Magic Cards commercial in any program they wished, day or night. After some negotiation with Don the station agreed to place the spots in two programs of his choice, *Get Smart* and *The Dick Van Dyke Show*— the two most popular syndicated shows of the day.

The original shipment of cards sold out in the first ten days the commercials aired. Stancraft Playing Cards was called to make two more print runs of TV Magic Cards and ship them air express to guarantee arrival in the drug stores before Christmas. Another 100 spots were scheduled. "The sales were overwhelming," Don says, "surpassing the old Christmas record set by Mattel's Hot Wheels. Before the New Year rang in, we had sold 110,000 decks of TV Magic Cards."

The cards continued to sell moderately well even after the holidays, due to the purchase of additional commercial time on another Los Angeles station, KHJ-TV. On January 28, 1971, the last order of decks was shipped to the participating Thrifty stores, and by the end of April, when the campaign was considered over, a total of 135,000 decks had been sold.

• • •

The coast-to-coast wheeling and dealing in TV Magic Cards didn't hinder Brodien from continuing with his regular appearances as Wizzo on WGN-TV's *Bozo's Circus*. His five-a-week appearances on the program, which he started doing in 1969 while Bob Bell was sidelined with surgery, had been streamlined to a comfortable two or three shows a week. This new schedule

Capitalizing on the popularity of their television characters, Marshall and Roy Brown were constantly making outside appearances with their Marshall Brodien & Cooky Show. *Photograph by Bolber/Chicago, courtesy Marshall Brodien Collection*

not only allowed Marshall to get back into doing two or three trade shows per month, it also gave him the freedom to make numerous lucrative personal appearances as Wizzo the Wizard.

From the beginning, Larry Harmon Pictures Corporation, holders of the Bozo the Clown copyright and licensing rights, always demanded a percentage of any fees charged for Bozo's outside appearances. This bothered Bob Bell little, as he never cared for making appearances away from WGN-TV — he believed the character was a creature of television and should rarely be seen outside the studio-circus environment.

On the other hand, Wizzo and Cooky, the other clown stars of the show, were free to take their characters anywhere they pleased. "We did all kinds of personal appearances," Marshall says, "from grand openings of shopping centers to headlining festivals and fairs. Over the years, Roy Brown and I made some extremely good money on the side being Cooky and Wizzo." And on top of Marshall and Roy's riches was a genuine and sincere friendship that money could not buy.

The popularity of *Bozo's Circus* in Chicago had soared. It was the top-rated children's show in the Midwest. When the 500,000th studio audience member showed up for the show on June 7, 1971, there was a major celebration that made network news and nationwide headlines. The reservations list for show tickets stretched for seven years. It was reported that hundreds of women wrote for tickets the moment they knew they were pregnant, assuring that their six-year-old children would be able to see the show.

23

Eicoff Enters the Scene

About the same time Don Sandburg got TV Magic Cards into Thrifty Drugs on the West Coast, Marshall had a call from Ron Bliwas at A. Eicoff & Company, one of Chicago's biggest ad agencies. He said they had seen the commercials running on WGN-TV and Al Eicoff, the president of the company, wanted to talk with Marshall and Rick about some marketing ideas he had for TV Magic Cards.

Alvin Eicoff was a pioneer in the field of broadcast direct-response marketing. The legendary Eicoff-created TV commercials of the 1950s and '60s for such products as salad makers, rug cleaners, combination knife sharpeners/glass cutters, chrome cleaners, food slicers, handheld sewing machines, and do-it-yourself hair cutters, motivated consumers to spend more than $500 million with the various companies represented. Eicoff had an uncanny ability to introduce new products on television with ridiculously small advertising budgets and sell directly to consumers. He made his mark in broadcast advertising by producing successful commercials that used the techniques, as well as the jargon, of the fast-talking pitchmen at fairs and carnivals. Eicoff's early 30-minute commercials pitching the Hair Wiz, Vitamix, Tarn-X, and the Dexter handheld sewing machine were precursors of broadcast television's infomercials and harbingers of the round-the-clock shopping commercials of cable TV.

Marshall and Rick were a little reluctant to meet with Al Eicoff, mainly because they believed they were doing a fairly good job of marketing TV Magic Cards themselves. Marshall says, "I remember saying to Rick on the way downtown for the meeting that we shouldn't tell much, because it sounded like somebody was trying to figure a way to knock off our product and method of selling it."

23. Eicoff Enters the Scene

As Marshall and Rick sat in the mahogany-paneled conference room of Eicoff's offices high above North Michigan Avenue — with all of Eicoff's partners, Ron Bliwas, Manny Gutterman, Bob Berg, and Burt Babetch present — the first thing Al explained was the concept of key-outlet marketing and how his company could get them into every retail chain in America. He said, "We can put TV Magic Cards in retail stores coast to coast, from Eckerd Drug in Florida to Fred Meyer Drugs in Oregon to Thrifty Drug in California to Osco Stores everywhere."

"Hold it!" Marshall said, "We are *already* coast to coast with our product."

"Yeah," Rick said. "Marshall's buddy from WGN has successfully placed the cards in 200 Thrifty Drug stores in Los Angeles.

This was news to Al. He complimented the boys on their deal. Then he smiled and said, "But with the distribution network that we have in place," gesturing toward Manny Gutterman sitting beside him, "we can get TV Magic Cards into many more stores. We can place your product in literally thousands more stores, and..." Al paused and looked around, then continued his pitch in a soft voice, as if his own conference room was bugged, "We can buy advertising airtime *cheaper* than anyone else in the business. And because we know where and when to buy airtime, we can guarantee immediate results."

Marshall and Rick listened as Al told them how his agency had arrived at formulas for determining a "profitable advertising-to-sales ratio," no matter what part of the nation they wanted to peddle their product. They were soon convinced that Al was a master strategist when it came to media buying: he knew where to place the spots, when the most effective times were to run them, and he knew how to negotiate for the lowest possible media rates.

By the mid 1950s, Eicoff had joined forces with Manny Gutterman, the man who held reign over chain store distribution across America. "The chains worshipped Manny as if he were royalty," Eicoff would later write in his 1982 autobiography, *Or Your Money Back*. "The buyers loved Gutterman because when he gave the chains a product, he gave them something they could sell at a huge profit." When Manny teamed with Al to handle the distribution of all of A. Eicoff & Company's direct response and key outlet advertised products, the phrase "Available in these stores only" became formidable words for buyers everywhere. Their early sales triumphs with such products like the Salad Maker, Nu-Vinyl, Classic Nails, and the Roll-O-Matic Mop made not only the manufacturers wealthy, but Al and Manny as well.

Could Eicoff's company do the same with TV Magic Cards? Brodien and Carey agreed to a simple trial-run contract. The agency charged a 10% fee of the wholesale cost of the cards to get the merchandise into the retail outlets. The stores received a 30% discount off the retail price of $2, plus the "free" advertising (the where-to-buy tags on the commercials). With approximately 20% of the retail cost of TV Magic Cards going to the advertising budget, this meant almost $1-a-deck profit on each deck sold.

"During our first year of advertising exclusively through Eicoff, which was 1971," Marshall says, "we sold close to another million decks of TV Magic Cards." When Al suggested that Marshall come up with some other magic products to pitch on the airwaves, he filmed a one-minute commercial for the TV Miracle Deck (a Stripper Deck). When this spot aired on stations in six regional markets, it produced, as Eicoff promised, "instant results," selling over 200,000 decks. Then, after finding out they could obtain some reasonably priced plastic sets of Cups & Balls from Jules Traub of Fun, Inc., Marshall put together a TV Magic Cups commercial on November 15, 1971. This single trick release, promoted as a holiday season stocking stuffer, available only at Walgreens, sold remarkably well for $1.98.

Following TV Magic Cups, they rolled out the TV Magic Show, a boxed 12-trick magic set that included the Rice Bowls, Houdini Chain Escape, Cut-and-Restored Rope, Cups & Balls, Phantom Cards, Magic Coin Bank, and a half-dozen other effects. It retailed for $9.95. The set was pieced together from individual tricks manufactured by Fun Inc. And when strategically placed into the Eicoff/Gutterman direct-response advertising/distribution machine, along with an Eicoff-produced 90-second commercial, the new set sold nationwide by the hundreds of thousands.

"One of the things we learned from Al Eicoff was how to sell the concept of professionalism with the TV commercials," Marshall says. "Al believed that the commercial had to show the magician as a true professional; he had to be a working pro, not a hobbyist or an amateur who was trying to sell the product." Eicoff also maintained that only a pro could convince viewers that they could do magic tricks like the pros if, *and only if,* they purchased the product. "When we signed with Al, the first thing he had us do was videotape a new introduction for the TV Magic Cards commercial. I came out wearing white tie and tails and produced a fluttering white dove. There was applause. Then the camera cut to me in a business suit, holding the product. I said: *'Hi, I'm Marshall Brodien — a professional magician. Most magic tricks are easy, once you know the secret. And you don't have to be a professional.'* Then I went into the product demonstration."

Likewise, when the commercials were produced for the TV Magic Show set, the emphasis was on the fact that this was not just a box of tricks. This magic set was the creation of a magician, a working professional that viewers had seen on TV. The TV Magic Show commercials opened with a teaser shot of a pro such as Johnny Thompson producing a dove or Norm Nielsen vanishing a musical instrument. After the applause cue, there was a cut to

After selling another million decks of TV Magic Cards in collaboration with A. Eicoff & Co., in 1972, Marshall launched the TV Magic Show, a 12-trick box of magic that sold for $9.95. *Marshall Brodien Collection*

Marshall in a business suit, immediately establishing himself as a professional as he went into his rapid-fire demonstration of the tricks.

TV Magic's television direct-response sales campaigns were highly profitable because Eicoff's carefully researched marketing strategies assured the biggest bang for the advertising buck. "Al taught us exactly how much you needed to spend per product per market area for advertising," Marshall says. "For example, when we put 20,000 TV Magic Show sets in stores in the Omaha, Nebraska area that would sell for $10 apiece, we knew we had to spend $20,000 on TV advertising, a dollar a set." At the time, a $10-set cost Brodien and Carey $2.25 to put together, and Eicoff and Gutterman got 5% to 6% of that to place them in the retail outlets. Therefore, if they spent $1 to advertise it and the store received $3 each for moving them, it meant they were realizing $3 profit on each and every $10 box of tricks sold.

"We were making money like crazy and having to pay all sorts of sales taxes, business taxes, and additional personal income taxes. That was when Al sent us to see his accountant, Burt Babetch, who showed us how to make a budget and advised us to get incorporated." TV Magic, Ltd. was chartered on March 31, 1972.

Friends in the Biz

Marshall had moved to Rolling Meadows, a bustling suburban community northwest of Chicago, during the winter of 1969, about the time the sales of TV Magic Cards started to snowball. He and his wife Judy had filed for a separation and he was living in an apartment on Algonquin Road. Even though the headquarters of TV Magic, Ltd. remained on Grand Avenue in Fox Lake, and it was an hour commute from the apartment to the office, Marshall liked being back in Rolling Meadows every night. That's because his place was only two blocks from the Lancer Restaurant, an upscale steakhouse on Algonquin Road in nearby Schaumburg.

Marshall discovered the restaurant two or three months before his move. A friend at WGN-TV mentioned to him that Bill Anastos — the owner of the Cairo Supper Club where Marshall had headlined as a hypnotist until the place closed after the 1964 bombing — was working as a bartender at the Lancer. Late one afternoon when Marshall happened to be in the area, he stopped in to see if Bill was there.

Bill was behind the bar and was both surprised and glad to see Marshall. They spent the rest of the evening reminiscing and laughing about the crazy things that happened when Marshall did his hypnotic show at the Cairo. Bill had completely forgotten about the dancer who volunteered to be hypnotized and as soon as she got onstage shocked the audience by tearing off her dress and revealing she wasn't wearing anything else. Marshall had to be reminded of Armelia Greca, the belly dancer that Bill had booked. She was a crazy lady who claimed she suffered headaches and couldn't remember her belly dances because Brodien's act "disturbed her and caused her mind to wander," so Marshall had to put her in a hypnotic trance before she could do her act. The stories had everyone in the lounge in stitches. Every time someone came in and sat at the bar, Bill insisted that Marshall retell "the one about the hypnotized guy who went into the men's room and when he heard the band playing 'Night Train' he peed all over himself." The laughs went on past midnight.

A couple of weeks later, when Marshall was back at Lancer's (as the regulars called it) to have dinner, Bill introduced him to the owners, Nick Tselos and Perry Kapos. Also that evening, Marshall met Dominick Volpe, a gentleman in his mid 60s who was introduced as "a good fellow who comes in here all the time." As soon as Dominick was told that Marshall was a magician, he told Perry, "I thought I recognized dis guy. I knew him when he was a kid workin' at the Magic Lounge in Cicero. He's damn good."

Dominick was retired, but had once owned Premium Beer, a company that was the exclusive distributor of Foxhead 400, a beer brewed in Waukesha, Wisconsin. In the 1950s and '60s, the brand enjoyed a prominence in select restaurants, taverns, and retail liquor stores throughout Chicagoland.

• • •

By spring of 1972, unless Brodien was out of town doing a trade show in Dallas or Boston or Las Vegas, the chances were extremely high you'd find him evenings at Lancer's. "I went there practically every night for dinner," Marshall says. "A lot of the time I would meet clients at the restaurant instead of at the office in Fox Lake."

One night on his way home from the airport, after returning from a week-long trip to Washington, D.C., Marshall stopped by Lancer's for a drink. Dominick was there. As they sat at the bar talking, Marshall noticed something unusual. "Perry and Nick had been working several months on some additions to the place—two new meeting and banquet rooms downstairs and a huge ballroom upstairs—but as I sat there looking around, it was apparent the work had stopped."

When Marshall asked Dominick if he knew why, he learned that Perry and Nick had reached the limit their bank would lend them for the expansion. Even though the restaurant was doing good business, they didn't have the $10,000 needed to keep the construction going.

Marshall wanted to help. He called Perry the next day and offered to do so. Rather than suggest he go to the bank and co-sign on the construction loan, Marshall said he'd personally loan them the money. "I wrote out a check for ten grand because I knew they would be receiving the next draw in 30 days. They were happy, the work was completed on schedule, and they paid me back in three months. Perry wanted to include the interest, but since they had been paying for my dinners all during the construction, I told him to forget it."

∙ ∙ ∙

When Marshall's divorce became final in June 1972, he decided it was time to abandon apartment living in Rolling Meadows and buy a house. He'd met Sue Olson, an attractive real estate agent in the neighborhood, and he called her asking for some assistance finding a new home. Sue started taking Marshall out on house hunts every morning; in turn, he starting asking her out on dates almost every evening. Because business came before pleasure with the ever-professional Ms. Olson, finding Mr. Brodien a new home was her priority ... at least for the moment.

"It took her two weeks, but Sue finally found a house about eight miles from Schaumburg that I really liked. It was in Medinah and close to the Medinah Country Club and its beautiful championship golf courses. The house was brand-new, had never been lived in, and because it was the first spec house this developer had built, I got it for a great price."

Marshall and Sue became friends during the Medinah real estate transaction and, only months later, they were negotiating to purchase another property—this time as partners. It wasn't a residential property; instead, a piece of commercial property for investment purposes. Together, they bought two parcels of land within the Centex Office Park development in Schaumburg. And a week after closing, they'd started the construction of two buildings that would have a total of 10,000 square feet of leasable warehouse space.

The completion date for the warehouse project fit perfectly with expansion plans for TV Magic, Ltd. The company was in the midst of another manufacturing-run of its top-selling TV Magic Show set. "We had added some color to the graphics on the box," Marshall says. "It contained the same 12 tricks, but now Peacock Packaging in Itasca, Illinois was assembling the sets for us." Peacock was only two weeks away from delivering the order of a 100,000 units, as well as 50,000 units of the new TV Magic Tricks kit, which was a $5.95 15-trick set that included a 33–1/3 RPM record with instructions. "Because we couldn't even start to store this new inventory at our warehouse in Fox Lake, Rick called and suggested that we rent some space in one of the new buildings that Sue and I had built."

Schaumburg Mattress Makers had pre-leased one of the warehouses, so the other was immediately leased to TV Mystery Products, the new company that Marshall and Rick formed to handle the receiving and shipping of TV Magic, Ltd. merchandise, including the mail-order business generated from advertising material that was distributed with TV Magic products. The partners shut down the office in Fox Lake and moved into the new office/warehouses at 529 Lunt Street in Schaumburg.

The business relocation necessitated Marshall taking some time off from the *Bozo's Circus* show. Magician friend Johnny Thompson, who'd worked trade show dates for Marshall whenever his busy schedule prohibited him from doing them, came to the rescue again. Johnny created a clown character called Clodhopper, and although Clodhopper performed no magic, he filled in for Wizzo the Wizard for almost four months.

Spring 1973 marked the beginning of Marshall and Rick's second year with A. Eicoff & Company. They had sold enough TV Magic Ltd. and related catalog products to declare a net profit of $700,000. In the process of moving that much magic merchandise via key-outlet marketing, over $1.2 million was spent on television advertising time. When it was time to write a check to Eicoff for that amount, both Rick and Marshall wanted to be the one to sign it. "We sort of fought over whose signature would be on that check," Marshall laughs, "It meant that only one of us would be able to say he'd signed a check for over $1 million." Brodien was never able to brag about being the big spender — Carey won the coin toss.

• • •

As Marshall was leaving Lancer's late one night, his friend Dominick stopped him and said, "Bodean [that's how he pronounced Brodien], we're having a party for a few of the fellas over at Mr. C's [Jackie Cerone's] house this Saturday. I think it would be good if you was there. Maybe do a few tricks for Jackie's friends. They'll love it. If you'll meet me here at da restaurant on Saturday afternoon around four, I'll drive you over."

It was a 22-mile ride from the parking lot of Lancer's to the front driveway of Jackie Cerone's home in Elmwood Park. As they approached the block where the house was located, Dominick said, "Bodean, don't you ever bring your car here. I'll always drive you. Mr. C's place is watched by the friggin' FBI, 24 hours a day, and you don't want your car to ever be seen here."

Cerone had just gotten out of the federal pen and, at the time, was second in command to Chicago mob leader, Joey "The Doves" Aiuppa. Prior to that, from 1966 through '69, Jackie "The Lackey" Cerone had served as the boss of the Chicago Outfit; however, in 1970 he was convicted on racketeering charges when Sue Bombacino turned state's evidence and ratted on numerous mob figures.

Dominick parked his car in front of Cerone's two-story brick house. As they walked through a gateway beside the house, Dominick pointed toward a brick bungalow. "Jackie's out here," he said. "It's where he likes to cook for his friends. I hope you're hungry."

They didn't knock, just walked right in the door, which was slightly ajar. The air was thick with the aroma of sweet garlic and simmering sauces.

Dominick introduced Marshall to everybody by first names: "This is Jackie, of course ... over there is Willie ... that's Geno ... Frankie ... Anthony ... and Nicky over by the bar. Everybody, this is Marshall Bodean, da magician I've been tellin' you about."

Jackie reached out to shake Marshall's hand. "Pleased to meet you, Mr. Brodien," he said. "Nicky, fix our guest whatever he wants to drink."

"I was a little nervous at first," Marshall recalls. "After all, these guys were well-known members of the Outfit. But as soon as I did a couple of tricks and they were all laughing and having a good time, I was at ease. They kept asking to see 'one more trick.'"

After dinner, Jackie told Brodien that his barber, Carmen D'Amico, was quite adept with a deck of cards. "Carmen is the kinda guy you'd never want to play cards with, if you know what I mean ... and I think you do. But what bothers me is that Carmen's always trying out his new card tricks while he's cutting my hair. Mr. Brodien, I'm sure you've heard of Carmen?"

"Yes, I've met him," Marshall said. "He and his friend, Ed Marlo, a magician all the magicians call 'The Cardician,' used to come in the Magic Lounge regularly. They'd sit at a table in the corner and exchange card tricks for hours."

That prompted Jackie to pull open the drawer of a side table and take out a pack of playing cards. Tossing the box toward Marshall he said, "See what you can do with these cards. Somebody brought 'em back from Vegas." It was a brand-new deck from the Stardust and the seal hadn't been broken. But that didn't matter to Marshall. He removed the cards, shuffled them up, and was astonishing everyone with card tricks, just as if the Stardust deck was a gimmicked deck of TV Magic Cards. As Marshall started a fourth card trick, Jackie raised his hand signaling a stop, and he asked, "Mr. Brodien, how's about a little Louie the 13th?"

"I don't know anything about Louie the 13th," Marshall said. "But I'll give it a try."

Nicky poured generous jiggers of the vintage cognac for both men. Marshall cautiously sipped his; Jackie belted his. "Not a bad nightcap," he said.

"Yeah," Marshall said, taking another sip, "I think I like it."

"Hey, Nicky, make sure Mr. Brodien gets a bottle of Louie the 13th when he leaves."

Fifteen minutes later, after Jackie knocked down his third shot of cognac, the party was over. He suddenly got quiet and sat staring into space. The guys started saying, "Good night" and started filing out the door. Dominick leaned over to Marshall, and said, "I think it's time we leave, too."

As they drove past the Elmwood Park town-limits sign, Dominick looked over to Marshall and said, "Hey, Bodean, Jackie likes you. That Louie da 13th is $800 a friggin' bottle. In a bar, it costs $150 a shot." He drove another mile and said, "You know somethin' else... The bottle is made outta real crystal... Yeah, Bodean, Mr. C. likes you."

Marshall laughed, looked down at the metallic gold label of the Louis the 13th bottle sitting in his lap, and said, "Maybe I should have had him sign the bottle."

"Hey, Bodean, Jackie don't sign nothing.'"

As they got a little closer to Schaumburg, Marshall asked, "Dominick, how is it you were able to walk inside Jackie's house? You didn't have to knock. We just walked right in."

"I never knock. What's wrong with dat?"

"Well, anybody could have come in." Marshall said, "What's to stop somebody that's crazy from walking in, right in the middle of Jackie's party?"

"Bodean, nobody's dat crazy."

25

The Best Partner Is No Partner

After signing that $1.2 million check to the Eicoff agency for a year's worth of television time, Rick Carey developed an aversion to advertising. By late summer of 1974, he was grumbling and complaining that TV Magic, Ltd. was spending too much money on advertising. He told Marshall, "You're already so well known as a magician on television that we could save a lot of money by running fewer commercials."

Advertising wasn't the only thing Marshall and Rick disagreed about. They were having arguments over the directions they wanted to take the company. "Since we still wanted to remain friends," Marshall says, "I suggested that one or the other of us should buy out the business. I told him that I was interested in purchasing TV Magic, Ltd., but if he didn't want to sell, then he should make an offer to buy it."

In November 1974, Carey agreed to pay more than a half-million dollars for Brodien's interest. Marshall signed a non-compete agreement and the buyout was contingent on the condition that Marshall remain on the payroll as a consultant to TV Magic, Ltd.

Brodien and Sue Olson had just completed the construction of a new 15,000-square-foot building on an adjacent lot, so Marshall set up his own private office in a 2,500-square-foot space in that building. He would continue to create and develop new products that bore his name and image, as well as remain on retainer for the production of any new TV commercials.

Once at the helm, Carey started releasing some of the TV Magic products that had been on the drawing board. The first was the TV Money Magic Set, a 15-trick set where all the effects involved coins and currency. This $9.95 box of tricks even included the classic Money Maker Machine, a plastic roller press that magically transformed blank pieces of paper into real dollar bills.

The company that was fabricating and assembling the sets somehow convinced Rick this set was destined to be TV Magic's all-time bestseller. He placed an order for 1 million of the TV Money Magic Sets. Marshall warned him not to do it unless he was planning to spend significant money on advertising, suggesting that they put together a commercial as soon as possible.

Eicoff's creative staff produced a razzle-dazzle one-minute spot, and Marshall was the magical pitchman who enlightened viewers, "The remarkable TV Money Magic Set — money not included — can be found in participating stores for only $9.95." The week Rick took delivery of the new sets, Manny Gutterman unleashed a massive distribution campaign, placing them in hundreds of stores in just about every state in the union. But when it was time to give Al the go-ahead to purchase the airtime to announce the new product, Rick balked. He refused to follow Eicoff's game plan. Rick actually believed the set would sell without commercials hyping it "As seen of TV."

After the Christmas season of 1976 was over, Rick's unadvertised TV Money Magic Sets sat gathering dust on drug store shelves across the nation. The Eicoff/Gutterman success formula for key outlet marketing had been violated. Without television advertising, no demand was created for the new product. Since key outlet marketing is based on guaranteed sales, Rick was forced to take back all the unsold TV Money Magic sets — over 600,000 of them. He had overextended himself. Any profits were tied up in inventory. And you can't pay bills with inventory, even if you have a warehouse full of Money Magic Sets.

To alleviate Rick's cash flow problems, Marshall offered to buy back TV Magic's mail-order business, calling his new company the TV Magic Catalog Company. Orders generated from advertising inserted with TV Magic merchandise had always provided lucrative ancillary income for the partners. Flyers described 10 or 12 more tricks that could be ordered. But the operation had turned to total disorder because Rick couldn't afford to keep the ordered items in stock.

When the ever-ambitious Brodien took over the TV Magic Catalog Company, he made sure the back orders were filled, he reprinted the flyers offering fascinating new tricks, and he created and distributed a fully illustrated catalog that listed hundreds more items that could be ordered. In three months, the size of the mail-order business tripled.

• • •

In the early 1970s, Al Eicoff helped make a few fortunes for Columbia House, a division of CBS Broadcasting, when the company decided to market hi-fi recordings through direct-response advertising. The Eicoff agency created the now legendary commercial for an LP recording called *Best of the Big Bands*. Famous bandleader Harry James came on camera with a handful of old 78-RPM records, saying, "These priceless records are collector's items." Then he dropped them on the floor. "Well, don't worry. Now you can get them all on high-fidelity 33-1/3 RPM records." A nostalgia craze was sweeping America, and Eicoff's recognized people's inherent longing for the good old days and the music of the era. Sales were, as Al himself said, "record-breaking," and they soared higher for the Columbia House hits that followed: *The Fabulous '50s, Glenn Miller Favorites, Italian Love Songs, Top of the Hit Parade*, and *The Incomparable Brook Benton* (which sold to the tune of 400,000 units at $6.95 in five months).

Collaborating again with Columbia House, Eicoff came up with *Music Masterpieces*, an album of symphony and opera classics that became the second biggest-selling record offer in television history. (Number one was the Elvis Presley album offered immediately after he died.) Over 1.8-million copies of *Music Masterpieces* were ordered from the well-placed TV commercials.

When Eicoff helped Columbia House promote their Record Club on television, "support advertising" was born. The commercials created an awareness of Columbia House's print and direct mail advertising campaigns, where new members could pick and choose from the hundreds of records offered for sale. Memberships in the Record Club increased by the thousands, turning the art of selling subscriptions on television into a statistical science.

In the spring of 1978, CBS worked with Eicoff and Rick Carey to set into motion a similar support-advertising venture for TV Magic, soliciting subscriptions to the Columbia House of Magic's Magician's Secret File. The Columbia House magic club was envisioned as being like a record club, except, instead of a record a month, sets of 24 instruction cards plus a trick a month were to be mailed out monthly for a year. Participants in the plan would be entitled to examine all 38 sets of 24 cards of the Magician's Secret File on a ten-day, free trial basis. Only the sets kept would cost $1.89 each (plus shipping and handling).

Continuing in his capacity as a consultant to Rick, Marshall worked with writer Clarence Sutton to create the 936 illustrated instructions that comprised the Magician's Secret File. The tricks were easy enough for youngsters to learn and the categories were all encompassing. Marshall posed for dozens of colorful photos to illustrate each of the Secret File categories. Rick's job was to provide the dozen or so tricks-of-the-month that were to be sent as bonuses with the instruction-card sets.

CBS shot a two-minute commercial at a studio in New York City. Despite the insistence by both Marshall and Al that the commercial begin with the appearance of a professional magician, the director bucked the duo's

A promotional photograph of the contents of the Columbia House of Magic's "Magician's Secret File" that turned out to be an unsuccessful venture in support-advertising marketing. *Marshall Brodien Collection*

tried-and-true convention and opened with an 11-year-old performing tricks in a living room setting. A half-dollar changed to a penny when covered with a playing card; when the penny was covered with a glass, instead of the penny changing back to the half-dollar, the glass disappeared. After the applause from friends and family, an announcer's voice dropped in, saying: "You know, mystifying magic tricks like the one's you've just seen are really easy, *once you know the secret.*" Marshall's tease line was there, but there was no follow through by a seasoned pro. The studio announcer continued, "Magic is lots of fun, helps a youngster develop poise and confidence, and makes him the center of attention." On screen, the birthday party crowd watched the boy magician levitate his younger sister. "Now, at last, the secrets of hundreds of mystifying tricks are revealed. Here on these handy cards from the Magician's Secret Files from the Columbia House of Magic."

Those who sent in a dollar and signed up for the first set of 24 cards of the Magician's Secret File received — "with no obligation to buy anything now or ever" — the following gifts: 1) The *Six Secrets of Being a Good Magician* LP record. 2) A 12-inch Magic Wand that could be used for a number of spectacular effects such as the Rising Wand, the Rubbery Wand, and the Climbing Wand. 3) A 4- by 7-inch File Tray, "a $5 value sturdy tray to store your magic cards in." 4) 24 Colorful Category Cards, "to help organize your Magician's Secret File." 5) And a Lifetime Membership in the Magician's Secret Society. If after ten days the kids or parents wanted their money back, all they had to do was send back the cards. The five gifts could be kept.

The Columbia House of Magic commercial aired in test markets in the Midwest for only three weeks, then it was discretely pulled. Rick could not deliver the bonus tricks that were to be included with the card sets. CBS got nervous about their deal with TV Magic, Ltd., and when they heard the company was on the verge bankruptcy, they canceled the campaign. Less than 1,000 sets of the first 24 cards were mailed out. Columbia House refunded any installment payments that were made by the parents of the wannabe young magicians.

Old Chicago

A Southern California developer by the name of Robert R. Brindle had been telling the media, since 1973, of his plans to build what he touted as "the world's largest completely enclosed amusement park." He held an option on a piece of land in the Chicago suburb of Bolingbrook, directly off Interstate 55. Brindle announced there would be over two-dozen rides, an arcade and a haunted house, restaurants and a beer garden, and boutiques and specialty shops galore—$120-million worth of "recreational retailing." And, unlike the long-gone Riverview Park, which always closed for the winter, the 545,000 square-foot, beneath-a-dome facility would be open year round, rain or shine. The innovative theme park was called Old Chicago and was slated to open in the summer of 1975.

Marshall first heard about Old Chicago one night at Lancer's, when he bumped into his friend "Ernie the Magnificent." Ernie was a clown who performed magic shows for school assemblies and children's birthday parties, but he was also the "wizard of odds" around Schaumburg. He was the friendly bookie who'd cover a bet, big or small, on football, baseball, boxing, horseracing, or just about any event where something moved. "Ernie had just done a birthday party in one of the private rooms at the restaurant and he came into the bar to have a drink. He told me he'd been hired to work at this new indoor amusement park under construction in Bolingbrook. He said the developers were looking for retail tenants and suggested I go out and talk with the owner, because it would be a great place for a magic shop. So, a few days later, I contacted Robert Brindle and made an appointment to see the place."

From the day of its premature groundbreaking, Old Chicago was plagued with legal hassles and construction complications. Mr. Brindle stepped off on the wrong foot with officials of the Village of Bolingbrook when he began pouring foundations and putting up concrete exterior walls before filing for building permits. When Marshall arrived for his tour of the site, he was told that the financial backers were holding back construction funds until Village officials approved the zoning and issued permits. None of the architectural, mechanical, or engineering plans were approved, yet, construction crews had started ride installations and were erecting storefronts.

After talking with Brindle and his partners, it was apparent to Marshall that the Old Chicago project lacked a primary lender. He was able to set up a meeting with Brindle and Arlington First National Bank, where some financing possibilities were discussed. As a result of this gesture, Brodien was given his choice of a lease location — a prime corner at the front gate of the indoor theme park.

June 26, 1975 marked the first day of business at the Marshall Brodien Magic Shop at Old Chicago. A crowd of over 15,000 turned out for the grand opening. For publicity, a girl tap-danced non-stop atop the 72-foot-high dome structure. The half-completed parking lot couldn't accommodate all the cars, and traffic backed up on Interstate 55 for seven miles. Later that summer, as the place started drawing 30,000 to 40,000 people a weekend, much to the dismay of the highway patrol and the Village police force, Old Chicago had literally put Bolingbrook on the map.

In order to get the Marshall Brodien Magic Shop up and running, Marshall made a deal with an East Coast magic dealer by the name of Fred Wren to train the demonstrators and manage the store. For the first nine months of operations, the shop boasted of healthy per-capita-sales figures. However, as Old Chicago entered its second year, the bottom lines of Wren's sales reports became abysmal. Suspecting some hanky panky, Marshall talked with a couple of the demonstrators. Not only was it disclosed that Fred was tampering with the cash register, he was selling merchandise other than what was in the store's inventory. "He was putting together his own line of tricks in the backroom, easy-to-make tricks like the Three Card Monte and the Three Rope Trick. His helpers sold these tricks under the counter, never putting the money in the till."

After setting Mr. Wren free, Marshall picked up the phone and called his friend Jay Marshall — who with his wife Frances Ireland Marshall owned and operated Magic, Inc. (formerly Ireland's Magic Co.), the granddaddy of Chicago magic dealers — asking for some advice on how to run a retail shop. At Jay's suggestion, Marshall called Billy Bishop, a semi-retired professional magician who, along with his son Glenn, ran a little magic shop in a mall in Oak Park.

Billy Bishop & Anne (his wife) burst onto the show-business scene after World War II, playing top nightclubs coast-to-coast. They enjoyed extended engagements at Billy Rose's posh Diamond Horseshoe in New York City, played the stage of the famous Palace Theatre, were repeaters on *The Ed Sullivan Show*, and they continued to be an in-demand club date act into the 1960s and '70s.

Billy was excited about the possibility of operating the shop in Old Chicago. Yet, when Marshall asked if he was interested in buying it, he had to say no, admitting that he didn't have the cash. "I really liked Billy and wanted him to have it," Marshall says. "And aside from the fact I wanted to get out of the retail business, I felt Billy was the guy who could make a go of it."

Marshall, as he often did, made Bishop an offer that couldn't be refused. "I told Billy there was a note for about $4,000 on the place, and that was for the display counters and fixtures. If he would assume the loan and pay it off, the shop was his, lock, stock, and barrel — all the merchandise, everything." Billy couldn't believe it, but shook Marshall's hand, cinching the deal.

By this time, Robert Brindle was out of the picture, and Illinois Central Railroad had taken over the property management. Billy Bishop renegotiated his lease, paid off the note within a year, and was forever grateful to Marshall for the opportunity. A year later, Billy was offered and accepted a position as director of merchandising and entertainment for Old Chicago, but the recreational-retailing venture would only last a couple more years.

In 1980, the rides were removed and the building was converted to the world's largest indoor discount mall. By that time, Billy had moved on, relocating his inventory and fixtures to his former magic shop in Oak Park. Old Chicago would eventually be demolished in 1986 to make way for the Arena Auto Auction.

The Restaurateur

One Saturday afternoon while Marshall was at the Catalog Company office/warehouse, catching up on some paperwork, the phone rang. It was Dominick. "Bodean, am I glad you're there. Don't go no place. I'm on my way over." Since he was calling from the Lancer Restaurant, Dominick was at the front door of the office in less than ten minutes.

"It's my grandson's birthday," he said. "And since da kid loves magic, I thought maybe you got a magic set he'd like." Marshall took Dominick back into the warehouse and they picked out a couple of magic sets and some assorted tricks. "You know, da kid's only seven years old, but he's gonna love this stuff. He's already got a thee-ater in the basement where he puts on his shows. I tell you, Bodean, he's da greatest."

When Marshall showed up at Lancer's for dinner that night, Dominick was there and thanked him for the magic sets and the tricks. "Da grandkid killed 'em at the party. He did all them tricks with the class of a friggin' Houdini. And like I says, he's only seven."

"Maybe when he grows up, he'll be good enough to work Vegas," Marshall said.

"Hey, Bodean, whether da rabbit comes outta the hat or don't come outta the hat, the kid will be in Vegas! Understand?" (This was at a time when the Outfit had a stranglehold on four major hotels in Las Vegas, skimming untold millions of dollars from casino gambling operations.)

• • •

After enjoying a late dinner one evening at Lancer's, Marshall went into the lounge to see if Dominick was there. He was and he signaled for Marshall to join him at the end of the bar. Dominick said he might have to excuse himself for a moment to end an argument between the restaurant's two owners.

For the past few months, Nick Tselos and Perry Kapos had been having a few more fights than usual. Nick was going through a divorce and Perry felt that his partner's personal problems were affecting their business relationship. Some of the restaurant's habitual customers thought that Nick simply wanted Perry out. They felt Nick was trying to make it so uncomfortable for Perry that maybe he'd sell out for next to nothing. On this particular night, Nick was making a flap about enforcing a ridiculous new rule he'd just made up: Women wearing slacks would not be permitted in the dining room.

"Dominick never really cared too much for Nick," Marshall says. "So, that night when they were arguing and Nick pushed Perry across the room, it made him extremely angry."

Dominick, who was as many years old as the combined ages of Nick and Perry, grabbed Nick by the shoulders, lifted him off the floor, and slammed him against the brick wall of the lounge. Nick slumped to the floor. Dominick leaned over and asked, "You ever try to walk around with your head in your hands?" Nick was unable to speak, so Dominick said, "Lemme tell you what happens… You can't walk too far."

In addition to having marital problems, Nick was being pressured by creditors and individuals he owed money to. Threats were made that he'd be "out of the picture" if he didn't come up with the cash quickly. It was an ideal time for Perry to buy him out, but he didn't have the money.

Marshall wanted to help Perry, so he went to his banker to see if a loan could be arranged. The banker said that there was no way his bank could or would loan money to Perry. On the other hand, if Marshall was interested in borrowing money to acquire an interest in the Lancer Restaurant, they would loan him whatever money he needed to buy out Nick. Brodien walked out of his bank with a letter of commitment: they would loan him the $150,000 that it took to pay off Nick's creditors and purchase a 50 percent interest in Lancer's.

Two weeks later, a sales contract was drafted and a closing date of March 2, 1976, was set. When the day arrived and all the parties met at a bank in Arlington Heights, the president of the bank pulled Brodien aside and informed him they couldn't let him borrow that amount of money. "I was told I had already gone over my limit because of some recent investments I'd made in my other businesses," Marshall says. "I couldn't believe it, and I told my banker that the team of attorneys assembled in his conference room were there because of the letter of commitment he'd given me. He excused himself and told me to wait while he ran downstairs to another office."

27. The Restaurateur

In lieu of living up to the terms of his letter, it seems that the bank prez had located a customer in the trucking business that was willing to make the $150,000 loan happen right then and there. The owner of the trucking company (someone who would later be called a "banking connection") wired the $150,000 directly to the banker, who direct-deposited the funds into Brodien's account. Because of this "friendly transfer," it became a simple matter of issuing cashier's checks for the monies necessary to close the deal.

All Marshall was aware of was the fact that he had to sign an affidavit agreeing to pay back the $150,000, a document that was notarized and co-signed by the bank's president. And because Marshall was now the 50% owner of a restaurant appraised at $2.5 million that was doing great business, he foresaw no problem taking care of the note — at least, not for the moment.

• • •

Soon after the papers were signed and Brodien was an official owner of the Lancer Restaurant, his partner Perry hired a couple of new bartenders. Marshall had been out of town that week, working a trade show in St. Louis, and when he stopped by the restaurant he found an unfamiliar face behind the bar. The new bartender had no idea he was about to serve the owner of the establishment.

"The new guy was nice and treated me like a normal customer," Marshall says. "He told me a couple of jokes, so I did some tricks for him. After a while, he asked me, 'Sir, do you know that magician called Wizzo that's on the Bozo show?' I told him that I knew Wizzo, and I asked him if he watched the program. He said, 'Yeah, I tune it in every now and then, and I gotta tell you I think that Wizzo is sorta weird.'"

The bartender excused himself to refresh some drinks at the other end of the bar. When he returned, he said, "Yeah, like I was saying, that Wizzo is a strange dude."

"That's an interesting observation," Marshall said, as he stood up to leave. "It was nice talking with you. My name is Marshall Brodien. I'm Perry's new partner, so, I'll be seeing you around."

Two nights later, when Marshall looked into the bar, the new bartender greeted him with a "Hello, there, Mr. Brodien." The fellow appeared a little embarrassed, but walked over and said, "Pardon me for asking, Mr. Brodien, but are you Wizzo?"

Marshall grinned and said, "Yes."

"How come then, a couple of nights ago, when I said I watched *Bozo's Circus*, you didn't tell me you were Wizzo?"

"Well, you just asked me if I *knew* Wizzo," Marshall said. "And I said I did."

"Oh, yeah ... you're right, I just asked if you *knew* him," he said, as he shook his head, and went back behind the bar. "You're right, Mr. Brodien, you did say you *knew* Wizzo." No doubt, the slightly confused employee thought Mr. Brodien was weirder than his incarnation of Wizzo the Wizard.

• • •

In 1978, WGN-TV began broadcasting via satellite. Every weekday, *Bozo's Circus* was beamed into millions of households from Canada to Mexico. Wizzo, who continued with his two-and-three-times-a-week appearances on the show, now found he had fans in Alaska, Hawaii, and the Caribbean. In Chicago, at WGN-TV's Studio One, show tickets were as scarce as a clown's frown. The reservations list for *Bozo's Circus* stretched to seven years.

The unavailability of Bozo tickets was something that the guys who hung out at Lancer's didn't seem to understand. One night, Dominick approached Marshall and said that it was absolutely imperative that he get some Bozo tickets for friends of Joey Aiuppa's family. It was a Tuesday and they wanted to come to the studio for the Thursday taping. Marshall told him that it was next to impossible, but he'd see what he could do.

"Marshall, just remember," Dominick said, "if Joey does a favor for you he forgets it, but if you do a favor for him he never forgets it."

Marshall pulled all sorts of strings at WGN to get the four tickets. Then on the day before the show taping, Dominick called and said they needed one more. Marshall told Dominick there was no way, and warned him that if they showed up at the studio with five kids and only had four tickets, the ushers wouldn't let them in.

The next morning brought a phone call that let butterflies loose in Wizzo's stomach. The WGN receptionist called back to the studio where Marshall, Roy Brown, Bob Bell, and producer Al Hall were rehearsing. "Mr. Brodien, I think you better come up here," she whispered. "There's a big black limousine parked outside the front door, and the driver says that his boss needs to speak with you."

"I went out to the car a little nervous," Marshall recalls. "But when the tinted-glass window lowered I was relieved to see that there was only a party of four sitting inside. They'd just showed up early. So I directed them to a nearby McDonald's and told them to come back at eleven o'clock when the studio doors opened."

On a later occasion, when Dominick was favored with the exact number of Bozo show tickets he'd requested for a friend, he was extremely appreciative of Marshall's efforts. "Thanks, Bodean!" he said as he put the tickets in his inside coat pocket. "Getting these tickets has made me the happiest guy, 'cause they're for my very closest friend, a real friend who's like my brother. I can't tell you how friggin' happy this is gonna make my friend. I sincerely thank you from the bottom of my friggin' heart."

But the heart has reasons that reason doesn't understand. Dominick saw Marshall the next day at the restaurant and said. "Bodean, I was showing those tickets to my daughter-in-law, and she went outta her mind. She had to have them. So I gave 'em to her. She's taking her kids to the Bozo show tomorrow."

"What about your good friend?" Marshall asked.

"Hey, Bodean, screw him! Blood's thicker than water."

• • •

Early one Saturday evening, after spending the entire day on his boat with friends on Fox Lake, Marshall drove home to Medinah, not even stopping by the restaurant to check on things. He was dead tired and had already taken off his clothes and was ready to go to bed when the phone rang. It was Dominick. "Bodean, whatta you doin' tonight? Jackie is havin' a party at Dino's, starting about nine o'clock. He's got 20 people coming, and he wants you to be there and do some tricks."

Marshall tried to explain that he was so tired he could barely move and he couldn't imagine having to entertain a bunch of Jackie Cernone's friends. But Dominick wouldn't take no for an answer. "Bodean, you know how much Jackie likes your magic," he said. "Hell's bells, you're only 20 minutes away. Hey, Bodean, Jackie loves you. Dat's what we're really talkin' about here. So, get your friggin' clothes back on and come on over Dino's. It'll be loads of fun."

It was pouring down rain when Marshall pulled into the parking lot of Dino's. The Italian restaurant and bar in Melrose Park was a favorite gathering place for leaders of the Outfit and it had become Jackie Cerone's unofficial headquarters.

As Marshall walked in, he was escorted to a secluded dining room in the back of the restaurant. The first person he recognized was Jackie who was sitting at the head of a huge U-shaped banquet table. Over the din of merrymaking, he heard him shout, "Hey, Mr. Brodien, come sit over here and have something to eat. How 'bout some of this chicken Vesuvio? Or you have to try the cacciatore with escarole. Or take a look at the menu. Order anything you want. Dino will fix it."

Marshall thanked Jackie for the invitation and, as he sat down, noticed the tailored sport shirt that Jackie was wearing. "That's a beautiful shirt," Marshall said. "I like it." The deep purple silk shirt had the initials "JC" embroidered with gold thread on the cuffs. Jackie yelled down to the end of the table, "Hey, Nicky. When my tailor comes to town, three shirts for Mr. Brodien."

After dinner, Marshall performed a 30-minute stand-up show. The trick that had them all talking was the Invisible Deck. One of the guests sitting in the back of the room was handed an imaginary deck and asked to take out any card, remember what it was, then reverse it in the deck. Everybody was laughing as the guy went through the moves as if he was holding 52 playing cards. The so-called Invisible Deck was passed up toward the stage. When it got to the front row, Marshall reached out and took a real Bicycle-brand deck from the spectator's hand. He asked the person in the back of the room who'd selected the imaginary card to call out the name of the card that he saw in his mind. It was the Jack of Hearts. Sure enough, when Marshall thumbed through the deck, there was one card reversed. It was the Jack of Hearts.

By midnight just about everybody had left Dino's. Marshall was showing Jackie and Dominick some dice-stacking tricks, when Jackie stood and said, "Gentlemen, let's adjourn to the bar and have a little drink."

"As we were sitting at the bar," Marshall says, "Jackie asked if I had any funny jokes. So I asked him, 'Do you know what you get when you cross an Italian with a Polack?' He said, 'No, Mr. Brodien, tell me what you get when you cross an Italian with a Polack.' When I said, 'A hit man that misses,' I thought he was going to fall off his barstool. When Dominick repeated the punch line, 'A friggin' hit man that misses,' they laughed again, and when Jackie, who rarely used the F word said, 'A friggin' hit man that friggin' misses,' they roared."

Marshall glanced over his shoulder and into the deserted dining room. It was past one o'clock in the morning. Through the doorway, the only cars Marshall could see on the puddled-up parking lot were his, Dominick's, and another that must have been Jackie's.

"What time does this place close?" Marshall asked.

Jackie said, "When we leave is when it closes." He turned to the bartender and said, "Play my favorite song three times, then we're leaving. Okay?" The bartender nodded and went over to the jukebox to punch the B2 button three times. Frank Sinatra started crooning "Strangers in the Night," as Jackie gave the command to crack the seal on a bottle of Louis the 13th.

It was almost two A.M. when they walked toward their cars. Jackie was in a good mood, asking Marshall, "How the hell did you know that chump was going to pick the Jack of Hearts? You gotta teach me that one, Mr. Brodien."

"I can't do that, but I can show you a pretty amazing trick that I'm going to do on television next week." Marshall opened the door on the driver's side of his car and pushed a button, causing the trunk lid to yawn open. He brought out a two-foot-square piece of glass that was surrounded with a decorative frame. "Gentlemen, this is the world famous Dove Through Glass illusion."

The Dove Through Glass is an apparatus trick where the magician causes a live dove to penetrate the center of a sheet of Plexiglas. And even though Marshall didn't have a bird, he proceeded to give a convincing demonstration using his fist. He asked Jackie and Dominick to tap on the glass to make sure it was solid. Then he said, "Imagine that I am holding a fluttering white dove in my hand. Watch closely as I push that live bird right through the center of this piece of glass." Suddenly, Marshall's arm was sticking through the solid glass as if there were an invisible hole in its center.

Jackie couldn't believe what he saw, and asked, "Are you tellin' me you can do that with a real dove? Huh? Wait till Joey sees this one! You know how he goes for doves! Dominick, be sure we get Mr. Brodien over to Joey's house to do that trick."

Dominick nodded and said, "Yeah, Joey'll go outta his friggin' mind when he sees that trick done with a live dove!"

Jackie was referring to Joey "The Doves" Aiuppa (a.k.a. "Joey O'Brien"), the mob leader whose only run-in with the law had been for shooting doves. There was a city park near his home in Oak Park, and when he started whacking a covey of ring-neck doves with his snub-nose .38 one Sunday afternoon, a park ranger wrote him a citation for disturbing the peace. Of course, Marshall remembered Joey as the man who put an end to his run at the Magic Lounge in Cicero, when the mob decided to turn the place into a strip joint.

As Marshall drove out of the parking lot at Dino's he thought to himself, "I sure hope Joey doesn't show up with a gun when I show him the trick."

Visit from the FBI

Brodien's secretary was on the intercom telling him there was a gentleman on the phone who said he was with the FBI. His name was Smith and he needed to make an appointment. Marshall told her to set up a meeting the next day, because he was leaving that weekend to do a show in the Virgin Islands. His old WGN-TV buddy Don Sandburg was producing a circus extravaganza in St. Croix, and he'd booked Marshall to perform.

"This Mr. Smith who showed up at my office was just like the Colombo character on TV," Marshall says, "complete with the trench coat. He showed me his business card and FBI badge and said he wouldn't be taking too much of my time."

Smith removed his rumpled raincoat, opened an attaché case, and took out a handful of file folders, which he spread on the desk. "Mr. Brodien, I'm sure you recall signing a note about a year ago ... at the offices of the bank in Arlington Heights ... I believe it was with a trucking company of sorts? For the amount of $150,000?"

"Yes, that was the amount, but I don't know anything about a trucking company," Marshall said. "It was the bank that gave me the money."

"You say, they *gave* you the $150,000?

"Well, they loaned me the money..."

"Mr. Brodien, if you don't remember anything about a trucking company, could there have been a silent partner involved?"

"No," Marshall said. "It was just a loan for $150,000."

"Not to change the subject, Mr. Brodien, but these documents show there was no collateral put up for this loan."

"That's correct. There was no collateral."

"I'm puzzled," Smith said. "This bank loans you $150,000 and there's no collateral... You say you know nothing about a trucking company being involved... And you also tell me there's no partner... Like I say, I'm puzzled. Do you ever get puzzled, Mr. Brodien?"

"Well, in my business," Marshall said, "I puzzle people all the time."

"Yes, sure. Mr. Brodien, we already know you're a magician. And we know about your magic business. And we know almost everything about your restaurant business, too." Smith paused as he picked up another file folder and took out a document. "We just don't understand this loan."

"What do you not understand?" Marshall asked.

"Did you pay back this $150,000 loan?"

"Yes. I delivered a check to the bank when the note was due."

Smith shuffled through more papers and said, "There's a letter here that shows that a vice president at the bank in Arlington Heights signed on the note with you... This must be your partner, right?"

"No, he's not a partner. He is a friend."

Smith stood up and took a few steps around the office, looking at the framed magic posters on the walls. Then, in true Colombo form, he swiveled around and said, "I'm more puzzled, Mr. Brodien. This gentleman's an officer of the bank and he signs on the note for $150,000, and you say he's not a partner ... just a friend."

"That's right."

Smith sat back down. "Well, we do know that you paid back the money." He gathered up the file folders and slid them back into his attaché case. "However, if you happen to have that canceled check, I'd like to see it."

At this point in the interrogation, Marshall was getting nervous and concerned. It was beginning to sound like the loan hadn't been reported to the bank officers. Yet Marshall told the FBI agent he'd be glad to get him a copy of the check.

"That will be fine," Smith said, putting on his raincoat. "Now, I must tell you that I'm going over to talk with your friend at the bank."

"Not to change the subject," Marshall said, "but do you have children?"

"Yes. I have a girl and two boys."

"Would you like to take them three of these magic sets?"

"No," Mr. Smith said. "No, but thank you. I can't take something like that from you. No gifts of any kind. Not when I'm meeting with you over business matters."

"I understand," Marshall said, stacking the magic sets behind his desk.

"But, you know something? My kids watch you all the time on the Bozo show. They like it when you do the magic as Wizzo. If you have a photo, an autographed photo of Wizzo, I could take that."

Marshall asked his secretary to bring in some 8 by 10s and he started signing them, asking for the childrens' names.

"Now, an autographed picture isn't a gift is it?" Smith asked, sticking the photos inside his brief case.

"No, I give them away all the time for publicity purposes," Marshall said.

"Next time ... *if* there is a next time and I have to come back to see you, I'll buy those magic sets. My kids would like that." He started toward the door, but turned and said, "I know as soon as I walk out that door you're going to grab the phone and call your friend and say the FBI is on the way to talk to you ... and you know something?"

Before Marshall could answer, Smith continued, "Legally, you can call the bank and warn him I'm coming and there's nothing I can do about it. But, Mr. Brodien, I'd appreciate it if you didn't pick up that phone." As soon as the agent left the building, Marshall called his attorney, who listened to the story and told him to just get the copy of the check to the FBI and don't worry about it.

"Actually, back when that loan was due," Marshall remembers, "I didn't have the cash. But luckily, it was at the time my realtor friend and investment partner, Sue Olson, wanted to become a part owner of Lancer's. So she offered to pay off the $150,000 if I gave her a 25% interest in the restaurant. That was all right with me. Now I owned 25% of the $2.5-million restaurant for absolutely no money at all."

Shortly after the visit from the FBI, the vice prez at the bank was indicted for a string of "creative banking" endeavors. Marshall never heard anything more from the FBI. And Mr. Smith never returned to purchase those three magic sets.

• • •

Marshall's June 27, 1978, appearance on Don Sandburg's *Circus Stage Show* in St. Croix was a huge success. Don had relocated to the Virgin Islands when he signed a contract to produce shows and events for the Island Center Theater for the Performing Arts. For two years, Don booked big-name talent, then changed to a circus-theme show, which gave him the opportunity to hire many of the acts he'd worked with while producing *Bozo's Circus*.

Marshall enjoyed doing the show because he got to work as Marshall Brodien, rather than Wizzo. And he was such a hit he was invited back for two more appearances, in February and September of 1979. Flying off to the Caribbean became a great getaway from Chicago, but getting his magic props to the islands posed a problem more than once.

The first time he flew to the Virgin Islands, because there was barely enough room for the passengers on the small aircraft that flew between San Juan and St. Croix, Brodien's Substitution Trunk illusion had to wait until the next flight. By the time it was delivered backstage the show was practically over. The trick was performed as an encore.

"Marshall's sword-box illusion never made it back on the plane after his second appearance," Don recalls. "So, we ended up keeping it on the island until I booked him back for a third time." But after that show, an airline fiasco almost sealed the fate of the Temple of Angee, the treasured illusion created by Marshall's idol, Jack Gwynne. It disappeared somewhere in the friendly skies between St. Croix and Chicago.

After repeated calls to airline's baggage handlers, Brodien had to resort to the power of the press. He asked WGN-TV director Al Hall to call the airline's PR department, and tell them how valuable the prop was that they'd lost. Al spoke with the director of public relations and told her that the illusion was part of a show that would be featuring Chicago Mayor Michael Bilandic. "I think you will agree that it's ultra important that we find this prop," Al told her. "So, we wondered if it would help if we sent a couple of reporters and a camera crew from WGN News to assist in the search for it..."

"The next morning," Marshall says, "the airline called and said they'd found the Temple. It was delivered to my house by noon."

29

DBA Marshall Brodien Magic Co.

A week before Rick Carey filed bankruptcy for TV Magic, Ltd., Brodien got a call from Al Eicoff: "Marsh, you never should have sold the business to Rick. You were the only one who knew what magic would sell. You knew how to run the company. Why don't you buy it back?"

When Marshall said he was totally opposed to doing anything like that, Al said, "Why don't *we* buy it back? You, me, and the Guttermans could make it work. Together, we'll buy the assets of the company. You do the commercials and create the products with your name on them, and we'll buy the TV airtime and handle the advertising and distribution."

"I didn't want to do it, but they talked me into it," Marshall says. "And thank God they did." When the bankruptcy court put the business on the auction block, a price was agreed upon for the new partnership of Brodien, Eicoff, and the Guttermans (Manny and sons, Art and Steve) to buy everything. Eicoff immediately arranged for the same auctioneer to hold another auction. The trucks and company vehicles, lifts and machinery, office furniture and equipment, as well as the entire line of TV Magic products, were sold. The new owners realized enough money from the assets auction to pay for the company they'd bought in the first auction. "We basically got the business back for nothing," Marshall says.

On December 21, 1979, the Marshall Brodien Magic Company was chartered and offices were set up at 520 North Michigan Avenue, in the same building occupied by A. Eicoff & Company. The first product released was the old reliable, millions-selling TV Magic Cards — now packaged as "Marshall Brodien TV Magic Cards." New commercials were produced, again using that familiar intro, "Hello, I'm professional magician Marshall Brodien. Most magic tricks are easy, once you know the secret..." The next product released was the Marshall Brodien 25 Trick Magic Set. Then came the Marshall Brodien 12 Trick Magic Set, the Marshall Brodien Card Box and Deck, and the Marshall Brodien Magic Show with Magician's Table. The Brodien name on the box, coupled with the AS SEEN ON TV graphic on the packaging made the difference. The re-born company realized a profit of $300,000 in its first year.

• • •

Brodien made a trip to the West Coast in 1981 to visit his friend Norm Nielsen. Norm's sophisticated manipulative act had become a perennial favorite at the Crazy Horse Saloon in Paris, yet his contract allowed him to take part of each year off for engagements in Reno and Las Vegas. Nielsen had received an invitation to attend the grand opening of Siegfried & Roy's new show *Beyond Belief* at the Frontier Hotel in Las Vegas, and a quick call was all it took to be assured that Marshall was also invited. Marshall looked forward to meeting the German illusionists, and hoped he might have the opportunity to plant the seed for the possible design of a Siegfried & Roy magic set sometime in the future.

In 1961, magician Siegfried Fischbacher was employed as a steward aboard the Bremen, a German ocean liner sailing between Bremerhaven and New York. When the ship's captain learned of Siegfried's talents he had him performing for the passengers. Siegfried needed an assistant and he asked another steward, Roy Horn, to help, soon learning that Roy possessed a cheetah he'd smuggled on board. Siegfried had the ship's carpenter build a special illusion, they worked the cat into their show, and thus was born the act of Siegfried & Roy. In 1965, while touring Europe, they got a big break performing at a gala in the presence of Princess Grace of Monaco, which led to an offer to work in Las Vegas in 1967.

The team was booked as a ten-minute novelty act in the *Folies Bergere* show at the Tropicana. Casino boss K.J. Houssels took them aside and warned, "Boys, I gotta tell you, magic don't work in this town." It would take Siegfried & Roy a few years to prove Houssels wrong. After three months at the Tropicana, they went back to Europe and wouldn't return to Vegas until 1970. They brought more exotic animals and were given a 12-minute spot in the *Lido de Paris* show at the Stardust; this time the three-month booking turned into a three-year run. This success led to their triumphant five-year engagement as the closing act of *Hallelujah Hollywood!* at the MGM Grand.

By 1977, Siegfried & Roy had returned to the *Lido* show at the Stardust and were performing an unprecedented 35-minute headliner spot in the show, with the million-dollar marquee sign of the Stardust proclaiming them the

"Superstars of Magic." Ringling Bros. and Barnum & Bailey circus impresario and producer Irvin Feld and his son, Kenneth, were so impressed with their spectacular spot that they agreed to produce two Siegfried & Roy primetime television specials. When *Siegfried & Roy with the Lido de Paris* (February 1, 1980) and *Siegfried & Roy Superstars of Magic* (November 11, 1980) aired on NBC, the dynamic duo's name and fame spread far beyond the Las Vegas Strip. The Felds became the illusionists' producer when *Beyond Belief* debuted in '81 at the Frontier. The new 100-minute spectacle became the first ongoing magic show in Las Vegas history.

At the *Beyond Belief* premiere party, Marshall was introduced to the Felds. Even though Irvin knew of Brodien's TV Magic Cards and his success producing the TV Magic line, he was surprised to hear that Marshall had put together a magic set for another television personality. When TV sitcom actor Bill Bixby (*My Favorite Martian and The Courtship of Eddie's Father*) starred in the 1973 NBC adventure series *The Magician*, its producers, Paramount Television, authorized Brodien to bring to market the 25-trick Bill Bixby's *The Magician* Magic Set. Feld was interested in the story of how easy it was to get Bixby's merchandise on the shelves of retail chains, but what piqued Feld's interest even more was Marshall's offer to do the same for Siegfried & Roy. Irvin and Kenny insisted that Marshall fly to New York in the next month or so to "seriously discuss the possibility of doing a magic set for the boys."

"When I met with the Felds," Marshall says, "the first thing Irvin wanted to know about was my background in the magic business. I explained how I started at 14 as a demonstrator in a Chicago Loop magic shop. But as soon as I mentioned I had worked in the sideshow at Riverview Park he told me to stop." It wasn't because Feld had heard enough; it was because he wanted to know exactly what Marshall had done with the sideshow. Irvin was fascinated with anything that was connected with circus or carnival, and the sideshow certainly was. "I told him that I was the talker and I started doing the freak show spiel. He loved it. He told me, 'You're my kind of a guy, a real pitchman, the kind of a guy I like to work with.' He practically said, 'You've got the deal.' I left New York that day with Irvin's orders to put together a prototype magic set to take out to Vegas and show Siegfried & Roy."

There were no big magic sets on the market at the time, and because Marshall felt the Las Vegas Superstars of Magic were larger than life, he assembled a 60-trick set in a photographically illustrated, jumbo-sized box and called it "The Siegfried & Roy Spectacular Magic Set." A commercial was produced that chroma–keyed his image onto the stage where Siegfried & Roy were performing. "Hi, I'm Marshall Brodien, here at the fabulous Frontier Hotel in Las Vegas, the home of the Superstars of Magic, Siegfried & Roy..."

29. DBA Marshall Brodien Magic Co.

Then prefacing his pitch with the ever familiar, "Most magic tricks are easy, once you know the secret," Marshall went through a show-'n'-sell of the many magical items in the $24.95 set. The commercials were originally aired in Chicago and on the West Coast, with 50,000 units placed in Walgreens, Thrifty Drugs, and Toys 'R' Us stores. In addition, a 12-trick Siegfried & Roy Pocket Magic Kit was produced. Two hundred fifty thousand units of this $9.95 set were placed in retail outlets everywhere. Another 250,000 Siegfried & Roy Magic Card Box & Deck sets were produced and distributed in Toys 'R' Us stores everywhere.

Circus Daze Over

By the early 1980s, WGN-TV had changed the name of the *Bozo's Circus* show to the *Bozo Show*. The program was expanded to 90 minutes and was videotaped and broadcast weekdays at seven A.M. The 13-piece Big Top Band was long gone and replaced with a trio, and the policy of booking paid circus and variety acts was dropped. Guest magicians and novelty acts were given a videotape of their performance as compensation. An in-the-round stage replaced the circus-ring set and scenery, and Frazier Thomas of *Garfield Goose* fame who was the circus manager, was now "master of ceremonies." The only visage of circus that remained was the clowns — Bozo, Wizzo, and Cooky — who appeared in skits produced by Al Hall. More cartoons (and commercials) were added. Roy Brown's puppet character of Cuddly Dudley, originally created for a *Chicago Tribune* subscription promotion and later turned into a talking puppet for WGN's *Ray Rayner and His Friends*, appeared regularly. Bob Bell provided live time-checks, weather, and sports reports for the pre-recorded program.

While the *Bozo Show* never claimed to be setting standards or raising the bar for excellence in children's programming — *Sesame Street* it wasn't — the critics usually panned or pooh-poohed the show for having little, if any, educational value. Burning questions of who'd get a cream pie in the face or which kid would win the bucket-toss game provided the program's principal continuity. Michael Arlen of *The New Yorker* criticized the show's "carnival cheapness and its almost primitive exploitation of children and parents."

Yet, by 1983, the *Bozo Show*, despite the early morning timeslot, had a

Opposite: The legendary Harry Blackstone Jr. joined forces with Wizzo for the *Bozo Show 30th Anniversary Special* in 1981. *Marshall Brodien Collection*

30. Circus Daze Over

Circus manager Frasier Thomas, Bozo, and Wizzo conduct the ever-popular Grand Prize game, a feature of the show since 1962. *Courtesy WGN-TV Chicago. Bozo the Clown® & ©Larry Harmon Pictures Corporation. All rights reserved.*

viewership that could not be denied. "Its local at-home audience of 300,000 just about equals that of the three major networks' morning news shows combined," reported *The Wall Street Journal* of October 31, 1983. "And at least twice that many watch it on cable-TV systems around the country." The front-page article revealed that the hottest ticket in Chicagoland wasn't the Bears, the Lyric Opera, or even *Donahue*— it was for the studio tapings of the *Bozo Show*. The waiting list was now ten years long. Many children who got to watch the show being taped were there because their parents had written for tickets before they were born. *Time* magazine told of a mother in Kankakee, Illinois, who'd written for five tickets in the 1970s when "she expected to give birth a few times and didn't want any of her not-yet-conceived children to miss out on the chance to be part of the beloved TV show." When the tickets were mailed out, eight years later, the woman and her husband had three daughters, and they spent a happy 90 minutes together at WGN-TV's Studio One watching a Bozo taping.

The Wall Street Journal story attributed the popularity and the longevity of the *Bozo Show* to the focus on audience participation — the interaction with live clowns and kids. The skits and comedy bits were a contrast to the animated cartoon content of children's programs being produced in the 1970s and '80s. Producer Al Hall always felt the show's acceptance and success was no more than it was due. "Kids tuned in to have a good time," he says. "And we gave it to them. We were fast-paced, alive, upbeat, and while a lot of the gags were old to adults they were new to the kids." When Cooky asked, 'What do you get when you cross a parrot with a gorilla?' then said, 'I don't know, but when it talks, everybody listens," the parents may have groaned, but the kids roared.

The skits were equally innocent and uncomplicated. For example, when Bozo and Cooky were having a disagreement over different colored napkins at the kitchen table, Wizzo's magical powers were called upon. Bozo insisted, "All the napkins should be blue." Cooky said, "I want 'em all yellow!" With a magical touch of the Stone of Zanzibar and a "Doody, doody, do," Wizzo produced yellow-and-blue-polka-dotted napkins.

The high spot of the *Bozo Show* remained the Grand Prize Game, a Bob Bell/Don Sandburg creation played on the show since 1962. Originally called Bozo's Buckets, a boy and a girl from the studio audience tried to throw Ping-Pong balls into six lined-up and numbered pails, each one farther away than the last. In the beginning a silver dollar was added to bucket number six every day until someone won. A Schwinn bicycle was soon added for hitting number six, and by the '70s a $50 bill was thrown in, too. In the years when the show was broadcast live at noon, the Grand Prize Game was a big favorite in bars and saloons, with customers placing bets on which numbered bucket the kid would hit that day.

31

Home Shopping

Al Eicoff was eager to tune into the profits of cable television with Marshall Brodien Magic products. Al loved the immediacy of selling via satellite broadcasts — sales were actually counted while the commercial was still on the air.

"Al wanted to come along when I flew to St. Petersburg, Florida, to do some segments on the Home Shopping Network in 1983," Marshall recalls. "He wanted to find out which timeslots — morning, afternoon, or late night — got the best sales responses."

Eicoff was definitely in his element at HSN. After all, the televised sales demonstrations, pitching product for 20 to 25 uninterrupted minutes, were a resurrection of the direct-response advertising techniques he'd pioneered 35 years prior. Only now, instead of needing to film or videotape the commercials, they were broadcast live. And rather than having to mail in the cash, check, or money order to make a purchase, shoppers merely dialed a toll-free number.

The Home Shopping Network got its start in Clearwater, Florida, when a radio station there had an advertiser that couldn't pay his bills. In lieu of cash, the station owner accepted 112 electric can openers, which were auctioned over the air. A complete sellout gave birth to *Suncoast Bargaineers*, a regularly scheduled program. By 1981, the concept had moved to a Tampa Bay-area local-access television station. Launched as the Home Shopping Channel, it was soon changed to the Home Shopping Network and was broadcasting 24 hours a day by satellite, providing advertisers with commercial time beyond what was offered on traditional broadcast television.

A Marshall Brodien Magic Show set was especially designed for the initial HSC offering. There were 50 classic magic and card tricks, and the price of $49.95 was prominent in the graphics on the front of the big box, although the set would be "reduced" on-air to $24.95. "There really was $50 worth of magic," Marshall says. "They were all premium tricks and if you tried to buy them separately, they would cost $60 to $70."

At Al's insistence, Marshall pre-recorded a two-minute video clip with a non-stop demonstration of at least 20 of the tricks: "Watch this ball as I place it on top of the cup. It penetrates and appears under this cup. Lift the other cup and the ball's there. The card in this box is clearly the Ace. Snap your fingers and it changes to the King. Pour some rice into a bowl. Cover it with another, and you have twice as much rice. Now all the rice has changed to bowls of water ... it's all so easy, once you know the secret." The plan was to run this tape in addition to live on-camera demos.

A huge display had been set up in the studio with every one of the 50 items spread out on an eight-foot-long table. It looked impossible that all the tricks would fit back into the box. When it was time to go on camera, the Home Shopping host introduced Marshall (Al stayed in the control booth) and he went into the familiar "Most magic tricks are easy, once you know the secret" spiel, chatting with the host about the value of the magic set and the amazing number of items that it included. All the while, he would be demonstrating tricks for the host, items like the Sponge Rabbits or the Cut-and-Restored Rope. Between expressing her awe, the host confirmed that this $49.95 magic set was being offered today for only $24.95. The toll-free lines were opened. The $24.95 price scrolled across the screen. The host advised that operators were standing by to take orders. An additional toll-free line would be opened to answer questions viewers might have. Then the director cued the rapid-fire performance videotape, after which Marshall would return live to explain, "You receive all 20 of the tricks you just saw performed, plus 30 more! Also supplied are easy-to-follow instructions that teach you step by step how to do all 50 tricks." The countdown was well under way, with the host advising there were only 17 minutes left to take advantage of this sensational Home Shopping offer: "All 50 magic tricks in this $49.95 Marshall Brodien Magic Show set for only $24.95!" In the background telephones were ringing with operators taking orders. Marshall kept pitching, demonstrating more tricks, and answering questions from callers. The video was cued again. "Only three more minutes to take advantage of this chance of a lifetime offer...."

A sales-per-minute minimum is established for merchandise offered on the Home Shopping Network. A running score of units sold and the total dollar volume per minute appears on an off-camera monitor. Advertisers continue to peddle their item until the tally falls below the minimum. When sales taper, the host moves on to another offer from another merchant. The first time Brodien and Eicoff traveled to Florida to debut a custom magic set, they sold 2,600 units. Eicoff wanted to experiment with timeslots and obligated for a cheaper past-midnight spot. Going on at one in the morning, they sold another 2,400 sets in 29 minutes.

Some of the phone-ins from viewers added a bit of levity to the arduous task of pitching product against the clock, especially when the spots were scheduled after midnight. There were the expected weirdos and drunks, but many calls came from night owls who saw they had a chance to talk with a television celebrity. With his hours upon hours of pitching TV Magic Cards and two decades of appearances on WGN-TV's nationwide broadcasts, Marshall Brodien had become quite the household name.

A middle-aged lady from Charlotte, North Carolina, phoned and asked, "Isn't that magician selling the magic sets the same one that's Wizzo on the *Bozo Show*?"

"Yes, I play that character," Marshall answered, as he did Wizzo's signature "Doody, doody, do."

The woman cackled and asked, "Wizzo, could you *doody* on my husband?"

"Yes, is he there?"

"Yeah, he's right here on the couch," she said.

The director signaled to a cameraman to zoom in close on Marshall's face, and when he did a double "Doody, doody, do ... Doody, doody, do," viewers could hear a jolly man in the background, yelling out, "Thanks, Wizz, I needed that."

Over the next decade, Marshall would return to the Home Shopping Network at least 20 times, as well as make numerous appearances on QVC (the Quality Value Convenience home-shopping channel chartered in 1986). Al Eicoff was of the belief that these infomercial-style, direct-marketing spots did a lot more than just move 5,000 or 6,000 units of merchandise each time Marshall went on. The live demos perpetuated the Marshall Brodien brand name. Every time he went on the shop-at-home networks, in the days and weeks that followed, there were noticeable jumps in sales of merchandise that was already positioned in stores across the nation.

Ships Ahoy

Marshall's numerous trips to St. Petersburg to appear on the Home Shopping Network led to the purchase of a place in Florida. "My brother Charles, who lived in Fort Lauderdale, was a realtor and was always trying to get me to buy a second home there. Finally, when he called and told me about a condominium in Pompano Beach that was 'too good a deal to pass on.' I bought it, remodeled the interior, and turned it into a nice place to stay and bring people. But after three years, I found I wasn't using it that much, so I sold it to someone from Chicago who I thought was a friend."

The "friend" started acquiring more real estate in Florida, and when he bought a hotel on Hutchinson Island to convert to condos, Marshall was talked into investing in seven of the units, with the intention of renting them out as apartments. It wasn't long before Marshall and the other investors discovered the deal was turning bad. False loan documents had been filed and the bank was about to foreclose on a man that Marshall now knew for sure was not a friend. As soon as he heard the FBI was investigating, Marshall called his attorney, telling him he wanted out.

Brodien decided to invest his money not on land, but instead, on something seaworthy. He bought *another* boat. "I was in love with boats most of my adult life," Marshall says. "And the moment I heard my friend Don Sandburg had moved from the Virgin Islands to Fort Lauderdale and was dealing in boats, I had him start looking for a cabin cruiser that I could dock in Florida."

• • •

The very first boat Marshall owned was the speedboat he bought with Eddie Kosmer, his friend who helped convert the Boston Nocturne into the

Club Mystic after Marshall got out of the Army. "Eddie kept the boat at his place in Ingleside, which was on Duck Lake. We'd go boating and water skiing in the Fox Lake area and sometimes take the boat to Lake Michigan."

When Marshall got married in 1963 and moved into the house that Kosmer built for him on Duck Lake, he bought another boat. Naturally, it was a bigger boat. It was docked practically in his backyard, enabling him to be on the water at the drop of a captain's hat. But it wasn't until after his divorce in the '70s, when Brodien and Rick Carey were riding on the crest of success marketing TV Magic Cards, that Marshall decided he needed a party boat. He bought his third boat, a 25-foot Rebel Craft cabin cruiser, which was christened "WIZZO." However, because fans were constantly in the wake of the craft trolling for autographs and "Doody, doody, do's," even during the business meetings that Brodien frequently held on board, he was forced to repaint a smaller-lettered "Wiz" on the stern, minimizing the visibility.

The fourth boat Brodien owned was a 26-foot Trojan, a sleek Fiberglas cabin cruiser. "Al Eicoff loved this boat," says Marshall, "and he always wanted to go out on it, sometimes for the whole weekend." It had a complete galley and dinette, a head with a shower, and the cabin space to sleep four. But by 1981, Brodien's boats had become canoes by comparison to the whopper that Al Eicoff purchased and kept on Lake Michigan. The yacht was so big that the salesman who sold it to Al quit his job to become Al's captain. Then, two winters later, as icy artic winds transmuted the sky-blue waters of the lake into a gray lackluster slab, Al decided it was time to haul his boat to Florida.

• • •

It was only a month after Al had moved his yacht to Lighthouse Point Marina in Pompano Beach, when Don Sandburg called Marshall with the news that he'd located the boat he was searching for. "Don found me a great deal on a previously owned 32-foot Carver Mariner, which I parked right across the slip from where Al's boat was." The yacht-like motorboat became Marshall's hotel afloat. The spacious forward cabin provided comfortable living quarters for two, another six could be accommodated in the main cabin, and two more could sleep in the enclosed fly bridge. Marshall's monster craft was christened the "Sleight of Hand" and he would end up keeping the boat, as well as another cabin cruiser at Fox Lake, until well into the 1990s.

33

Mansion for Sale

During the six weeks it took Don Sandburg to track down Marshall's Florida dreamboat, the two *Bozo's Circus* buddies spent quite a bit of time together, brainstorming a concept for a new television series. The program would be called *Magic Mansion*, and it was envisioned as a half-hour situation comedy aimed at family audiences.

Each week viewers would be transported to the stately Victorian castle that was the slightly haunted home of the wealthy, retired, and eccentric master magician, Marshall Brodien. Here they would encounter not only the unpredictable antics of the mischievous household staff, they would be privy to the regular visits of different guest magicians who would exhibit their diverse talents before a live audience in the mansion's grand ballroom. Though magic and fantasy would provide the overall theme for *Magic Mansion*, both Marshall and Don were in agreement that the appeal and staying power of the series would depend upon the strength of its guest artists, the inventiveness of the running gags (of which Don was a master at creating), and the memorability of the characters.

In addition to Marshall, who would play the bemused magical host, the cast would include Roy Brown, who would portray Orville the Handyman, the proverbial Jack-of-all-trades and master of none. Whether Orville was fulfilling the duties of chauffeur, gardener, carpenter, or dog walker, his ineptitude and childlike manner turned each task into disaster. Nathan the Butler, would be a "proper English gentleman who behaved like a Damon Runyon racetrack tout." Other regular characters were to be Hildegard the Cook; Mimi the Upstairs Maid; John D., the eccentric and seldom seen founder of the estate; Constable Barnes, the town sleuth who constantly pried into Brodien's affairs, hoping to uncover magic secrets; and Puddles the Puppy (actually Roy Brown in a dog suit).

Don sat down at his typewriter and created a 20-page production treatment for *Magic Mansion*, which would serve as a proposal that Marshall could take back to WGN-TV to seek out potential investors. It took Don four pages just to describe the studio set that would serve as Marshall's library, "a place where anything and everything imaginable can happen." Secret passageways were inhabited by a family of friendly ghosts, Shakespearean statues whispered and winked, the fireplace ignited when someone said, "I'm cold," and a revolving bookshelf revealed a rusty suit of armor that cracked Henny Youngman one-liners. Everything in the library at the Magic Mansion — be it a Tiffany lamp, an ornate mirror, a dumbwaiter, or a doorknocker — had a weird and wacky persona. Adjacent to the library set was the Grand Ballroom, which would serve as the seating area for the studio audience, as well as the theater where Brodien's guest magicians would perform.

Sandburg's proposal pointed out parallels between the *Magic Mansion* program and the highly successful *Bozo Show*. As with the *Bozo Show*, the studio audience would be a key element. Families would be invited to the studio to watch the show being taped, and their reactions would become a part of the show. The characters would constantly break the "fourth wall" to deliver asides and interact directly with the audience. Sometimes kids would be invited on camera to assist with magic effects and participate in bits with the characters and guest artists. The philosophy (if there was indeed such a thing in producing a situation comedy for children's television) was that viewers at home would accept the *Magic Mansion* as representing, at one moment, a real place, and the next, merely a theme and décor for a fun TV show.

"Readiness is all," wrote William Shakespeare, centuries before television producers were scheming for the opportune season to debut their newest situation-comedy series. Being ready at the wrong time may have been the reason the *Magic Mansion* pilot never had a fair shake at being produced.

At the time when Brodien submitted Don's well-crafted proposal to WGN-TV's programming execs, *Chicago Sun-Times* columnist Robert Feder had just spilled the news that Bob Bell would be retiring from broadcasting at the end of the 1983-'84 season. While the station was usually interested in producing new programs such as *Magic Mansion* to pitch to potential advertisers, the big concern at the station became "How do we keep the *Bozo Show* alive?" While they sought a replacement for Bell, WGN needed Marshall and Roy Brown to keep the daily show together, and not be expending their energies developing a new weekly show. *Magic Mansion* became a property that WGN-TV would put on hold ... unfortunately, forever.

A New Bozo

He was 62 and had played the role of Bozo the Clown for 24 of those years. On Wednesday, April 4, 1984, local and national media jammed WGN-TV's Studio One to cover Bob Bell's final taping as Bozo. Wizzo, Cooky, and Circus Manager Frazier Thomas were part of the finale sketch that ended with the inevitable pie fight, with Bob getting more than a lion's share of the sailing shaving-cream confections.

Bob retired from broadcasting while the *Bozo Show* was still rated number one in its timeslot. The nationally syndicated *Entertainment Tonight* produced a feature segment on Bob Bell and his contributions to children's television. WGN-TV produced and broadcast a 30-minute primetime documentary, *Bozo: The Man Behind the Makeup*. The Chicago Chapter of the National Academy of Television Arts and Sciences presented Bob with their highest award, The Governors' Award, during the live broadcast of the 26th Annual Chicago Emmy Awards. All of these now historic programs, including Bob's farewell *Bozo Show* can be viewed upon request at the Museum of Broadcast Communications in Chicago.

During the summer of 1984, a nationwide search was set in motion to find a replacement for Bell, who left behind a pretty big pair of shoes to fill. Roy Brown and WGN-TV producer Al Hall viewed the numerous audition tapes that arrived on a daily basis. They reviewed resumes and photos from established circus clowns, as well as actors, drama students, and a few TV personalities who wanted to be a clown. There were letters from individuals who had no show biz experience whatsoever, but claimed it was a lifelong dream to don the yak hair wig, red nose, and trademark grease-paint smile of Bozo.

Meanwhile, as the *Bozo Show* went into summer reruns, Marshall, who hadn't performed at a trade show in almost five years, got a call from Bethlehem Steel, asking if he was available to go back on the trade show floor. He hemmed

The 1984 season of the *Bozo Show* started with Joey D'Auria joining the cast as the new Bozo. Marshall and Roy Brown continued in their regular roles of Wizzo and Cooky, and musician Andy Mitran became show's official one-man band as "Mr. Music." *Courtesy WGN-TV Chicago. Bozo the Clown® & ©Larry Harmon Pictures Corporation. All rights reserved.*

and hawed and told the secretary who called, "I'm working at WGN-TV three days a week and trying to keep a restaurant open, and to tell you the truth, it's just not worth $500 a day to go out and do 20 shows a day for four to five days."

That response prompted Bill Ladshaw, Bethlehem's director of advertising and promotions who'd worked with Brodien for years, to fly to Chicago, take a cab to Lancer's, and see what it'd take to make a deal. "Bethlehem really wants you to do these shows," Ladshaw said. "How much do you want?" When Brodien suggested $1,000 a day, plus travel expenses, and they supply a girl to work the shows, Bill said, "No problem, how about all expenses, the girl, and $1,500 a day?" Within a week, the scripts and the contracts arrived, with the first trade show being the Off-Shore Technologies Exposition, staged at Astrohall, next to the Astrodome in Houston. After that, there was another five-day show in St. Louis and two more trade shows for Mastick and Caradco, two subsidiary companies of Bethlehem Steel.

After the run, there was a call from Bill Ladshaw, who wanted to personally thank Brodien for doing such a great job. Marshall, in turn, expressed his gratitude to Bill for making the work financially rewarding. But he had to ask, "How come when I did all those trade shows for Bethlehem back in the '60s and '70s, you never offered me that kind of money?"

Ladshaw laughed and said, "You never asked for it."

• • •

By late summer, WGN-TV was closing in on finding a new Bozo. After returning from a West Coast trip to audition about a dozen people, Al Hall received a call from Joey D'Auria, a stand-up comic from Pasadena, California. "He saw a story in the *Christian Science Monitor* about the show looking for Bob Bell's replacement," Hall remembers, "and he wanted the job." D'Auria's outrageous act of playing musical candles as "Dr. Flameo" had won him a first place on Chuck Barris' infamous *Gong Show*. This whacky award led to an appearance on NBC's *The Tonight Show* starring Johnny Carson. When Roy Brown and Al viewed D'Auria's videotape, they liked what they saw and arranged for an interview. Joey's act played well for late-night audiences, but how was he with kids?

Roy gave Joey a crash course in clown makeup. An audience of screaming kids was assembled, and he scored big-time laughs with his portrayal of Bozo. After the tryout, Roy walked into the room and told Joey, "You were great, but I have to tell you, I have broken my arm in three places." When D'Auria answered, "Don't go in those places," Roy and Al knew they had their man. They signed Joey on the spot. He moved to Chicago and taped his first *Bozo Show* on September 5, 1984.

Check, Please!

By mid–1985, Marshall wanted out of his deal at the Lancer Restaurant. It had been a profitable venture for close to eight years, but he desired to devote more of his energies to selling and performing magic.

When Marshall talked with his original Lancer's partner Perry Kapos about leaving, he learned that Sue Olson, his investment partner, was also ready to sell. The co-owners agreed to put the restaurant on the market for $2.8 million. If they got an offer anywhere close to $2.5 million, they'd take it. Sue wanted to have the exclusive listing and that was okay with Marshall and Perry. However, after six months, and even after co-listing Lancer's with another Realtor who specialized in restaurant properties, a buyer could not be found.

Marshall asked his friend Dominick if he could suggest any friends or associates who might be interested in purchasing the restaurant. One Saturday night when the place was doing especially good business, Marshall said to Dominick, "This place has got to be an ideal operation for the right people. It has a 400-seat restaurant that's usually packed, and the 1,000-seat banquet room is always turning over big parties..." He point-blank asked, "Tell me the truth, Dominick, wouldn't this place be a good money-laundering machine for the Outfit?"

"Bodean, dis joint would be a top loader," Dominick said with a chuckle. However, he didn't know of anyone who'd be interested in buying Lancer's.

On New Year's Eve that year, Sue suddenly changed her mind about selling and offered to buy out Marshall and Perry. She wanted to be the sole proprietor—maybe even give the place a new name. But the hitch was she couldn't come up with the cash required.

Finally, Marshall and Perry offered to lease her the place. Sue took over the operations, agreeing to pay Perry $4,000 a month and Brodien $2,000 a month. "She also traded me some real estate she owned for all my stock in the corporation," Marshall says. "For the second and final time, I was out of the food and beverage business, and I was a happy man."

Because Dominick wanted to make sure Marshall and Perry continued to receive their lease payments, he suggested that Sue get a chef who could "really make this joint go big time." Dominick told her, "Talk with my friend Vic Giannotti. He could give this place some personality, some good food, too."

But Sue was involved in opening Toucan Charlie's, a trendy little lounge she'd created on the front corner of Lancer's, and apparently too preoccupied to give Vic a call. Completely frustrated, Dominick gave Giannotti's phone number to Marshall, and said, "Bodean, get Vic out here! You gotta hook her up with him before it's too friggin' late."

Vic's father, Nick Giannotti, had been the head chef of the Armory, a "private" Italian eatery in Forest Park. The Armory was actually headquarters for mob consigliore Sam Giancana until 1964, the year he was incarcerated in Cook County jail. Nick and his son Victor took over the operation of the restaurant, which was opened to the public as "Giannotti's." Not long after Sam Giancana's 1975 gangland slaying at his Oak Park home, the building was sold, and Vic opened his own place on the south side of Chicago.

When Vic eventually met with Sue and she learned what a success he'd experienced serving fine Italian cuisine to influential people, she was sure that "going Italian" was going to be her restaurant's salvation. She even asked Giannotti how he felt about changing the name of the place to "Victor's."

Vic laughed and said, "I like the location. It has potential. Maybe we can make some sort of arrangement. But, let me have 60 days or so to think about it." Assuming this meant negotiations were under way and a deal was in the works, the overconfident Ms. Olson called a sign company and ordered the name out front changed to "Victor's."

Sue and Vic, however, would not become partners. After two months of meetings they were never able to agree on even the most preliminary of terms for a deal. And, despite the fact there was never a handshake agreement for the venue to become a signature restaurant for Mr. Giannotti, Sue went ahead and printed menus with the Victor's name and was advertising and promoting the place as Victor's Italian Restaurant.

• • •

Without the worries of running a restaurant, Marshall was free to devote more time and creative energies toward developing new and different magic products. The Marshall Brodien Magic Company had moved from Al Eicoff's office on Michigan Avenue to the more spacious offices of Gutterman & Associates in nearby Lincolnwood. The first new set introduced had the incredibly long name of "Marshall Brodien's World's Greatest Mind Reading Secrets Revealed for the First Time." Then, deciding to capitalize on the popularity of their TV celebrity characters of Wizzo and Cooky, Marshall and Roy Brown put together a Wizzo the Wizard Magic Set and a Cooky the Clown Makeup Kit. New commercials were produced for these two products and they were test-marketed in the Chicago area.

By mid 1986, Marshall and Al had collaborated on a concept for a syndicated television program that, in a somewhat sneaky way, would serve as a free advertising vehicle for products of the Marshall Brodien Magic Company. Starting with Al's premise that the appearance of professional magicians helps sell magic to the masses, Marshall put together a pilot episode of *Wonders of Magic*. The show was shot at the Medinah Country Club, and featured the professional magicians David Seebach, Bob Higa, Mark the Magnificent, Tim Balster, Ken Mate, the juggling August Brothers, Cooky the Clown, and international magic star, Norm Nielsen. Marshall, and Ken Mate, who also wrote the script, hosted the show. Close-up magic segments were shot on location at three Chicago-area restaurants — Schulien's, Gilardi's, and Victor's — and included the talents of Terry Veckey, Tom Niesen, Chuck Schulien, Al James, Mr. Ash, and Tom Spera.

Producing a one-hour program for commercially sponsored non-primetime television meant you only delivered 46 minutes of actual show content. Fourteen minutes of the 60-minute timeslot would be filled with commercials.

Wonders of Magic was offered to independent stations and cable channels free of royalty charges or usage fees. If they chose to schedule and broadcast the show in their local markets, they could realize the revenues from selling eight minutes of advertising airtime. Why only eight and not the total 14 minutes allotted for commercials? TV stations got the show for free, but they had to give the Eicoff Agency six minutes of airtime for Marshall Brodien Magic Company commercials.

When stations obligated to run the program, Eicoff's agency would make sure that the Marshall Brodien Magic spots — usually positioned midway and near the end of the show — were pitching items that Manny Gutterman's distribution people had placed in retail outlets in the area or region where the program was televised.

Broadcast tapes were edited and ready for distribution by the beginning of 1988, but the show didn't air until later that summer, and it was only on two cable-access channels in Chicago and two independent stations in Peoria and New Orleans. Test marketing of *Wonders of Magic* was soon tabled and eventually abandoned. That's because Marshall had been recruited to work on a challenging new project, an attraction promoted as "the hottest nite spot in America." It was a place called ToTo's, and the press releases promised "an adult nightclub that makes you feel like a kid again."

36

ToTo's

Brodien had been away from the restaurant business for almost a year when Sue Olson called and said that she was thinking about opening a theme nightclub at Victor's. She wanted to know if he'd like to get involved. The concept was to take the 10,000-square-foot ballroom above the restaurant and convert it into a dance club with a circus and carnival theme. To create atmosphere, Sue wanted to hire trapeze acts, clowns, fire eaters, sword swallowers, jugglers, and magicians. A rock-'n'-roll circus band would play for patrons who danced in the center-ring. There would be two bars. Peanuts, popcorn, and cotton candy would be served. Games of skill would add to the midway experience.

Sue had visions of becoming the impresario of the greatest showplace on earth. She had no idea how to implement her grand plan, but she did know that Marshall would know how to pull it off. She offered Marshall a share of the profits if he'd design and help put together the place she wanted to call ToTo's.

Marshall, who vowed never to ever get back into the restaurant or nightclub business, says, "It was a dangerous thing to do, but I thought this concept might fly." He not only invested his time and talent, he was enticed into subsidizing the development of ToTo's to the tune of $125,000. "I still owned a piece of investment property with Sue, so we sold it and used the money to partially finance the nightclub."

After nine painstaking months of specialty construction and pouring in a couple hundred thousand more dollars, the ballroom above Victor's was transformed into a carnival midway, and ToTo's officially opened in December 1988.

The walls were decorated with colorful circus and sideshow bally pan-

Bozo was recruited to join Wizzo and Cooky and make a rare out-of-the-studio appearance for a special Easter show at ToTo's in 1988. *Courtesy WGN-TV Chicago. Bozo the Clown® & ©Larry Harmon Pictures Corporation. All rights reserved.*

els painted by WGN-TV scenic painter, Bob Hedberg. Using Marshall's snapshots of the old sideshow banners from Riverview Park, Hedberg, who also created scenic backdrops for the Chicago Lyric Opera, painted a series of original posters for the walls of ToTo's — the Knife Thrower, Sword Swallower, Fire Eater, Snake Charmer, the Strong Man, Fat Lady, Cooky the Clown, and more.

When it was showtime on the main stage of ToTo's, Andy Head juggled Indian clubs, balls, and rings. The August Brothers manipulated flames, balanced a flaming barbecue grill atop their heads, and produced a slithering six-foot-long boa constrictor. Among the magicians who performed were Brett Daniels, Terry Evanswood, Tim Balster, Ken Mate, and Paul Lee. And the stage was a dream for illusionists because of the slew of special effects built in, including the secret trappings for the famous De Kolta Vanishing Lady illusion.

People screamed and laughed at their grotesque reflections in the funhouse mirrors. They had fun trying to knock down the stuffed cats or tossing a ring on a bottleneck to hopefully take home a big fuzzy plush animal. The Girl in a Fishbowl illusion, where a live girl swam about in a 12-inch-high glass bowl, created a sensation during opening week. Roving Channel 2 newscaster Bob Wallace, whose popular "Where's Bob?" segment was featured on the WBBM-TV evening news, filed his review of the circus nightclub from inside the fishbowl.

As with any exciting new nightspot, funseekers flocked to ToTo's during its first months of operations. However, the wave of popularity crested in less than a year. By fall of 1989, there were weeknights when only a handful of people showed up. The entertainment staff outnumbered the patrons. Marshall and Ken Mate, who'd been helping Sue book the talent, tried to convince her that during these slow periods the nightclub should be marketed as a party venue, leased out to private groups, and promoted as the ideal place for corporate events. Their show-business advice fell on deaf ears.

ToTo's was originally designed as "The adult nightclub that makes you feel like a kid again," but owner/operator Sue was on a mission to change that game plan. Because she couldn't afford to keep the circus and variety acts on the payroll, her son's head-splitting, ear-piercing rock-'n'-roll band was the only featured entertainment. A totally different crowd now frequented ToTo's. The good-times theme disappeared when the circus-art bally panels were painted over. Marshall got disgusted and walked from the deal. Sue dealt with the undesirable and dwindling turnout for another year before folding the tent.

Ventures in Toyland

"Magic's not going anywhere, anymore."

That was the sentiment expressed by Al Eicoff in January 1991, when the partners of the Marshall Brodien Magic Company met to work on a business plan for the year. "Last year was the worst year in the 12-year history of the company," Eicoff said. "And for all the work involved in keeping the company going, it's not worth it." Manny Gutterman and his sons, Steve and Art, who were one-third partners, also expressed their dissatisfaction with the company's performance. Corporate accountant Burt Babetch informed everybody that it was indeed true that the business was operating in the red and still owed the bank $70,000.

"What do we do?" Al asked.

"The partners personally pay off the loan, and you dissolve the company," Burt suggested.

Marshall disagreed with the doomsayers. He believed the company still had potential. He felt sales had slipped because the products could only be found in drug chains such as Walgreens, Eckerd's, Thrifty Drug. Marshall asked, "Why don't we bring some toy salesmen on board, people who know how to place our merchandise in stores like K-Mart, Toys 'R' Us, and Target?"

Eicoff fired back, "Why don't *you* buy the company, and *you* hire some toy salesmen?"

"Buying the company would take a lot of cash," Marshall said.

"Well, if you think you can make it go," Al said, "pay off the $70,000 note we have with the bank, and we'll give you our stock." The only proviso Al posed was that the loan be refinanced at a different bank. The offer appealed to Marshall and he shook hands with the partners and told them he'd let them know something within the week.

Marshall went to see his friend Bob Hoge, the president of a bank in St. Charles, Illinois. Hoge's son was an aspiring young magician who Marshall had helped along with his career. When Marshall told his banker of the path he wanted to pursue with the Marshall Brodien Magic Company, he was pleased to have the opportunity to provide the needed financial assistance. "Even though I offered all the merchandise in the warehouse and the costly injection molds as collateral," Marshall remembers, "Bob said that wasn't necessary, my financial statements were sufficient, and he made the loan anyway."

That February, Marshall went to the Toy Show in New York City by himself. He set up an exhibit in the Al Gilly & Associates' showroom, and Al Gilly assigned a sales rep to the Marshall Brodien Magic Company. For the next three days, Marshall was introduced to several buyers as he demoed his merchandise. As a result, they ended up taking large orders from BJ's Warehouse Club and Toys 'R' Us. "From those orders alone I was able to pay off the $70,000 note," Marshall says. "And I grossed well over $100,000 that year, managing to make a profit of $20,000. And I owned all the stock in the company."

As much as Marshall enjoyed winning new accounts and getting product into the stores he wanted to be in, he did not like the business part of the business. Writing the orders, the reorders, the backorders, the invoicing, and the follow-up paperwork had him bound to a desk for more hours than he cared for. It was putting a strain on his first love — performing. Brodien absolutely lived for the three-times-a-week that he could escape the office and become Wizzo the Wizard.

• • •

Things were going full tilt with the *Bozo Show*. The ten-year tickets reservations list had run out, and WGN-TV announced that on St. Patrick's Day, they would be taking five more years of reservations via a special hotline. There was pandemonium at the switchboard. Illinois Bell reported that in five hours there were 27 million dial-ups in Illinois alone, peaking at 120,000 call attempts per minute. The story made the front page of the *Los Angeles Times* and was featured on the *NBC Nightly News*.

The "Take a Vacation with Bozo" contest — where 20 families were flown to Walt Disney World in Florida while a week of shows were taped with Bozo, Wizzo, and Cooky — had become a perennial promotion, and, in 1991, while the WGN-TV gang was taping the program in Orlando, Marshall Brodien, a.k.a. Wizzo the Wizard, was made an Honorary Citizen of Walt Disney World.

Not long after the crew returned from Disney World, Roy "Cooky" Brown

When Marshall traveled to Orlando, Florida, in 1991 to tape the *Bozo Show* for the third time, Wizzo was made an Honorary Citizen of Walt Disney World. *Marshall Brodien Collection*

was hospitalized for heart-related problems, and Don Sandburg was recruited to fill in as Sandy the Tramp while Roy recuperated. This gave Marshall and Don the opportunity to revive some of the classic Bozo, Wizzo, and Sandy sketches that hadn't been done since the 1960s. And the slapstick and inside gags even got larger — Sandy and Wiz knew that Cooky was watching from home.

All *Bozo Show* fans born on September 11, 1961, were automatically entered into a drawing to win a chance to play the Grand Prize Game on the *Bozo Show 30th Anniversary Special*. George Palmer of Roselle, Illinois won the drawing, but only made it to bucket number five, claiming a cash prize of $1,500. Returning to appear on this primetime program with Joey D'Auria and Marshall, were veteran ringmaster Ned Locke, Ray Rayner, Don Sandburg, and popular actor Adrian Zmed. Magician Harry Blackstone Jr. made a guest appearance, performing his legendary Vanishing Birdcage, as well as an illusion where a beautiful lady was magically transformed into a Bengal tiger.

Roy Brown was back on the show by January 1992, and early that spring the treacherous trio of Cooky, Wizzo, and Bozo revived a magic skit with the Substitution Trunk illusion that hadn't been performed since the days when Bob Bell was Bozo. Just as the classics improve with age, this old comedy sketch when dusted off and given a few new patter lines would win the *Bozo Show* an armful of Emmy Awards.

Marshall received an Emmy in 1992 for his orginal skit with the Substitution Trunk that featured the magical antics of Wizzo, Bozo, and Cooky. *Photograph by Spellman Studios, Geneva, IL, Marshall Brodien Collection*

37. Ventures in Toyland

As the scene opens, Cooky is sitting on a wardrobe trunk. The phone rings. He answers it and tells the kids, "It's Bozo." Cooky cups his hand over the receiver and says, "Hey, kids, Bozo wants to know if anybody has seen his trunk here at the circus. He wants me to lock it up and move it over to his tent..."

Of course, the kids in the studio audience are screaming and shouting, "You're sitting on it! You're sitting on it!"

Cooky hangs up, telling Bozo that he'll look around for the trunk. He stands up, muttering, "I'm so tired and overworked, I don't have time to look for Bozo's trunk...."

The kids are going wild, yelling, "It's right there!"

"Maybe Bozo's trunk is in here," he says, actually opening the lid of the trunk. "Say, it's nice and dark inside here. The perfect place to hide and take a nap." Cooky crawls in the trunk and pulls the top shut.

Bozo and Wizzo walk on the set together. "Where's that Cooky?" Bozo asks. I just phoned him and told to lock up this trunk and get it over to my tent. Wizzo, lock it up for me. I'll go find Cooky to help us move it."

Bozo exits and Wizzo proceeds, with much "Doody, doody, doing," to secure the trunk with a huge padlock and some leather straps. He holds up the big key and warns the kids, "Keep an eye on this trunk while I go help Bozo look for Cooky."

Only seconds later, Bozo comes back on, carrying a scenic flat with a big red star and "Cooky" painted on it. "Hey, kids, look at this new dressing room door to welcome Cooky back." He stops in front of the trunk and says, "Now where did Wizzo go? I see he's got my trunk locked up, but now I need him to take the trunk over to my tent."

The phone rings. Bozo picks it up. "Cooky, is that you? Where are you? Stay there, I'm bringing you your new dressing room door." Bozo hangs up the phone and tells the kids, "That was Cooky, and he says he's over at his tent."

"No! He's not!" cries the studio audience. "Cooky's in the trunk!" The parents have joined the clamor. "Open the trunk!" "He's hiding in the trunk!"

Bozo asks, "How can he be in the trunk? He was just on the phone. I'm going to find Wizzo. He has the key to this trunk. I need to find Wizzo to open it."

About that time, Cooky strolls into the scene. The silence is deafening as he circles the trunk. The studio audience is completely stymied. Cooky is smiling and holding the big gold key high above his head. Bozo turns around and shouts, "What's going on here? The boys and girls are telling me you're inside this trunk! And where's Wizzo? I thought he had the key. You clowns are driving me crazy!"

Bozo grabs the key, unlocks the lock, opens the lid, and inside, wearing a Cheshire Cat grin, is none other than Wizzo the Wizard!

Not only would Marshall, Roy, Joey, and the show's musical director Andy Mitran, receive an Emmy apiece at the 34th Annual Chicago/Midwest Emmy Awards that year, the statues and certificates were passed out at the by none other than *Bozo Show* producer Al Hall, who at the time was serving his third term as President of the Chicago/Midwest Chapter of the National Academy of Television Arts and Sciences.

• • •

Numerous are the amateur magicians and established pros who attribute their beginnings in magic to a deck of TV Magic Cards or a Marshall Brodien magic set. Lance Burton — the world champion magician who, in 1995, signed a $100-million, 13-year contract with the Monte Carlo in Las Vegas — is one of those whose interest was definitely fueled by a deck of TV Magic Cards. In the mid '70s Lance's mother, Hilma Burton, bought him a deck at a local Walgreens as a birthday present.

However, Lance went further than most and got extremely serious about his card manipulations. He developed an act that won the first-ever-awarded Gold Medal at the 1980 International Brotherhood of Magicians Convention. Traveling to Lausanne, Switzerland, in 1982, Burton won the coveted Grand Prix of the Fédération Internationale des Sociétés Magiques and, at 22, became the youngest magician as well as the first American to earn this prestigious world championship. His sophisticated cards and doves act, which had garnered a feature spot in the *Folies Bergere* at the Tropicana in Las Vegas, would be held over for nine years. During the extended run, Lance developed numerous show segments with illusions, which the show's producers allowed him to try out regularly on the ever-changing audiences. By 1991, he had created and assembled enough material that he was able to produce, direct, and star in his own show at the Hacienda in Las Vegas. The production was called *Lance Burton: A Magical Journey* and it opened in July that year.

That fall, Marshall was on a business trip to the West Coast and stopped by Vegas to see Lance's new show. He was duly impressed. *A Magical Journey* had all the facets of the traditional full-evening shows of Thurston, Dante, and Blackstone — the grand masters associated with the glorious Golden Age of Magic — yet it was presented within the context of a sparkling high-tech Las Vegas spectacle. The element of the show that was the talk of the town and winning the acclaim of the media was Lance's infectious Southern hospitality. Never before had a magician charmed a Las Vegas crowd as did Lance.

Marshall's forever-marketing-magic mind had visions of Lance Burton becoming a sensation on television and selling millions of magic sets as a result. Although Lance had made several successful guest appearances on *The Tonight Show* with Johnny Carson, he felt Lance was now ready to have a network special. However, Marshall would have to wait a while before encouraging him to pursue fame and fortune on the tube. After the show, Lance wanted to talk with Marshall about supplying a Lance Burton magic set, something that could be sold in the gift shop at the Hacienda. Marshall told him he would put together some numbers when he got back to Chicago, however, when he returned home, all he could do was talk about how great Lance's show was and how he was destined to be magic's next TV star.

• • •

One morning without warning, Toy Show manufacturers' rep Al Gilly called Marshall and said, "There's someone on the East Coast who's interested in buying your company. If you are interested in selling, you ought to go talk."

The C.E.O. of Harmony Toy, Ltd., flew Marshall to Boston to talk about acquiring his company. "He picked me up in his Jaguar at Logan Airport and drove me out to Harmony's headquarters in Burlington," Marshall tells. "It was actually the company's president, Jimmy Baum, who'd convinced the C.E.O that Harmony needed a line of magic products." Up until that time, the firm had specialized in board games and educational toys. Baum was well aware of Marshall's successes with marketing magic to the masses and hoped the Brodien brand could do the same for Harmony.

The meeting was short and sweet. A deal was struck almost immediately. Harmony Toy agreed to pay $300,000 for the assets and the manufacturing rights to all Marshall Brodien Magic Company products. Harmony got the entire inventory, all the injection molds for fabricating the plastic parts of the items, and they got Brodien.

"In addition to acquiring the exclusive use of my name on all the new magic products manufactured," Marshall says, "Harmony wanted to keep me on a retainer as their magic consultant. I signed a five-year non-compete contract that specified they could stop using my name at anytime, only as long as they paid me for the full term of the agreement." The beauty of the deal was that Brodien consulted with Jimmy Baum and Harmony's designers from his home office in Chicago, which allowed him to continue performing as he pleased, including doing the regular tapings of the *Bozo Show* at WGN-TV.

In April 1992, Brodien flew to the Magic Castle in Hollywood to receive the Academy of Magical Arts "Special Fellowship Award." At the same ceremony, the Academy honored Lance Burton as "Magician of the Year." After the awards banquet, Marshall met with Lance and told him of his new contractual arrangement with Harmony Toy. Since he'd been working on a classy black-and-red-boxed, gold-lettered "Lance Burton 12 Amazing Magic Trick Set" at the time he sold his company to Harmony, Marshall let Lance know if he was still interested that the new president, Jimmy Baum, was willing to honor the order. Because an order of 5,000 custom-assembled sets was a relatively small order compared to the quantities that Harmony shipped to distributors and retailers, they asked that Lance take delivery of the total order at once. This was okay with Lance. It just meant he'd be parking his Corvette in the driveway for awhile, as his shop at the Hacienda dwindled down the inventory stored in the garage.

Harmony Toy didn't dillydally that summer when going to market with the new magic line. Items released for the Christmas season were the Marshall Brodien Magic Show set; a Marshall Brodien 50 Amazing Tricks set; the Marshall Brodien Classic Magic Tricks set with 100 tricks; and various trick decks, including the ever-popular TV Magic Cards repackaged as Magician's Magic Cards. Harmony got Lance's order out in time for holiday sales at the Hacienda gift shop, and the company even had time to crank out an order for the design and delivery of a colorful eight-trick set for Siegfried & Roy, who were in the second year of sold-out performances of their extravaganza at the Mirage in Las Vegas.

Viva Las Vegas

When Marshall flew to Las Vegas that fall to visit with his friend Norm Nielsen and take a look at the new house Norm was buying, he was introduced to Peter Reveen. Australian-born Reveen was a hypnotist and illusionist who moved to town in 1975, when he headlined in the *Folies Bergere* at the Tropicana. He had long since earned a Realtor's license and was assisting Norm in the acquisition of his sprawling ranch-style estate on the outskirts of the city. Because both Reveen and Brodien had experienced successful careers as stage hypnotists, they hit it off immediately.

In the greater part of the last half of the 20th century, Reveen enjoyed enormous successes touring with a theatrical hypnotic show. His sold-out performances across Canada from the 1960s into the '80s established theater-attendance records that have yet to be topped. Interspersed among the years of box-office triumphs with his hypnotic show were a series of full-evening magic shows that Peter produced and toured. They cost small fortunes to build and take on the road and, inevitably, each one caused him untold financial grief. He could fill theaters again and again with his astonishing show of hypnotism, but even his diehard fans would not buy tickets when he brought his spectacular magic shows to town. By 1990, after a magic extravaganza that Peter had taken to Australia failed, he managed to unload the entire production on a wealthy Australian amateur magician, vowing to forever stick with hypnotism and never again touch an illusion.

However, as it is with most magicians who've experienced a modicum of success trouping the world with a stage full of illusions, Peter couldn't stay away from the big stuff. He found himself spending more and more time with his friend Lance Burton who, with the exception of Las Vegas pioneers Siegfried & Roy, had the only other illusion show in town. Peter told Lance that he deserved a better showplace than the Hacienda. The 40-year-old property was of a bygone era. The shiny glass towers of the new MGM Grand and the Luxor now eclipsed the rancho-style casino. One evening, Peter intimated to Lance that he wanted to work on finding him a new resort, help him negotiate a long-term exclusive showroom deal, and maybe even become his business manager one day. Lance grinned and said, "That could be very interesting...."

• • •

It'd been four months since Marshall and Peter met at Norm Nielsen's house when Marshall received a call from Peter. He was excited to tell that he'd just signed as Lance Burton's personal manager. He rattled off the things he wanted to do to advance Lance's career, and at the top of the list was a new hotel on the Strip with his own theater and bigger promotion and advertising budgets. Peter remembered that Marshall had once expressed an interest in seeing Lance do something big on TV. And from that day forward, Peter would relentlessly campaign for Marshall to put together some investors to produce a network special for Lance.

Now that Peter was on the bandwagon to steer Lance toward stardom, Marshall was convinced more than ever that a well-produced special would skyrocket Lance's celebrity, and who knew, it might make Lance wealthy as well as famous.

Marshall had been telling Al Eicoff about Lance's Las Vegas show for almost a year, and he finally convinced him to go see it. Marshall wanted Al's opinion. With nearly a half-century of television advertising and marketing successes to his credit, Eicoff would be the one who'd know if the concept of a Lance Burton special was something that could be shopped around to TV producers and sold to one of the networks.

Al had the time of his life on the trip to Las Vegas, and of greater importance, he liked Lance's show so much he took friends to see it three times. But was Lance ready for primetime? Did Al think they would like him in Peoria?

When Eicoff got back home, he called Marshall and said, "Marsh, here's the dilemma — few people outside the Las Vegas city limits know who Lance Burton is. I called my friend Al Masini with *Entertainment Tonight* to see what he knew about Lance Burton. And you know what? He said he'd never seen him. He said producing a show with a relatively unknown entertainer without a commitment from a network is a bad idea. Why don't you call Masini and let him talk you out of this?"

Alfred Masini was the Hollywood television writer who created the syndicated show-biz tabloid program *Entertainment Tonight*. When Marshall telephoned him he heard the same words of discouragement. "I don't know if you are thinking about putting your money into the show," Masini said, "or if you are planning to get others to invest, but either way, don't do it. I haven't seen Lance Burton's show, but it's dangerous to attempt anything like a special without some sort of go-ahead, a commitment, or as we call it in the business, a 'green light' from a network."

But Brodien took little heed of Masini's caution signal. "At the time, I didn't think we could miss," Marshall says. "I went back to Al and argued that the fact that nobody knew about Lance was what would make it work. I said, 'When people see the special and realize how great he is, what a sensational performer he is, we'll have a hit on our hands.'" Marshall's persistence and determination soon won out. Al was convinced they could make money with the show if they put it together themselves. Al set up a meeting with his attorney and accountant, and it was decided that the formation of a limited partnership would be the best approach.

Marshall called the partners the next day to tell them they would have a little extra time to work out the legal details. Lance was putting a temporary red light on the project and entering into a partnership of a different sort. Lance and Melinda Saxe, Las Vegas' self-proclaimed First Lady of Magic, were getting married on August 30, 1993.

Melinda had studied dance while in high school, learned most of her magic from Las Vegas magicians Gary Darwin and Geno Munari, and got her first job dancing in the Siegfried & Roy show. She also received support from her mother Bonnie Saxe, a former showgirl and choreographer who'd hung up her dancing shoes to produce and direct her daughter. From the mid 1980s and into the '90s, Bonnie was successful in getting the First Lady of Magic onto the stages of the Landmark, the Sands, the Sahara, and after a stint in Atlantic City, back to Vegas for an indefinite run at the Lady Luck.

After the hoopla of the "Royal Wedding"—as the 600-guest-listed event was declared by *MAGIC* magazine—subsided, and Melinda and Lance settled back into their respective two-a-night grinds at the Lady Luck and the Hacienda, Marshall got Lance's TV special back on schedule by starting to put together a production budget.

Marshall's son-in-law, Paul Torrey, an account executive with Motivational Media, a video production company that had delivered some impressive regional and national television commercials, had his company work up a shooting cost estimate. By fall, they had a budget that boasted of a bottom line of $400,000. When this document was paired up with Lance's script outline, Marshall was ready to present the package to the investment partners who'd incorporated as Magic Moments, Inc. It was now a matter of deciding how shares would be distributed among the stockholders. And since this was something they wanted to give some careful considerations, it was agreed to wait until the start of the New Year to begin the project.

• • •

Harmony Toy, Ltd. was pleased with the manner in which Marshall Brodien merchandise had moved during the holidays. In a short span of 16 months, sales of magic sets and magic products completely overshadowed Harmony's board games and puzzles business. But as Marshall and Harmony approached the end of the second year of their five-year contract, the toy company started introducing fewer new items with the familiar Brodien hallmark. And it wasn't because they were busy supplying custom items for Lance or Siegfried & Roy, important accounts that Marshall had brought to the table at Harmony.

Harmony Toy's chief executive officer fancied himself a financial wizard who had the power to shape market trends and was convinced the Harmony name was stronger than the Brodien brand. He made a move to remove Marshall's identity from the packaging. "Suddenly, the C.E.O.'s wife was put in charge of design," Marshall remembers. "She was a commercial artist and set out to change the look of all the magic sets. She thought everything should be more child friendly, have lots of bright, primary colors." However, the kindergarten-like graphics did nothing to convey to parents, the ones usually buying the magic sets, that the boxes were chock full of intriguing magic tricks.

Fortunately, only a small number of the new packaging designs made it to the shelves of toy stores. That's because the buyers didn't buy into the change. At the International Toy Show in New York that February, there were few new orders. Harmony's magic business, which had pegged over $5-million the previous season, dropped almost 50%.

"Because they had taken my name and picture off the products, it was apparent that the C.E.O. was trying to ease me out of the company," Marshall says. "But it was also evident that the company realized it had made a big mistake by not letting me do my thing."

Brodien went to the Harmony Toy's president, Jimmy Baum, to express his concerns. He pointed out that he'd been hired because he brought to Harmony a household name when it came to marketing magic. Jimmy agreed that Marshall's successes selling magic via key outlet marketing certainly gave him the expertise to know what a magic set should look like. Jimmy also listened to Marshall's philosophy that he'd adopted years ago from advertising guru Al Eicoff— even if the customer was a total novice he wanted to feel like what he was buying was a product endorsed by a pro. Consumers, be they seven- or eight-year-old kids or 78-year-old grandparents, wanted to see a photo of a real magician — even better, one that they'd seen on TV — on the box of tricks.

Jimmy set out to get things back on track. Marshall's smiling photographic likeness was returned to all of Harmony's magic products. On the box of the new Marshall Brodien 100 Trick Set with Video, colorful images of various tricks surrounded a photograph of Marshall, clad in tuxedo, pulling a videocassette from a top hat. The VHS tape that was included with the set featured Marshall performing and explaining at least 25 of the effects. The teaching of traditional tricks had gone high-tech at Harmony Toy.

39

A Shot at Producing

By February 1994, a production crew had assembled at the Hacienda showroom in Las Vegas and was on standby to begin shooting the special now called *Lance Burton: World Champion Magician*. Marshall assumed the position of executive producer for Magic Moments, and Motivational Media had hired Randall C. Young to direct.

In addition to the five days allocated for taping Lance's stage production, three days were scheduled for an on-location shoot at McCarran International Airport, filming an original illusion designed for the show finale. The script called for Lance and his six female assistants to take their final onstage bows then head for the airport, as they purportedly embarked on a world tour. Because the women had forgotten their passports, the master magician would employ a little trickery to get them through customs and security. After the half-dozen ladies crawled into Lance's three-foot wide, one-foot deep suitcase, he would snap the lid shut and nonchalantly lift it onto the conveyor belt for baggage check. As the suitcase passed though the X-ray machine, the camera would cut to the monitor, showing that the suitcase was mysteriously empty. The security guard would give Lance a thumbs up and say, "I see you're traveling light, Mr. Burton." Lance would carry the bag to a table around the corner, open it up, and out would step the six ladies, all excited about going on a world tour. Northwest Airlines agreed to assist with the shooting expenses of this segment. The airline would provide the roundtrip airfares of the Chicago-based production crew, in exchange for a promotional tag as Lance and his assistants flew off into the sunset.

Disillusionment arose on the first day of production. Shooting for television on the Hacienda's four-decades-old stage was a nightmare, as far as lighting was concerned. The lighting instruments were antiquated and not

Las Vegas magician Lance Burton, his dancers, and Marshall (as executive producer), shooting the one-hour special that never made it to network television. *Marshall Brodien Collection*

up to par for TV, and to compound matters the lighting director had zero out-of-studio, on-location experience. The test scenes turned out extremely dark. Additional lighting instruments, including programmable Vari-Lites, were ordered; however, they were not installed until the next-to-last day of the shoot.

Complications grew when Lance talked the director into shooting not by a production schedule, but instead, in the order of his Hacienda stage show. The special would open with a major part of Lance's award-winning dove act. Because it was a pantomime and music act, this meant that the star would not utter a word for the first seven minutes of the show.

The quality of everything videotaped during the first three days was questionable. Nothing was up to network standards. Yet the clock was ticking and there was no time to re-do anything, even though Motivational Media assured Marshall that the scenes could be fixed in the editing suite.

"It was my fault for not hiring a more experienced production company," Marshall admits. "It was a disaster." Television actress Ann Jillian was signed to appear as the guest host, with her talents to be used in at least one illusion vignette with Lance. However, her taped introduction of Lance and three ins-and-outs for commercials were the only times she appeared on camera. The girls-in-the-suitcase illusion slated for shooting at the airport never happened. The director claimed the permits obtained by Northwest Airlines were revoked. "I later found out that wasn't the truth, and he just didn't want to do it," Marshall says. "I should have told everybody, 'If you want to do this special it has to be done *my* way.' But I didn't, and that was when I realized I was not a TV producer."

As soon as the videotaping wrapped and Motivation Media went into editing and post-production, Peter called his friend Gary Ouellet — a high-powered Canadian attorney who served as a government lobbyist, but had recently resigned to produce television specials — to see if he could persuade NBC to take a look at the show. Ouellet, who had gained invaluable TV-production experience working for David Copperfield for five years, went to long-time NBC producers Gary Pudney and Bob Jaffee for help. They said that John Miller, the President of Special Events, was interested and an appointment was scheduled.

Marshall and Peter flew to NBC's offices in Burbank for the screening. After the presentation, the producers confided that NBC was not going to buy it, but they said they might be able to make parts of it work. Several of the segments had the sparkle of a network special and they said that perhaps the darkly lit and poorly directed scenes could be re-shot and re-edited. Yet, after reviewing the tape a second time, Ouellet came back to tell Marshall that Lance would be best served by completely starting over.

This was the last thing Brodien and his investors wanted to hear. Magic Moments had paid out close to $180,000 to Motivational Media, and basically they had a turkey on their hands. The investors' attorneys insisted that Motivation Media had simply not delivered the network-standards product promised in the contract. A lawsuit was initiated.

After Marshall returned to Chicago, Gary Ouellet called and expressed an interest in "starting over." He wanted to know if Marshall was interested in assigning the rights for a future Lance Burton TV special to Jaffee and Pudney's production company. Lance had signed a five-year exclusivity agreement with Marshall. But Marshall was so fed up with TV execs and deal making that he gave them a go-ahead, without asking for any compensation or remuneration.

"The final settlement with Motivation Media took about two years, and it was for only $50,000," Marshall says. "By the time the attorneys got their $25,000 and the investors split up the balance, there was little the partners could do but write off the investment experience as a loss."

It would be two years before Jaffee, Pudney, and Ouellet would get around to producing a NBC special for Lance Burton. That's because, during the summer of '94, they started a new project called *The World's Greatest Magic*.

NBC had respectable experience with magic programs. The network pioneered the genre of the ensemble magic special in 1957, when it broadcast its *Producer's Showcase Festival of Magic*, a 90-minute program featuring Cardini, Robert Harbin, Sorcar, Milbourne Christopher, and others. In 1975, *Doug Henning's World of Magic*, produced by David Susskind, was broadcast live, and remains the highest-rated magic special in history. Seven more Henning specials were produced, but none of them drew as many viewers as the first. And it was not until *The World's Greatest Magic* aired on November 26, 1994 that NBC had another magic hit on its hands. The two-hour special received such high ratings that the network would give the production team the opportunity to try it again for four more years, with new specials airing the night before Thanksgiving.

Marshall's 1994 pitch may not have rung the right chimes at the network of the peacock, but it did open certain producers' eyes to Lance's popular Las Vegas show, as well as dozens of other rising young stars on the magic scene who, over five years, were invited to appear on the different *World's Greatest Magic* specials. Jaffe, Pudney, and Ouellet would eventually deliver a 1996 NBC special, *Lance Burton: The Legend Begins*, followed by *Lance Burton: The Encounter* in '97.

Marshall Meets His Match

Marshall's good friend Roy Brown, who'd appeared on the *Bozo Show* since 1968 as Cooky the Clown, announced his retirement in 1994. Heart-related problems had forced him to take a three-month leave of absence midway through the 1993-94 season. As he recuperated, Michael Immel filled in with his clown character of Spiffy Q. Fahrquahrrr. When Roy did return, a stash of 28 new clown sketches that Don Sanburg had written during the 1992-93 season were produced. Producer Al Hall had the skits shot in such a manner that they could be aired intermittently to finish out the season. Cooky could miss a live show taping and viewers at home wouldn't know it; the only people aware of his absence were those in the studio audience.

Through the spring of 1994, Marshall continued reporting to WGN's Studio One, donning the Wizzo costume and makeup, and taping two to three new episodes of the *Bozo Show* every week. "But it just wasn't the same without Roy there day to day," he says. "And when I heard that his doctors were not going to let him come back that fall, it was basically all over for me. I'd made up my mind to leave, but I didn't say anything to anyone until after our last show in April. We were sitting there in the dressing room, taking off our makeup, when I told everybody, 'I'm not coming back next season. I just don't have it in me anymore.'"

• • •

"Vanishing Act: After 30 Years, Wizzo Steps Back" were the headlines of a full-page feature article in the *Chicago Tribune* of July 17, 1994. The story about the retirement of Brodien's Wizzo character carried the byline of "Mary K. Doyle, Special to the *Tribune*."

Mary was a copywriter for Mozdren & Associates, a design and advertising agency in St. Charles, Illinois. She also served as the administrative assistant to the president of the firm — which had Motorola, Arthur Andersen, and First Card among its major clients — so her writing for the *Chicago Tribune* was done at night and on weekends. "I had been working as an independent contractor, writing features and profiles for the Sunday edition of the newspaper since 1990," Mary says. "That title of 'Special to the *Tribune*' was a fancy name for freelancer."

Her profile of Wizzo the Wizard was an assignment by choice, as were all the articles that she did for the paper. She had heard the news that Marshall was leaving the show, and because he'd been an integral part of the WGN-TV children's program that nearly three generations had watched, she knew it would be a wonderful human-interest story. "Chicago kids grew up watching the *Bozo Show*," she says. "When I was a child, the show was on at noon, and my brother, sister, and I would walk home from school and watch it during our lunch. We never wanted to return until we could see the winner of the Bozo Buckets game."

Mary called to set up an interview the day after her supervising editor approved her story proposal. Marshall immediately remembered her from an earlier conversation they'd had. "She had called me about a year before, checking some facts for an interview she was doing with Terry Evanswood, a young illusionist who got started with one of my magic sets." This time, the writer from the *Tribune* was calling to check out some facts on Marshall.

"I was looking out the window of my office when I saw her car pull up," Marshall says. "And when she got out I said to myself, 'Wow, she's a cute gal for a newspaper reporter.' As she sat across the desk from me, asking her questions, I couldn't take my eyes off of her." It was difficult to tell who was in the spotlight that day.

"Honestly, I was amused by Marshall's reactions during the interview," Mary recalls. "Here he was, the television star, yet I felt I was making him nervous. He was fumbling with the window blinds and items on his desk. He had trouble remembering dates and places. Towards the end of the interview, he walked around his mammoth desk and sat down next to me. It was a Sunday afternoon and getting late. I was a single parent working two jobs, raising three children, and I wanted to get home. I had my information, so I gathered my things and decided it was best for me to leave."

Typically, it took Mary four to six weeks to complete one of the *Tribune* profiles. While all of her subjects were usually interesting, she found Marshall's experiences to be engaging. "I knew that the activities of his life would take a lot of ink," she says. "It wouldn't be hard to write an interesting article to fill 50 column inches, which is a full-page article." But Marshall was worried that she didn't have enough information. She'd left her business card, so he called.

"It wasn't unusual for people to contact me after the initial interview to verify a fact or straighten out some details, but Marshall called more than any other interviewee I ever had in the past. He always had a great excuse. He had forgotten to tell me something about a certain event or he had just remembered another important reference for me to talk to." The truth be known, Marshall was smitten with the wordsmith. He was hoping another meeting might be required.

Thus came the ploy of the pictures. He told Mary he had some photographs that she had to look at. He said that once she saw them, she would want to use them with her story. "I suggested that he stick them in the mail," Mary says. "But he told me they were irreplaceable; he couldn't take the chance of losing them in the mail."

Marshall was persistent and determined to personally hand her the photographs. He says, "There was this restaurant in St. Charles, near the ad agency office where Mary worked. I told her I could drop the pictures off there. She could pick them up on her way home."

They met in the reception area of the restaurant. Marshall had assembled a packet of photos — early snapshots of him working at Riverview Park, a picture of him doing the straitjacket escape while in the army, his appearance on *The Mike Douglas Show* with Bill Cosby, and some location shots of the *Bozo Show* cast when they taped shows at Walt Disney World. The one showing him levitating Cosby on a broomstick would eventually find its way into Mary's *Tribune* story. As she gathered the stack of photos, Marshall looked at his wristwatch and said, "Gosh, it's past five o'clock. Do you have time for a bite of dinner, maybe a cocktail?"

"All along I realized that Marshall wanted to see me," Mary says. "However, I did not think it was ethical to become involved with him before the article was published. Nor was it a point in my life when I wanted to be involved with anyone. But, of course, Marshall's persistence and determination was flattering and fun."

A "first date" did precede the appearance of the story. They met at the Galleon, another restaurant in St. Charles. After dinner, as they stood in the parking lot saying goodbye, Marshall suggested they keep in touch. "That was when I told Marshall I had more information than I could ever use in his newspaper article," Mary says. "I suggested that he should have a book written about him and his magic life. Marshall got a little gleam in his eye and said, 'Okay. Why don't you stick around? You can be a chapter.'

"That response caught me off-guard. It was humorous, but the invitation to be a part of his life was much more appealing than an invitation to write his book, which is what I had expected to hear."

40. Marshall Meets His Match

After Marshall and Mary were married October 14, 1995, it wasn't long before she was attending magic conventions and soon became a integral part of Marshall's act. When not box-jumping and assisting Marshall, Mary Doyle Brodien is a busy writer, having published *Mentoring Heros* and *The Rosary Prayer by Prayer*. Photograph by Scott Lebin, Marshall Brodien Collection

A few weeks after the feature was out, Marshall invited Mary for dinner at a restaurant in Roselle. "I had my son, Joey, with me," Mary says. "During dinner I watched Marshall showing him tricks and laughing with him, and I remember wondering why I was resisting this man. I thought I should at least give a relationship with him a chance.

"Marshall was kind not only to me, but to my three children, which was very important. Whenever we got together he listened to them. He brought laughter to my life. I could be too serious, organized, and quiet. Marshall was playful. He told bad jokes and silly stories. He was like a mad-professor, not worrying about the time of day or deadlines of any kind. He lived in the moment. I realized a good dose of that attitude could be healthy."

The retired wizard and the writer were married October 14, 1995.

41

Magic Boom of the '90s

In the mid 1990s, the Walt Disney Company granted a license to Harmony Toy to design and manufacture a line of magic products promoting the releases of three new Disney feature films. The first was a "Magic of Aladdin" set that sold at retail as a tie-in with the premier of *Aladdin*, the feature-length cartoon featuring the comedic voice talents of Robin Williams.

When Disney Studios released the remake of their 1961 animated feature *101 Dalmatians* as a live-action movie in 1996, a "101 Dalmatians Tons of Fun 10-Trick Set" appeared on the shelves of Disney Stores nationwide. Filling out the line of *101 Dalmatians* promotional offerings were three four-trick sets with magical effects designed to fit the characters of Pongo, Wizzer, and Fidgit, three of the spotted pups from the movie.

Prior to the release of the animated feature *The Hunchback of Notre Dame*, Harmony distributed four different *Hunchback*-theme magic products. "The Hunchback of Notre Dame Magic Collection" contained "10 Tricks from the Court of Miracles" and included a colorful cardboard table for kids to perform the Cups and Balls on, themed versions of Grandma's Necklace, Color Vision, the Spike Coin, Multiplying Coin Tray, and five other effects. The smaller four-trick sets — Bell Tower Tricks, Festival of Fools Tricks, and Storyteller's Stage Tricks — were designed as rack-displayed merchandise and contained tricks totally different from the bigger set.

The original tricks and clever ideas that Marshall contributed to the movie-theme merchandise did not go unrecognized by his fellow magicians. In an article reviewing the magic products available to the general public for the Christmas season, *MAGIC* magazine of December 1996 stated: "Harmony Toy has brought higher quality and better ideas to Disney, and Disney has brought great artwork and more money to Harmony Toy: the simple equation makes good magic sets."

The following summer, Marshall received a call from Siegfried & Roy. Their top-ticketed Las Vegas magical extravaganza at the Mirage had been playing to twice-nightly sold-out houses since its premiere in 1990. *Forbes* magazine now reported the dynamic duo's annual gross income as being $46 million. Although they had a Brodien-designed eight-trick set that served as their mainstay magic merchandise for the last five years, they wanted something new.

Siegfried & Roy had just opened their "Secret Garden," a jungle-like walk-through attraction that was home to their rare white tigers and lions, and they desired to have a magic product that would promote both their collection of exotic creatures and the magic of their stage extravaganza. "But you must understand, vee vant our box of tricks to be different," said Siegfried. "No cups und balls or dee bowls mit rice like all dee others have. *"Ja, das ist richtig!"* Roy said. "Ours must be original und feature dee animals."

Fresh off the Disney project, Marshall had lots of original concepts still spinning around, as well as some new ideas, and he scheduled a session with Harmony's graphic artist and package designer. It took about a month to put together a prototype set, as well as a couple of specialty magic items.

All of the effects in the 12-trick set were themed around the show animals and the creatures living in the Secret Garden. Playing cards were printed with colorful images of lions, tigers, and panthers. The sponges for the standard Multiplying Rabbits trick were sculpted to represent a family of soft white tigers. The classic Color Vision trick had six varieties of jungle cats on its cube. The names of some of S&R's tigers—Neva, Mirage, Sitarra, and Shasadee—were revealed in mind-reading mystery. There was an Invisible Tiger Tube, a Magic Tiger Food trick, Striped Tiger Prediction, the Tiger Escapes, and a half-dozen other exotic cat theme tricks. Brodien was given the go-ahead by Siegfried & Roy and the Mirage's marketing staff to produce the magic kit.

Another item that met with instant approval was Marshall's design of the Siegfried & Roy Illusion Box & White Tiger, a mirror-box effect that produced and vanished a small plush toy tiger. A quartet of items from the twelve-trick set were packaged as a smaller S&R Four Trick Set for rack display, as were the S&R Magician's Card Box and Deck, and three trick decks customized with the S&R logo.

A striking portrait of Siegfried & Roy, shot by Annie Lebovitz, was integrated into the colorful package design and, by autumn of 1997, these six Harmony Toy items were displayed in the gift shops on the Mirage property. They would be reordered and restocked year after year, remaining the principal magic merchandise for Siegfried & Roy for over six years. Even when the show would be forced to close in 2003, after Roy Horn experienced a near-fatal bite by one of the show's white tigers, the sets and magic items continued to be stocked and sold, as they had now become highly desirable collector's items.

• • •

Despite the skyrocketing magic sales at Harmony Toy, word on the street was that the company was for sale. But Marshall wasn't too bothered when he heard this. Some months prior, when he noticed that his five-year contract was about to expire, he'd expressed an interest to stay on for another five years, but only if the terms were right. Harmony's C.E.O. was against it, but his attorneys advised otherwise. They renewed immediately to keep Marshall happy. Apparently, legal counsel realized that if was indeed the plan to sell Harmony, a company now worth millions, they desperately needed Brodien's branding to seal any sort of deal.

The first company to express an interest in buying Harmony was Pressman Toy Corporation, a family-owned games manufacturer that came into prominence in the 1920s when it acquired the rights to Chinese checkers. The company had recent successes with games that were adaptations of TV properties such as *Wheel of Fortune*, *Jeopardy*, *Double Dare*, and *Scooby Doo*.

A Chicago-based toy and games company named Cadaco (an acronym for its founders *C*harles *a*nd *D*on *a*nd *Co*mpany), a subsidiary of Rapid Displays, Inc., was also interested. Cadaco had been around since 1935, and Tripoley, All-Star Baseball, numerous chalk games, and Care Bears board games were among the many products it manufactured and distributed.

By late 1996, both Pressman and Cadaco were at the point of making offers for the purchase of Harmony. Either way, both companies were obligated to accept Marshall's existing contract. Although he had no say-so in which offer should or would be considered, Marshall did make it known that he was not interested in spending much time in New York, a stipulation that came with the Pressman offer. Because Pressman's factory was in Brunswick, New Jersey, it meant he would be required to make periodic trips to the East Coast.

Naturally, on January 1, 1997, when the buyer for Harmony turned out to be Cadaco, with its manufacturing operations in the Windy City, Marshall was pleased. "I continued working from my home office creating product as I always had, and if I was needed for a production meeting or a decision, it was a quick and easy drive to the corporate offices downtown." Cadaco also decided to retain the services of Jimmy Baum as their national sales manager.

So, it was business as usual when Marshall and Jimmy appeared at the Al Gilley & Associates showrooms at the Toy Show in New York, showing and selling the newest magical creations from Cadaco.

• • •

Two years before the Cadaco buyout of Harmony, Brodien detected a shift in the patterns of the mass-market buyers at the annual Toy Show in New York. "I noticed that the representatives for the smaller toy chains were not placing orders for the new Marshall Brodien magic sets. They would stop by the showroom, look at the latest stuff and ask, 'Is this product in Toys "R" Us or Wal-Mart or Costco?' And when we would say yes, they would tell us they were not interested in ordering it."

It dawned on Marshall that the reason the independent toy stores did not want to carry the latest Marshall Brodien magic sets was because their competition, the Wal-Marts and other discounters popping up everywhere, were heavily marking down these products. He went to Jimmy Baum and said that Cadaco needed to be able to supply something different for these retailers — magic items that couldn't be found on the shelves of the national mass marketers.

Marshall suggested that they should come out with a Lance Burton product line, magic sets offered only to the smaller retailers and regional toy chains. "Jimmy liked the idea of creating our own competition and was willing to gamble on it," Marshall says. "We designed a Lance Burton 25 Trick Set and a 50 Trick Set, as well as some Lance Burton trick decks and single-packaged tricks that were sold exclusively to the independents and mid-sized chains." The Lance Burton magic products sold well, and this allowed the Marshall Brodien sets to remain exclusive in stores like Sam's Club and Costco ... at least for a while.

Two Christmases later, after carrying Marshall Brodien magic sets for four years straight, Costco was receptive to the idea of marketing and promoting a specially designed Lance Burton set. Lance had become a hot property. He was into the second year of his $100-million contract with the newly opened Monte Carlo resort in Las Vegas, and NBC had broadcast his second special, *Lance Burton: The Encounter*. And in 1997, holiday shoppers at Costco stores across the nation purchased 100,000 of the new 100-tricks-with-a-video sets manufactured by Cadaco. For the next five years, Lance's line of magic sets, including a couple of 100 trick sets, would become a fixture at Costco, keeping Marshall busy designing and creating new items, as well as producing and directing the different teaching videos that appeared in the attractively packaged sets each season.

The instructional videos that accompanied the Lance Burton magic sets marketed through Costco were all taped in the green room of Lance's theater at the Monte Carlo. *Photograph by John Moehring, Marshall Brodien Collection*

• • •

At the turn of the century, *MAGIC* magazine published a one-year-long multiple-installment feature called "The Century." Each month, a series of tributes appeared saluting "The 100 significant people in magic who have influenced the performing art in America during the 20th century." The magicians acknowledged ranged from past masters like Houdini, Kellar, Blackstone, Thurston, Cardini, and Dai Vernon, to contemporary wizards such as Doug Henning, Lance Burton, David Copperfield, and Siegfried & Roy. In the September 1999 issue, Marshall was added to the prestigious list. Next to a photograph of Marshall holding a Lance Burton magic set was a paragraph that described how Marshall was responsible for getting multitudes of Americans interested in the art of magic: "The first prop that Mrs. Burton bought for her son was a deck of TV Magic Cards. And apparently she wasn't the only person making such a purchase after seeing Marshall Brodien's famous card trick commercials of the '70s. Multitudes were interested in becoming card tricksters, and over the years millions of decks of TV Magic Cards were

In addition to being chosen as one of "the 100 significant people in magic who have influenced the performing arts in America during the 20th century" by *MAGIC* magazine in 1999, Marshall also received the 2000 Merlin Award, "For Keeping the Dream Alive" from the International Magician's Society. *Photograph by Spellman Studios, Geneva, IL, Marshall Brodien Collection*

sold. Perhaps of greater importance was the fact that Brodien took the success of his electronic-era Svengali pitch and went on to market ever bigger and better things magical. With the establishment of the Marshall Brodien Magic Company he constantly reshaped the traditional box of tricks and through a determined and persistent campaign of direct-broadcast advertising cultivated millions more magic enthusiasts."

To cap off the century, the International Magician's Society presented Brodien with a 2000 Merlin Award "For Keeping the Dream Alive." The gold Oscar-like statuette carries the inscription: "Marshall Brodien has made more magic accessible to youngsters and aspiring magicians than any individual since educational toy maker A.C. Gilbert, the creator of the legendary Mysto Magic sets."

42

Farewell to 40 Years of Fun

The plug was pulled on the *Bozo Show* in 2001. But its fate had long been sealed. In 1994, not long after Marshall left the program, WGN-TV changed the five-times-a-week format to a once-a-week Sunday morning program. The program was later made "educational," following a Federal Communications Commission mandate requiring broadcast television stations to air a minimum three hours per week of educational and informational children's programs. The newly named *Bozo Super Sunday Show* hung on for five years. On March 23, WGN-TV announced that the program would not return and a farewell show would be produced that summer.

Bozo: 40 Years of Fun! was broadcast July 14. The primetime special paid homage to WGN-TV's legacy of having created the most popular, locally produced, fully licensed, longest-running, nationally televised Bozo show ever. The media had a heyday with the final studio event. CNN cameras captured the glorious goodbye and dispatched the news to the world via satellite. Bozo's farewell was Dan Rather's signoff on *The CBS Evening News*. The Associated Press wire services headline read, "Boomers Reminisce as Bozo Bows Out." Both *Newsweek* and *Time* ran full-color, full-page tributes. The show even made the Top Ten List on the *Late Show with David Letterman*.

Brodien donned the Wizzo the Wizard makeup and costume for the farewell show and asked his magician friend Mark Holstein to join him for an unconventional staging of the classic illusion, Backstage with the Magician. Wizzo and Mark allowed a camera behind the scenes as they "explained" how Mark's wife, Sue, was going to disappear from a cabinet. And just about the time the studio audience and viewers at home had surmised, "It's easy, once you know the secret," out popped Sandy the Tramp. A total magical

When Bozo show writer/producer Don Sandburg returned to appear on the *40 Years of Fun!* farewell special, he was magically produced by magician Mark Holstein (left). Marshall Brodien Jr. assisted and, as always, Marshall appeared as Wizzo (right). *Marshall Brodien Collection*

surprise! Sue had indeed vanished, and in her place was Don Sandburg, the show's original writer, producer, and performer, who'd flown in from the West Coast to appear as Sandy, the clown role he'd created 40 years ago.

The special was generously spiked with hilarious video highlights from the days when the show aired as *Bozo's Circus* and starred Bob Bell as Bozo, Ned Locke as Ringmaster Ned, Roy Brown as Cooky the Clown, Sandburg as Sandy, and, of course, Marshall as the "Doody-doody-doing" mystic from the far away land of Arobia.

The farewell fling saw juicy pies of shaving cream fly through the air with the greatest of ease. The famous Grand Prize Game was rigged making sure a toddler in the audience was the surefire winner. Joey "Bozo" D'Auria asked, "Whatta they gonna do, fire me?" All stops were pulled out as longtime producer Al Hall joined the cast, crew, and crowd, parading about the studio for the final signature "Grand March." Rather than a weepy tribute, the last *Bozo Show* on earth was a joyous celebration.

The cast of the July 14, 2001, farewell show (from left): Robin Eurich (Rusty the-Clown), Andy Mitran (Mr. Music), Joey D'Auria (Bozo), Marshall Brodien (Wizzo the Wizard), and Don Sandburg (Sandy the Clown). *Marshall Brodien Collection*

• • •

Beginning July 3, 2002, the Society of American Magicians held a four-day convention in New York City, celebrating the 100th anniversary of the founding of the organization. The 162-page printed program carried a letter of welcome to the 1,200 attendees. The executive director of the convention, Bradley M. Jacobs, wrote, "This week you will attend a number of 'firsts' for any magic convention. The U.S. Postal Service is dedicating a new 37¢ Houdini Stamp concurrent with our Centennial. Jay Marshall, the Dean of the Society of American Magicians, has a few stories of the Deans he has known. And Marshall Brodien, a member of the Society for three decades, will tell about his multi-faceted career in magic...."

David Copperfield showed up to take part in the First Day Issue Ceremony of the Houdini stamp. Jay Marshall who'd held the honorary title of Dean of the S.A.M. since 1992, recounted stories of the seven previous Deans: Harry Kellar, Frederick Eugene Powell, Al Baker, Jean Hugard, Herman Hanson, Werner Dornfield, and H. Adrian Smith. And remarkably, Jay had personal encounters and friendships of all of them except Kellar, who died when young Jay was only three.

On Thursday, July 4th, at 10:30 A.M., almost every one of the 1,000 seats in the Grand Ballroom of the New York Hilton was filled when S.A.M. Convention-show producer Hank Moorehouse introduced Marshall. While there were some scripted questions to get things rolling, Marshall's spontaneous and witty answers soon transformed the session into a rollicking funhouse ride.

"Is it true you were only 17," Hank asked, "when you worked as the talker for a ten-in-one-show at an amusement park?"

"Yes, for the freak show at Riverview Park in 1951," Marshall said, taking the microphone and sliding into his glib sideshow pitch: "Once inside, you'll see Priscilla the Monkey Girl with long shaggy black hair just like a monkey ... two rows of teeth in the upper jaw like the anthropoid ape ... pouches in the sides of her mouth where she can store food for days at a time if necessary...." Smiles in the audience full of tricksters turned to chuckles as Marshall went into his ballyhoo for Emmett the Alligator-skinned Man. And the chuckles became belly laughs as he told of Tiny Carter, the World's Fattest Man.

He then regaled the audience with his tales of working at the Magic Lounge in mob-controlled Cicero, Illinois, where he did tricks nightly for mob leaders. Because many members of the assemblage were unaware that Brodien was a stage hypnotist, they were in awe as he told of his years as a hypnotic headliner at his own Mystic Club and the posh Cairo Supper Club in Chicago. And most were surprised to learn that Marshall was a pioneer in the trade-show field, being the first magician to perform scripted shows with illusions.

When Moorehouse asked Brodien to tell about how he started pitching magic on television, it was the cue to run the very first 1969 TV Magic Cards commercial. This was followed by various vintage TV Magic Ltd. commercials. Viewing these 20- and 30-year-old commercials was nostalgic for many; a substantial number of the magicians present had their first interest in magic sparked by either a TV Magic set or a Marshall Brodien Magic Company product. And when Marshall revealed that the whole thing started with a risky investment of $5,000 to buy airtime to pitch trick decks of cards, it made the success story as inspirational as it was unbelievable.

Remarking that Marshall was too modest to tell exactly how many TV

Magic Cards had been marketed over the years, Hank said, "Marshall will tell you he's sold *a few million* decks. But I know for a fact that ten years ago the Academy of Magical Arts presented Marshall with a Special Fellowship Award and there was a plaque that stated: 'Marshall Brodien is probably best known for pitching his TV Magic Cards on television, and he is personally responsible for getting millions of people interested in the art of magic by selling over 15-million decks of his cards...'"

"That's sort of right," Marshall interrupted. "It's really *a few million* more than that." The crowd laughed, and then Marshall explained, "Over the years, the distributors for the shops would call and ask what part of the country TV Magic Cards commercials would be running. They knew that the magic stores in those areas would want to have Svengali Decks in stock. That's because the drug stores or retail outlets where we placed the cards would sell out. People would go to magic shops and ask if they had the trick cards that were being advertised on TV. Well, the dealers could say, 'We have this Svengali Deck which actually does the same thing.' So, there had to be millions more of the trick decks that were sold by magic shops across the country as result of the commercials all those years."

The session concluded with the screening of select segments of Brodien playing Wizzo on the *Bozo Show*, including a montage of bloopers where Wizzo's tricks went a little differently than planned. In answer to a question from the audience as to how many appearances Marshall had made on the *Bozo Show*, Marshall replied, "I did 38 shows as Marshall Brodien before I started doing Wizzo. But during the 27 years I appeared as Wizzo, I did somewhere between 2,800 and 3,000 shows, and performed magic on just about every one of them."

"I think it's safe to say," Moorehouse concluded, "that with the unbelievable amount of shows as Wizzo and with the thousands upon thousands of times that Marshall Brodien commercials aired nationwide, Marshall has been seen on television more than any magician in the history of magic." The audience responded with a resounding ovation.

After the session, the line of autograph seekers stretching into the hotel hallway was over an hour long. Many of the people wanted their programs personally inscribed with Marshall's words, "It's easy, once you know the secret...."

43

Sh-h-h-h... It's a Secret

One of Marshall's best-kept secrets — his understanding of the power of persistence and determination — is a secret weapon he didn't recognize until he was in his 30s. In 1964, Marshall was at the apex of his career as a nightclub hypnotist. It was the year he began his third one-year contract with the Cairo Supper Club, where the marquee proclaimed him AMERICA'S MOST ENTERTAINING HYPNOTIST. Then, five months into the return engagement, a firebomb was tossed through the front window of the nightspot. The club was forever shuttered. Its stellar hypnotist was out of a job.

The incident came at a time when Marshall was seriously considering dropping stage hypnosis in favor of seeking more work as a magician. He continued to do hypnotic shows at the Top of the Mark and the Prime Steak House in Chicago, while his booking agent Howard Schultz started lining up lucrative fair dates and corporate engagements for the magic and illusion act. Nightclub and stage hypnosis was becoming a part of Marshall's past.

One afternoon in late June, Schultz called and said, "Marsh, I've got you booked next Wednesday night for a good-paying private party. But you're not going to be too excited when I tell you the client is insistent that you do hypnotism. They say they don't want the magic. But, like I say, this one is for big bucks." When Marshall heard how big the big bucks were, he told Schultz that it was "no problem whatsoever" doing hypnosis. But he added that he'd bring along his close-up case, just in case somebody wanted to see some tricks.

"It was an after-dinner show," Marshall remembers, "so I didn't go to the Lake Shore Drive address that Schultz had given me until six after that evening. The building was a fancy high-rise overlooking Lake Michigan. When I pulled into the driveway a uniformed doorman told me that someone would look after my car." The elevator operator knew Brodien by name and took him directly to the floor where the party was. The doors parted and he stepped directly into the foyer of an elegantly decorated apartment that appeared to occupy a whole floor of the building. "A butler welcomed me and offered to take me to the bar, where he said I could relax while the guests finished dinner."

As the bartender poured Marshall a drink, he noticed what appeared to be a capital "M" etched on the cocktail glass. In fact, every piece of glassware on the shelf over the back bar had the same arched "M," which prompted Marshall to remark, "It looks like all your glasses are from McDonald's."

"Yes, sir," the bartender said with a smile, "I guess no one told you that you're in the home of Ray Kroc, the founder of McDonald's."

"Wow, I had no idea," Marshall said, as he picked up his jaw from the floor. "My agent only told me I was the after-dinner entertainment for a private party. He said nothing about it being for Mr. Kroc." He took a sip of his drink and asked how many people had been invited. When the bartender told him there were only 14 of Mr. Kroc's close associates, Marshall joked, "You better fix me another drink."

Marshall says, "It's difficult to do a show of hypnosis for a crowd that small. And it didn't help matters that the show was being kept a secret from the guests that night. It's always better if the audience knows they are going to be seeing a hypnotist. It builds anticipation and mentally prepares them for what's going to happen."

When it was showtime, he was escorted to the spacious parlor where the guests had assembled. He was formally introduced as the surprise entertainment for the evening. "I went into my usual explanation — 'It is *you*, the fine people who have gathered here this evening who will be the show.' — setting the stage for the hypnotism. Fortunately, two couples volunteered immediately and sat in the chairs that had been placed up front, and it didn't take long before two of the gentlemen were in a deep sleep." One of the subjects was Kroc's accountant; the other was the franchise manager for McDonald's stores in Florida.

The hypnotic bit that had the group laughing the loudest was the Hundred Dollar Test. The mesmerized accountant fervently attempted to pick up a $100 bill from the seat of a chair where Marshall had gently placed it, but couldn't budge the bill even when he was told it was a bonus from Ray Kroc. And the tried-and-true Bubbles La Rue bit, where the mild-mannered franchise manager shed his coat and tie and almost his trousers as he did an exotic dance, had them screaming for more.

Ray invited Marshall to join the party as they moved into the living room to have a nightcap. Marshall asked Ray if he thought his guests would like to see some magic; he only needed to take the elevator down to his car to get his attaché case full of tricks. For the next 40 minutes, Brodien was in the spotlight again, wowing the folks with trick after trick.

Ray had a fascination with show business. He told Marshall about his early days as a jazz pianist and how, as a young man, he had a yearning to make his living as a musician, hit the road and play with the big bands. "The closest I came to living that dream was in the 1930s," he said. "I was working for the Lilly Tulip Cup Co., and I got a job as musical director at WGES, where there was a piano in the studio. I sold cups by day and played piano on the radio at night."

When Ray Arthur Kroc was 14 years old, his father took him to a phrenologist, who said, "Your son is best suited to working in the food service industry." By 1954, Ray had cut a deal with San Bernardino, California drive-in restaurateurs Maurice and Richard McDonald to set up a chain of fast-food operations based on their assembly-line preparation of hamburgers and milkshakes. His first franchise opened in Des Plaines, Illinois. Six years later, when he bought out the McDonald brothers for $2.7 million, Kroc mortgaged his home and took out so many loans that the original $2.7 million cost $14 million to pay back. But in less than two years, he would make many millions more.

It was near midnight when Ray pulled Marshall aside, telling him he wanted to show him a secret that few people knew of. Walking over to an alcove adjacent to the living room, he pushed what looked like an elevator button. The oak wall panels parted to reveal a huge Wurlitzer pipe organ. After making sure his guests had a fresh round of drinks, it was the host's turn to entertain. Ray's mini concert started with the classics (Rachmaninoff as taught to him by his mother when he was five), segued to a Benny Goodman medley (with an abundance of jazz riffs), and ended with a rousing sing-along of "Take Me Out to the Ballgame" (a huge baseball fan, Kroc would buy the San Diego Padres in ten years).

When it was time to call it a night, Jane Dobbins Green, Ray's wife at the time, escorted Marshall to the elevator and thanked him profusely for making the party a rousing success. She gave him a kiss on the cheek and slipped a $100 tip into the breast pocket of his tuxedo jacket.

• • •

Three weeks after the evening of the party, a parcel was delivered to Marshall's doorstep. It was from Ray Kroc's office. There was no letter or note inside the box, only a gift-wrapped package that contained a simplistic crystal-clear glass plaque engraved with a familiar quotation:

> *Press on. Nothing in the world can take the place of persistence. Talent will not; nothing is more common than unsuccessful men with talent. Genius will not; unrewarded*

genius is almost a proverb. Education will not; the world is full of educated derelicts. Persistence and determination alone are omnipotent.

As Marshall reread the words, he presumed that Ray was sharing another secret, and deduced that the poetic message was a clue to Ray's success formula, perhaps a bit of entrepreneurial advice offered in appreciation for entertaining at the party.

In truth, those words on perseverance are attributed to the 30th President of the United States, Calvin Coolidge, who wrote, "The slogan 'Press on' has solved and always will solve the problems of the human race." That very quotation became a guiding light for Ray Kroc as he grew his business. When Marshall met him on that summer evening in 1964, there were 548 McDonald's restaurants across America that had sold over a billion hamburgers; by the time Kroc passed away in 1984, there would be 7,516 McDonald's worldwide and the 50 billionth burger had long since been served.

Marshall never again talked with or heard from Ray Kroc. Yet it's safe to say that the one encounter with the man, as fleeting as it may have been, was a mentoring experience — one that profoundly influenced the career path that Marshall ultimately pursued.

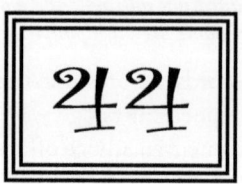

Pressing On

When Marshall answered his phone early one morning in March of 2004 it was his friend Steve Chezaday calling. Chezaday, a rock-'n'-roll illusionist who's also an accomplished magic craftsman, had been commissioned to build a new Blade Box for a fundraising performance that Marshall was doing that weekend.

"I've just given it the third and final coat of lacquer, and I plan to deliver it tomorrow as promised," Steve said.

"I can't wait to see it," Marshall said. "Why don't you bring it out to the house this afternoon?" He was anxious to see how the new design improvements for the metal blades looked and wanted to give the illusion a few run-throughs. But Steve advised that the paint should have at least a half-day to dry before attempting any kind of rehearsal.

Marshall countered with, "Well, the drive here is about an hour, right? So if you pack it up this afternoon and leave your place around five o'clock, that's more than a half-day, right?"

Marshall was steadfast. After all, he's kept that plaque he received 40 years ago—the one with the quotation exhorting "persistence and determination"—hanging next his desk and by the telephone.

Chezaday showed up at four, saying he wanted to beat the rush-hour traffic. He unloaded the new Blade Box and helped set it up in the garage. By sunset, Marshall had two successful rehearsals under his belt.

• • •

Brodien continued to consult with Cadaco, creating innovative new magic products and advising the company on marketing strategies, through the year he turned 73. Then, capitalizing on the popularity of DVDs as a teaching tool, he began releasing some of his select secrets to the magic fraternity. As the 40th anniversary of TV Magic Cards approaches, he's seriously considering returning to the tube with a flashy yet nostalgic commercial that pitches those wondrous magic tricks that guarantee, "You'll have hours of fun entertaining your family and friends."

The focus of Brodien's performing has been fundraisers and benefits. For five years in a row, he's headlined and, along with magician friend Mark Holstein, has served as the master of ceremonies for *Nothing up my Sleeve*, an annual fundraiser produced for the Rau Center for the Performing Arts in Crystal Lake. For some of these shows, Marshall's son, Marshall Jr., takes to the spotlight doing a magic act of his own, and on one show performed an illusion that produced Marshall's six-year-old niece.

Marshall's wife, Mary, who maintains a study in their home and enjoys a career of writing and producing inspirational books, has also become the "lovely assistant" and regular "damsel in distress" for Marshall's recurrent magic shows. Whether it be a fundraiser for the annual Make a Difference Day or a benefit for the Lions Club to raise money to buy wheelchairs for disabled children, Mary is there onstage with Marshall, slipping in and out of the Blade Box or jumping from one illusion to another with grace and aplomb.

In addition, Brodien diligently promotes these events. Because of his connections at WGN-TV, he's able to go on the *Morning News* program just about any time he wants, perform magic and talk about the upcoming production, and gain publicity that is truly invaluable.

• • •

If you look at the circled dates on the pages of Marshall's engagement calendar, it's apparent he's not considering slowing down anytime soon. So, how does he keep on keepin' on?

Of course, if you ask him, you'll hear his snappy patter line, "It's easy, once you know the secret." But that clever catchphrase that much of the nation believed was merely a slogan to sell Marshall Brodien and magic is the true key to his successful and happy lifestyle.

The real secret is there's *more than one* secret. Along the way, Marshall came to the realization that the traits of persistence and determination, as touted in that famous gentleman's quotation, are not always "omnipotent" as decreed. It takes more. For him to overcome obstacles and achieve his goals over the years, it's required an enormous amount of talent. He's had to cash in on a bit of that unrewarded genius he possesses. He's prevailed thanks to

Marshall's four children gather on Father's Day 2005. Seated in front are Anita Brazeau, who's a hairdresser and mother of three children, Anna, Michael, and Matthew; and Christine Torrey, mother of two daughters, Angel and Olivia. Standing to the left of Marshall is John Wanic, chef and restaurant owner; to the right, Marshall W. Brodien, an employee with United Airlines who regularly performs magic shows. *Photograph by Timothy Whaely, Lisle, IL, Marshall Brodien Collection*

his education, even if it's been an education of the "street-wise" kind, as Mary admiringly calls it. And, oh yes ... from time to time, it's been necessary to call upon the powers of Wizzo's Stone of Zanzibar and those magic words of "Doody, doody, do." Sure, it's been easy for Marshall, once he learned how to apply all those secrets.

• • •

Index

A. Eicoff & Company 162, 165, 170, 173, 192, 212
Abbott's Magic Company 12, 29, 74, 114
ABC Speaker (hypnotic stunt) 100–101
Academy of Magical Arts "Special Fellowship Award" 223, 249
Aiuppa, Joey "The Doves," *a.k.a.* Joey "O'Brien" 42, 49, 55, 170, 184, 187
Alan, Don 14, 62, 109
Amarico the Anatomical Wonder 26
American Gas Association (trade show) 144
American Museum of Magic 8
Anastos, Bill 98, 99, 104, 167
Arlen, Michael 196
Armando, Joe 126, 127
Arnold, Lieutenant General W.H. 79–81, 86
Ash, Ada 46, 47, 53
Ash, Mr. 212
August Brothers 212, 215

Babetch, Burt 163, 166, 212
Baer, Bobby 12–13, 18, 21–22, 28, 29, 31, 48, 62, 153
Balster, Tim 212, 215
Balzac, Eddie 97
Banning, George 38, 42, 43, 45, 47, 48
Barz, Mike 6
Baum, Jimmy 223–224, 228–229, 241, 242
Baumgarten, Robin 6
Beacon Inn 56, 59, 61, 62, 71
Bell, Robert Lewis "Bob" (Bozo) 108, 110, 146, 147, 149, 159, 161, 184, 196, 199, 206, 207, 209, 220, 246
Bennett, Tony 138–140
Berg, Bob 163
Berg, Joe 11, 29–30
Berks, Stewart v
Berland, Sam 11
Berman, "Silent Sam" 36

Best, Dick 21–22, 24, 28, 34, 36, 151
Bethlehem Steel (trade shows) 131–134, 148, 153, 207, 209
Big Top Band 108, 112, 121, 196
Bilandic, Mayor Michael 191
Bishop, Billy 59, 109, 179–180
Bixby, Bill 8, 194
Blackstone, Harry, Jr. 8, 196–197, 220
Blade Box (illusion) 22–24, 46–47, 52–53, 55, 59, 66, 133, 254
Blaine, David 3
Bliwas, Ron 162, 163
Bombacino, Sue 170
Boston Nocturne Club 88–94, 151, 203
Boyer, Ted 98
Bozo and His Friends (WHBQ-TV, Nashville) 109
Bozo: 40 Years of Fun 3, 245–46, 247
Bozo Show v, 1, 6, 196–199, 206, 207, 208, 218, 219, 223, 234, 235, 245, 249
Bozo Show 30th Anniversary Special 220
Bozo Super Sunday Show 245
Bozo the Clown 108–109, 148, 198, 207, 208, 215
Bozo the Clown (WGN-TV, Chicago) 109
Bozo: The Man Behind the Makeup (documentary) 207
Bozo's Circus (WGN-TV, Chicago) 108, 109–111, 114–115, 127, 128 143, 146, 148, 161, 170, 183, 184, 196, 205, 246
Bozo's Holiday Circus 129
Brindle, Robert R. 178, 180
Brodien, Anita Leah (daughter) 126, 256
Brodien, Arthur Olaf (father) 91–92
Brodien, Charles (brother) 203
Brodien, Christine (daughter) 148, 256
Brodien, Marshall Walter (son) 142, 246, 255, 256

Index

Brodien, Mary K. Doyle v, 1, 234–238, 255, 257
Brodien, Mildred "Millie" Genevieve Erickson (mother) 9, 91–92
Broomstick Suspension (illusion) 90, 91, 136, 137, 138, 160
Brown, Roy (Cooky the Clown) 6, 142, 143, 145, 146, 147, 184, 196, 199, 205–206, 207, 208, 209, 212, 218–222, 234, 246
Bruno 59
Bubbles La Rue (hypnotic stunt) 105–106, 251
Burton, Hilma 222, 243
Burton, Lance 8, 222–223, 224, 225–228, 242, 243

Cadaco 8, 241–242, 254–255
Cairo Supper Club (Chicago) 1, 4, 96, 98–107, 110, 113, 115, 120, 121, 126, 128–29, 167, 248, 250
Capitol Records 108
Capone, Al 42
Carey, Rick 151–152, 153, 154–155, 156, 158–159, 162, 165–166, 170, 173–174, 175, 177, 192, 204
Carnival of Wonders 59, 60
Carter, Tiny (World's Fattest Man) 26, 248
Cerone, Jackie "The Lackey" 7, 42, 170–172, 185–187
Chezaday, Steve 254
Chicago Magic Center *see* Treasure Chest
Christie, Tony and Joe 56, 58
Circus Stage Show (St. Croix, Virgin Islands) 190–191
Clay, Rodney 63–64
Cleveland, Dexter v
Columbia House (division of CBS) 174–175
Columbia House of Magic's Magician's Secret Files 175–177
Colvig, Pinto 108
Cooky the Clown *see* Brown, Roy
Cooky the Clown Makeup Kit 212
Coolidge, Calvin 253
Coon, George 11
Copperfield, David 232, 247
Cosby, Bill 136–138, 236
Costco 242, 243
Crandall, Clarke ("The Senator") 36, 38–42, 45, 48, 54–55, 59, 107
Crawford, General Joseph B. 77–78, 83–84, 86
Culp, Robert 137

D'Amato, Cus 115–118
D'Amico, Carmen 171
Daniels, Brett 215
Dante (hypnotist) 97
Darwin, Gary 227
D'Auria, Joey (Bozo) 208, 209, 220, 222, 246, 247
De Yip Loo 25, 109, 130

Dean, Dr. Michael 97, 98
Diamond, Frank "The Immune" 42
dice stacking 40–41
Dietrich, Bud 130
Dobritch, Al 46
du Maurier, George (*Trilby*) 150
Dunn, Benny 121

Ed Drane Company 157–158
Eicoff, Alvin "Al" 162–166, 174–175, 192, 200–202, 204, 211, 217, 226, 228–229
Electric Chair (illusion) 47, 55, 59, 140, 142
Electro the Human Dynamo 27
Ellie Frankel Quintet 137, 139
Elliott, Bruce 107
Emmett the Alligator-skinned Man 26, 248
Emmy (television award) 7, 220, 222
Ernie the Magnificent 178
Erikson, Carl August (grandfather) 92
Eurich, Robin (Rusty the Clown) 247
Evans, Ted (The English Giant) 36–37
Evanswood, Terry 215, 235
Everhart, Frank 107

Fah, Freddie 113
FBI 188–190
Feder, Robert 206
Feld, Irvin and Kenneth 194
Fields, Totie 140
fire eating 34–36, 47, 59, 64, 78
The 4811 (also The 4813) 42, 54
Fox, Karrell 135
Flaim Brothers 99
Francavilla, Captain Anthony F. 71
Frasier, Woody 136
Fun, Inc. 164

Galli the Gorilla 146
Gardner, Martin 61
Garfield Goose and Friends 145
Gem City Shows 56, 57
Giancana, Sam 42 82, 211
Giannotti, Vic 211
Gilbert, A.C. (Mysto Magic sets) 244
Gilly, Al 218, 223
Girl in Fishbowl (illusion) 216
Giuzio, Gene 80
Grand Prize Game 198–199, 220, 246
Greca, Armelia 167
Green, Brenda 117
Green, Jane Dobbins 252
Grippo, Jimmy 115, 117
Gutterman, Art and Steve 192, 217
Gutterman, Manny 163, 165, 174, 217
Gwynne, Anne 114
Gwynne, Jack 7, 36, 47, 61, 62, 114, 125, 191

Hackett, Bobby 138
Hall, Al v, 110, 112, 184, 191, 196, 199, 207, 209, 222, 234, 246

Index

Harmon, Larry 109, 161
Harmony Toy, Ltd. 8, 223–224, 228, 239–240, 241
Head, Andy 215
Hedberg, Bob 215
Hefner, Hugh 120–121
Hefner, Keith 120
Higa, Bob 212
Hogue, Bob 218
Holetite Pencil 84
Holstein, Mark and Sue 245, 255
Home Shopping Network 8, 200–202, 203
Hoover, Jeff 3–6
Houssels, J.K.
Hull, Burling 150

Ice Royals 124–126, 129
Illinois State Athletic Commission 115–118
Immel, Michael (Spiffy Q. Fahrquahrrr) 234
International Brotherhood of Magicians 59
International Magicians Society (Merlin Award) 244

Jacobs, Bradley M. 247
Jaffee, Bob 232–233
Jamboree on Ice 113
James, Al 212
Jenkins, Jackie Hoyt (The Armless Wonder) 26
John, Raymond 25
Johnson, Colonel Lawrence A. 65, 74, 77–78

Kaliban, Bob 80
Kapos, Perry 168, 182–183, 210–211
Karl the Bomber 95–96
Karris, Jimmy 88, 92, 95
Kennedy, John F. 126
Kitzing, Fred 131
Kitzing, Inc. 130–131, 134, 144, 147
Knoble, Ken 61, 71
Kodell, Jack 113
Konrad, Paul 5
Kosmer, Eddie 89–90, 92, 96, 121, 203–204
Kroc, Ray 251–253

Ladshaw, Bill 209
Lamb, Gil 109
Lance Burton: World Champion Magician (TV special) 230–233
Lancer Restaurant (also Lancer's) 167, 170, 178, 181–184, 190, 210
Lane, John 117
Lee, Paul 215
Leibovitz, Annie 240
Lennox Industries (trade shows) 134
Le Roy, W.D. 150
Lieberman, Don ("Mickey the Mook") 20–21
Liston, Sonny 115–119
Livingston, Alan W. 108, 109

Locke, Ned 108, 110, 146, 151–152, 154, 220, 246
Lund, Robert 8

Magic Cards 152–154
Magic, Inc. (Chicago) 179
Magic Lounge (Cicero, IL) 1, 7, 38–49, 50, 54, 56, 168, 187, 248
Magic Mansion (TV program proposal) 205–206
Magic Moments, Inc. 227, 230, 232
Manno, Carmen 44, 45
Marino, Tony 26, 34
Mark the Magnificent 212
Marlo, Ed 14, 171
Marshall, Jay v, 38, 10, 158, 179, 247, 248
Marshall Brodien & Company (illusion act) 123, 129
Marshall Brodien & Cooky (act) 6, 160
Marshall Brodien Magic Company 8, 148, 192, 200, 212, 217–218, 223, 244, 248
Marshall Brodien Magic Shop (Old Chicago) 179–180
Marshall Brodien Magic Show (set for HSN) 200–201
Marshall Brodien 100 Trick Set with Video 229
Marshall Brodien's World's Greatest Mind Reading Secrets Revealed for the First Time (set) 212
Masini, Alfred 226–227
Mastro, Frankie 117
Mate, Ken v, 212, 215, 216
McDaniels, Grace (The Mule-faced Woman) 27
McDonald's (restaurants) 252–253
McGraw, Bob 79
McIntire, Merl 75–77
McKnight, Doug v
Melinda *see* Saxe, Melinda
Meyer, Frank 151
The Mike Douglas Show 136–140, 236
Miller, Ed 11
Miller, John 232
Mitran, Andy (Mr. Music) 208, 222, 247
Moncrief, "Tex" 90
Montana, Montie, Jr. 129
Moon Magic (TV pilot) 142–143
Moorehouse, Hank 248–249
Motivational Media 227, 230, 232–233
Munari, Geno 227
Murphy, Stanley 20
Mystic Club 92–97, 248

National Association of Broadcasters 148
National Association of Homebuilders Show (Chicago) 130
National Magic Company 59
Nelson, Robin 113
Nielsen, Norm 164, 193, 212, 225, 226

262 Index

Niesen, Tom 212
Nye, Louis 138–140

Ogee O'Saturday ("The White Hindu") 34–35, 47
Okito (Theo Bamberg) 11, 29–30, 47, 59, 61, 62
Old Chicago (Bolingbrook, IL) 178–180
Olson, Sue 169, 173, 190, 210, 214, 216
One Hundred Dollar Test (hypnotic stunt) 99, 251
Orban, Dr. Thomas 72
Ouellet, Gary 232–233
Owens-Corning Fiberglas (trade shows) 130, 134

Palace of Wonders (Riverview Park sideshow) 20–21, 22, 24–25, 27
Pappas, George v
Patterson, Floyd 115–119
Paul, Johnny 38, 54–55
Paul, Rose 48, 49, 54
The Phoenix (magic publication) 107
Pillory Escape (illusion) 134–135
Pillsbury Sweet Cream Pancake & Waffle Mix (marketing film) 141–142
Pistone, Jumping Joe 42
Platt, Johnny ("Hadji Baba") 59, 107
Playboy (magazine) 120–121
Playboy Club 120–121
Pogo (boxing kangaroo) 47, 50–51, 52
Potash, Larry 5–6
"Press On" 252–253
Pressman Toy Corp. 241
Priscilla the Monkey Girl 26, 248
Professor Stevenson 18, 61
Pudney, Gary 232–233

Quartucci, Manny 42, 48, 59
QVC (cable shopping network) 202

Rainey, Tom 13, 29
Ray Rayner & His Friends 145, 196
Rayner, Ray (Oliver O. Oliver) 110, 111, 220
Reveen, Peter 225–226
Reversible Girl 25–26
Reynolds Metals (trade shows) 134
Richards, Dean 5
Richiardi Jr. 123
Rigid Lady (hypnotic stunt) 101–104, 105, 117
Riverview Park 4, 7, 20–28, 30, 33, 36, 41, 45, 46, 111, 134, 143, 178, 194, 215, 236, 248
Roach, Hal 109
Rocklin Irving & Associates 31–32
Rogue (magazine) 107
Romano, Chuck v
Rosen, Larry 136, 137
Rose's *Original* Magic Lounge (Cicero, IL) 49, 55

Rostenkowski, Daniel 129
Roy, Marvyn 113
Ryan, Dick 130, 135

Sandburg, Don (Sandy the Tramp) v, 110, 111, 112, 127, 142–143, 144, 145, 147, 148, 156–157, 162, 188, 190, 199, 203, 204, 205–206, 220, 234, 245–46, 247
Saxe, Bonnie 227
Saxe, Melinda 227
Saylor, Sid 108
Scarda, Judith "Judy" (first wife) 114–115, 118, 121–122, 123, 124–126, 136, 137, 142, 167
Schmidt, George 143
Schulien, Chuck 212
Schultz, Howard 109–110, 128, 130, 144, 250
Schultz the Undertaker 17
Sciortino, Joe 88, 92
Seebach, David 212
Serpentina the Snake Girl 22–24, 53, 59, 65
Sherman, Jim 11
Siegfried & Roy 8, 193–195, 224, 225, 227, 228, 240
Simplex Rising Cards 154
Siros, Bill 90
Smith, Lindsay v
snake-proofing army campsite 64–66
Society of American Magicians 35, 39, 40, 59, 247
Spera, Tom 212
The Sphinx (magic publication) 11
Stancraft Playing Card Company 158–159
Star, Hedy Jo 56–58, 84–85
Stone of Zanzibar 145–146, 199, 259
straitjacket escapes 74–77, 111–112, 236
Substitution Trunk (illusion) 136, 137, 191, 220–222
Super Circus Animal Acts 46–47
Sutton, Clarence 175
Svengali Deck 150–152, 154, 157–158, 249
sword swallowing 34–35, 36, 59
Szasz, Al 46, 50–53, 56, 136

Tellez, Roseanne 5
Temple of Angee (illusion), *a.k.a.* Temple of Benares 113–115, 125, 136, 191
Theobald, Don 13, 25, 62
Thomas, Frazier 196, 198, 207
Thompson, Johnny 147, 164, 170
Three Card Monte 16
Three-Legged Man 26
Thrifty Drug Company 156–157, 162
Tiny Carter (World's Fattest Man) 26
Tony Smith and his Aristocrats 126
Torrey, Paul 227
Torsberg, Vic 59
Torsen & Ellen 59
ToTo's 213, 214–216
Traub, Jules 164
Treasure Chest (Chicago Magic Center)

Index

13–19, 20, 21–22, 24, 25, 28, 29, 31–32, 36, 38, 41, 119, 150, 152, 153–154
Triner, Joe 117
Tselos, Nick 168, 182
Tullock, Eddie 130
TV Magic Cards 1, 4, 7, 150–159, 162–164, 167, 192, 202, 224, 243, 255; commercials 152, 153, 154, 156, 164, 171, 192, 222, 248–249
TV Magic Catalog Company 174, 181
TV Magic Cups 164
TV Magic Ltd. 8, 166, 169, 170, 173, 177, 192, 248
TV Magic Set 1, 222, 248
TV Magic Show 164, 165, 169
TV Magic Tricks 169
TV Miracle Deck 164
TV Money Magic 173–174
TV Mystery Products 169

Urban, Ron 109, 113
Vanishing Birdcage (trick) 2, 43,

Veckey, Terry 212
Victor's Italian Restaurant 211, 214
Vinnie "The Hat" 44
Vogt, Evelyn 90
Volpe, Dominick 168, 170, 181–182, 184, 185–187, 210–211

Wallace, Bob 216
Walt Disney Company (magic sets) 239

Walt Disney World 218–219
Wanic, John (Marshall Brodien's youngest son) 256
Westinghouse Electric (trade shows) 134
WGN-TV v, 1, 3–6, 31, 108, 111, 127, 129, 143, 146, 148, 151, 153, 155, 184, 196, 202, 206, 207, 218, 234, 245, 255
Whiting, Margaret 120
Wilhelm, Gene 12
Williams, Betty Lou (The Four-Legged Girl) 27, 37
Wizard Stripper Deck 154
Wizzo the Wizard 1, 3–7, 145–147, 160, 170–172, 183–184, 189, 196–197, 199, 208, 218, 219, 235, 247; Magic Set 212, 245, 249
WOC-TV (Davenport, IA) 50–52
Wonder Deck 154
Wonders of Magic (syndicated show) 212–213
Wren, Fred 179
Wyman, General Willard G. 7, 81, 82

X-Ray Cards 154
X-Ray Napkin (hypnotic stunt) 70

Young, Randall C. 230

Zmed, Adrian 220

www.ingramcontent.com/pod-product-compliance
Ingram Content Group UK Ltd.
Pitfield, Milton Keynes, MK11 3LW, UK
UKHW041933140426